Psychology Revivals

Clinical Psychology

Originally published in 1987, this book presents papers from the First Conference of European Clinical Psychologists, held at the University of Kent Canterbury in July of that year. It shows some of the most exciting and recent developments in research and innovations in professional practice from many European countries with an overall theme of the WHO strategy of 'Health for all by the year 2000.' The whole range of clinical psychology is covered, including: cognitive therapy, clinical psychology and WHO strategy, the mental health of ethnic minority groups, health psychology, care in the community, and many other topics. The book is likely to be of interest for anyone concerned with the recent history and policies in clinical psychology.

I0083937

Clinical Psychology

Research and developments

Edited by
Helen Dent

R Routledge
Taylor & Francis Group

LONDON AND NEW YORK

First published in 1987
by Croom Helm Ltd

This edition first published in 2015 by Routledge
27 Church Road, Hove BN3 2FA

and by Routledge
711 Third Avenue, New York, NY 10017

Routledge is an imprint of the Taylor & Francis Group, an informa business

Publisher's Note
The publisher has gone to great lengths to ensure the quality of this reprint but points out that some imperfections in the original copies may be apparent.

Disclaimer
The publisher has made every effort to trace copyright holders and welcomes correspondence from those they have been unable to contact.

A Library of Congress record exists under ISBN: 0709945442

ISBN: 978-1-138-81905-4 (hbk)
ISBN: 978-1-315-74483-4 (ebk)
ISBN: 978-1-138-81910-8 (pbk)

CLINICAL PSYCHOLOGY:

Research and Developments

Edited by
HELEN DENT

CROOM HELM
London • New York • Sydney

© 1987 Helen Dent
Croom Helm Ltd, Provident House, Burrell Row,
Beckenham, Kent, BR3 1AT
Croom Helm Australia, 44-50 Waterloo Road,
North Ryde, 2113, New South Wales

British Library Cataloguing in Publication Data

Clinical psychology: research and
    developments.
    1. Clinical psychology
    I. Dent, Helen
    157'.9   RC467
    ISBN 0-7099-4544-2

Published in the USA by
Croom Helm
in association with Methuen, Inc.
29 West 35th Street
New York, NY 10001

Library of Congress Cataloging-in-Publication Data

Clinical psychology.
    "Published in the USA by Croom Helm in association
with Methuen, Inc." — T.p. verso.
    Papers from the First Conference of European Clinical
Psychologists, held at the University of Kent at
Canterbury U.K. in July 1986.
    Includes index.
    1. Clinical psychology — Congresses. 2. Clinical
health psychology — Congresses. 3. Community mental
health services — Congresses. I. Dent, Helen.
II. Conference of European Clinical Psychologists (1st:
1986: University of Kent) [DNLM: 1. Psychology,
Clinical — congresses. 2. World Health — congresses.
Wm 105 C6412 1986]
RC467.C5866 1987   157'.9   87-15447
ISBN 0-7099-4544-2

Printed and bound in Great Britain by
Biddles Ltd, Guildford and King's Lynn

CONTENTS

Contents

2. Mental Health of Ethnic Minorities

Contents

3. Focus on Therapists

4. Focus on Therapy : Cognitive Aspects

Contents

Contents

2. Care in the Community: Chronic Psychiatry

3. Care in the Community: The Challenge
    of Ageing

Contents

4. Preparing Clients for the Community

PREFACE

It is now generally recognised that the
profession of clinical psychology has a great deal
to offer not only within the context of health care,
but within society at large. Recent years have
witnessed the steady growth of the profession,
particularly in Western countries, although the
distribution of clinical psychologists remains
uneven. The World Health Organisation and other
professional agencies have acknowledged the
importance of clinical psychology and have supported
the profession's development. Ultimately, however,
it is up to ourselves as individual members of our
profession to uphold the standard of our practice
and ensure that we continue to make a valued
contribution to the welfare of our fellow human
beings. How better to do this than by face-to-face
contact and discussion?
In the summer of 1984 the Division of Clinical
Psychology of the British Psychological Society
proposed that such a 'European event' be held. The
main aim of this proposal was to bring together
clinical psychologists from all over Europe to share
their skills and problems, exchange ideas and update
on new developments. As well as providing a
platform for scientific and clinical interchange,
the other important reason for holding a conference
was to support and meet professional colleagues,
particularly in the EEC countries.
The reader will see from the papers contained
in this volume the breadth of subject matter covered
by the conference; testimony to the vigour and
diversity of modern day clinical psychology. Many
papers, it will be noted, were products of
multinational collaboration, providing a rare and
gratifying glimpse into how well international
research can be made to work. In all over 260
delegates attended, from 21 nations.
In addition to the scientific programme, the
conference was a great success from the social and
interpersonal point of view. New friendships were
made and plans for exchange trips mooted. Everyone
involved expressed the desire for such a meeting of
European clinical psychologists to become a regular
event. Already, preliminary discussions for a
second conference of European psychologists are

under way. At the time of writing, it seems likely that the second conference will be organised by our colleagues in the Dutch Psychology Organisation, as part of the European Congress of Psychology to be held in July, 1989 in Amsterdam under the auspices of the European Federation of Professional Psychologists' Association.

It is fitting that the proceedings of the first conference are being published. It marks the final episode in this new and successful venture, and consolidates all of the good things that happened. It will stand as a reminder to all the participants of a very pleasant and fruitful week; for those not fortunate enough to be able to attend, it will stand as an overview of the best in clinical psychology in Europe, 1986.

As convenor of the conference it is my pleasure to acknowledge the hard work of my fellow members of the conference committee:- Frank McPherson, Anne Pattie, Annabel Broome, Helen Dent, Paul Alexander, Anne Green, Jackie Millington and Bruce Napier. To Helen Dent our grateful appreciation for taking on the mammoth task of compiling these papers and editing this book so competently.

Rooshmie Bhagat, Ph.D., FBPS,
Convenor, Conference Committee,
Department of Clinical Psychology,
Airedale General Hospital,
Keighley, BD20 6TD,
West Yorkshire.

Chapter One

INTRODUCTION

Helen R. Dent

        The papers in this book have arisen from the
First Conference of European Clinical Psychologists
held at the University of Kent at Canterbury, U.K.
in July, 1986. The need for such a conference was
prompted by developments within Europe on three
professional and political fronts.   In 1981, the
European Federation of Professional Psychological
Associations (EFPPA) was formed. The UK representative (and from 1982, EFPPA's president) Dr. Frank
McPherson, was involved on the conference committee
from the beginning. Secondly, the emergence of the
Directive on the Free Movement of Professionals
within the EEC which is likely to be implemented in
1987.   Thirdly, the publication of the World Health
Organisation's strategy of Health for All by the
year 2000 (WHO/HFA 2000) which emphasises the need
for collaboration between professional groups in the
European Region. As clinical psychologists, we are
- or have been - probably more aware of the work of
our colleagues in the USA, Canada and Australia than
of our geographically closer colleagues in Europe.
The   First   Conference   of   European   Clinical
Psychologists sought to redress this balance and to
lay the groundwork for harmonisation of methods and
standards of training and practice within the EEC.
        The conference was a great success and the
purpose of the book is to bring to a wider audience
the exciting research reported there.   Not all
papers presented at the conference are included
here; some were not submitted for publication and a
few could not be accommodated within the structure
of the book, which has been designed to stand alone
and is not simply a report of proceedings. One
important theme running through the conference, WHO/
HFA 2000, has been used to create a structure within
which individual papers are placed. Accordingly,

the book falls into three major parts.

Part One is directly concerned with WHO/HFA 2000 and the role that psychologists can play in this strategy. Dr. John Henderson, now Medical Director of St. Andrew's Hospital, UK, but formerly the Regional Officer for Mental Health at the WHO Regional Office in Europe, gives a clear account of that organisation and its objectives in chapter two. In chapter three Dr. Rene Diekstra details the skills and knowledge that psychologists have to offer HFA/2000, and the appendix to his chapter lists the specific targets of relevance to psychologists. Chapter four concludes this section with a detailed examination of the contribution that psychologists have made to one relevant area of health promotion – smoking prevention. This chapter highlights our shortcomings so far, and clearly points the way forward.

Part Two is based upon the theme of WHO/HFA 2000 Target 4 which states that:

"By the year 2000, the average number of years that people live free from major disease and disability should be increased by at least 10%."

Psychologists have many and varying skills to offer to this target and so this part of the book is divided into four sections each of which focuses on a particular approach presented in the conference.
General health psychology, which has been interpreted as the contribution of psychologists to illness that has a major physical component, comprises the first section. The chapters present work carried out in the UK, USA, Germany, France and Australia and deal with problems ranging from coping with severe physical disorders such as cancer or burns, to psychological sequelae of artificially induced pregnancy. The methodologies similarly range from international epidemiology through developmental and exploratory studies, to controlled experimental designs.
The second section in Part Two is concerned with health problems arising out of, or in the context of, cultural marginality. The papers were presented in a symposium convened by Professor Raymond Cochrane, to whom I am grateful for his assistance in editing this section and for writing, in chapter thirteen, a most helpful and informative

introduction to this area.

Section three contains chapters which examine the role of therapists, including medical practitioners, nurses and clinical psychologists, the interactions between therapist and clients and includes a rare glimpse in chapter nineteen of research carried out behind the iron curtain.

Section four in Part Two is concerned with the therapeutic intervention itself. The burgeoning interest in cognitive approaches to therapy made this an obvious choice for a symposium and workshops at the conference, and hence the focus in this section. Chapter twenty-four provides an introduction by the symposium's convenor, Paul Salkovskis, and the whole section constitutes a brief but wide ranging introduction to much of the important thinking in this area.

Part Three is based upon the theme of WHO/HFA 2000 Target 3 which states that:

"By the year 2000, disabled persons should have the physical, social and economic opportunities that allow at least for a socially and economically and mentally creative life."

Current concern with the drawbacks of institutional life and the move towards caring for disabled people within the community reflect the spirit of this target. Psychologists have much to offer to the care in the community movement and, indeed, many clinical psychologists are involved at all levels from planning through to 'hands on' care. The chapters in Part Three present this approach with various client groups throughout Europe.

The first section in Part Three provides a thoughtful introduction to the most important issues in community care. It represents a symposium convened by Dr. John Hall, to whom I am grateful for editing the chapters in this section. The following sections focus on care in the community with different client groups.

Section two is concerned with chronic psychiatric patients and contains contributions from Italy, Belgium, Norway, Israel, Germany and the UK. Included are some practical accounts of providing a service and some more detailed theoretical contributions which, I am sure, will provoke stimulating debate.

Section three focuses on providing a service for the elderly within the community. It neverthetheless contains a chapter on residential care in which Dr. Robert Woods and Professor Per Haugen argue that many elderly people cannot be adequately cared for in the community, therefore there is a need for psychologists to work towards improving the quality of life within institutions. Such work is quite consistent with the spirit of target 3.

The final section in Part Three follows the theme of preparing clients to return to or cope with the community. The chapters present the work of clinical psychologists with mentally handicapped and neurologically impaired clients and with those who have been detained following breaches of the law. The approaches described range from the clearly detailed therapeutic interventions of Dr. Barbara Wilson, to a comparison of services for the mentally handicapped in the Netherlands and England.

In addition to clinical and other professional psychologists, the contributors to the book include physicians, psychiatrists, paediatricians, social workers and a graphic designer. The wide spread of subject matter ranging from variables involved in the reporting of breast cancer to setting up a rehabilitation day centre in Northern Italy will give the book an appeal to a similarly broad range of professionals within the health service. Inevitably a book of this nature must lack depth in its consideration of the issues and hence its greatest value will be as an introduction to applied research and an update on clinical practice in psychology throughout the European Community.

In conclusion, I would like to thank the authors who submitted their papers for publication and the conference committee who placed their trust in my editorship. It has been a most enjoyable and rewarding task. My greatest debt of gratitude, however, goes to Mrs. Sheila Turner for her skilful typing, insightful comments and organisational ability. Without her hard work and dedication, this book would not have seen the light of day.

May I wish you good reading .....

PART ONE: WORLD HEALTH ORGANISATION (WHO)
             STRATEGY: HEALTH FOR ALL BY THE
             YEAR 2000 (HFA 2000).

Chapter Two

HEALTH FOR ALL IN EUROPE: THE WORLD HEALTH
ORGANISATION STRATEGY AND TARGETS

John H. Henderson

INTRODUCTION

The World Health Organisation (WHO) is a
specialised agency of the United Nations, with
primary responsibility for international health
matters and public health.

Throughout the Organisation, which was created
in 1946, the health professions of some 160
countries exchange their knowledge and experience of
health information of many kinds.   WHO's main
function is to act as a directing and co-ordinating
authority on international health work to ensure
valid and productive technical co-operation and to
promote international research.

The member states of WHO have set for
themselves a common goal "Health for all by the Year
2000" whereby at the end of this century all
citizens of the world shall have a level of health
that will permit them to lead a socially and
economically productive life.

The global strategy for health for all –
adopted in 1981 – represents a solemn agreement
between the governments and WHO with the aim of
making possible the attainment that people
everywhere should have access to health services and
that essential health care is planned with full
community involvement.   It means that health begins
at home, in schools and in factories, and that
people will use better approaches than they do now
for preventing disease and alleviating unavoidable
disease and disability.

It means that people will realise that they
have the power to shape their own lives and the
lives of their families, free from the avoidable
burden of disease, and aware that ill health is not
inevitable.

The WHO Regional Office for Europe is one of six Regional Offices throughout the world, each with its own programme geared to the particular health problems of the countries served. The European Region has 32 active member states and it is unique in that a large proportion of them are industrialised countries with highly advanced medical services. The European programme, therefore, differs from those of other regions in concentrating on the problems associated with industrial society.

In its strategy for attaining the goal of health for all by the year 2000 the Regional Office is arranging its activities in three main areas of work: promotion of lifestyles conducive to health; reduction of preventable conditions; and provision of care that is adequate, accessible and acceptable to all.

In 1978 the International Conference on Primary Health Care, held in Alma-Ata, U.S.S.R., declared that primary health care is the key to attaining the goal of health for all by the year 2000. Primary health care is based on practical, scientifically sound and socially acceptable methods and technology. It should be made universally accessible to individuals and families in their community through their full participation and at an affordable cost on a continuing basis. Primary health care takes place at the first contact between individuals and the national health system, as close as possible to where people live and work. It is the first element in a continuing health care process, and forms an integral part of a country's health system.

The European Strategy

The European countries, with their long experience and vast resources, have a special responsibility to the rest of the world as front-runners in exploring new avenues to solve health problems and reduce inequalities. Following the adoption in 1977 of "Health for All" as the main social target of governments and the WHO, the European Region WHO has taken important steps towards that goal with the formulation of a common health policy in 1980 and the adoption in 1984 of regional targets in support of the European regional strategy for health for all. The regional targets have been developed for the European member states through the active participation of experts and health and social institutions throughout the Region. These targets represent, therefore, a common view of what could and should be health for all in Europe, and are a challenge which the member states have set for themselves. The targets and their respective strategies propose possible health improvements, possible ways of achieving these, and the means for measuring progress and evaluating efficiency and efficacy. Obviously, the methods of operation proposed by the regional targets can be implemented only by the member states themselves, and any achievement will depend on the will of the countries to orient their own policies and strategies towards a common goal such as health for all. The essential step is widespread dissemination of the message through all levels of the community from policy makers to the people, involving the mass media, the health professions, consumer groups, and the educational system. It is hoped that such dissemination could stimulate wide debate around the major issues and create the necessary conditions for change.

Prerequisites for Health for All
In 1980 the Regional Committee for the WHO European Region approved their first common health policy, the European strategy for attaining health for all. This strategy called for a fundamental change in the countries' health developments and outlined four main areas of concern:-

Lifestyles and health;
Risk factors affecting health and the environment;
Re-orientation of the health care system itself;
The political management, technological, manpower, research and other support necessary to bring about the desired changes.

Although it seemed rather ambitious to formulate specific regional targets to supplement the implementation of this strategy, since member states differ so much in socio-economic development, in health status and in political orientation, the Regional Committee in 1984 endorsed 38 regional targets that reflect common needs, priorities and values in the health systems of all member states. However, it was unanimously agreed that there could be no effective action to secure health for all without strong political and public support - not-

9

withstanding the already high commitment from health services and health professionals alike. A high responsibility, nevertheless, lies outside the health sector. Freedom from the fear of war, adequate food and income, decent housing, safe water, sanitation and a satisfying role in society are all essential for health.

Equity in Health

Two other basic issues must also be tackled by political and social commitment. The first is to reduce health inequality among countries and among groups within countries. A second issue is to strengthen health promotion as much as to reduce disease and its consequential disabilities and handicaps. Thus a prospect for adding life to years is occasioned by ensuring the full development and the use of people's integral or residual physical and mental capacity in order to derive full benefit from, and to cope with, life in a healthy and satisfactory way. The reduction of disease and disability will add to the quality of health in life, and finally, by reducing premature deaths and thereby increasing life expectancy, will add years to life. Targets 1-12 cover these two basic issues of equity in health.

Lifestyles Conducive to Health

Targets 13-17 are intimately bound up with the values, priorities and practical opportunities or constraints of specific cultural, social and economic situations affecting lifestyles. A person's particular way of life is shaped by patterns of interpersonal interaction and social learning that inter-relate with and depend upon the social environment. Thus, lifestyles shaped by experience and environmental factors are not simply individual decisions to avoid or accept certain health risks. Many lifestyles enhance health, develop physical and mental well-being, and protect the individual from the effects of stress. Other lifestyles include behaviour that may damage health. Harmful practices such as smoking or excessive alcohol consumption are sometimes ascribed to personal stress, but they often become routine habits used by a majority of people to cope with life and ease social contacts. Cultural patterns of social interaction, symbolic behaviour and tension reduction are learned in childhood and reinforced through life. Lifestyle practices are increasingly influenced by public and corporate policies that control the production of goods and promote products that may damage health. To be effective, therefore, health programmes concerned with lifestyles must deal with structural influences on behaviour as well as its specific individual components.

There are ethical issues to be considered when lifestyle policies and programmes are being devised. This means that a delicate balance must be achieved between respect for individual rights of free choice and the duty of society to promote the health of the population.

Healthy Environment

The environment of the European Region is changing rapidly in terms of demographic structure, human lifestyles, consumer goods, energy resources, methods of industrial and agricultural production, transportation, tourism and migration. All these factors can cause, and can interact to produce, impacts on health. Improvements in human environment, including the upgrading of housing, the reduction of long-standing pollution, and the provision of better working conditions involve many aspects of government at central, regional and local levels, and require well-integrated, multi-sectoral planning and management. The development of new technologies in the areas of energy production or chemical manufacture must be such that it minimises potential adverse effects on human health, and this requires the establishment of mechanisms for assessment, monitoring and systematic evaluation. In all countries of the Region there is widespread interest in the quality of the environment and in its influence on human health. The targets for environmental health policies number 18 to 25.

Appropriate Health Care

Over the past twenty years, there has been a massive increase in the resources allocated to health services in the Region as a whole, and technological developments in medicine have been unprecedented. As a result, the quality of life for many patients with specific physical conditions or mental illnesses has improved significantly. Despite these real achievements, however, the health of people in Europe has not progressed as rapidly as might have been expected. We are presently faced with the dilemma of what to do in an increasingly complex situation characterised by the emergence of new health problems and challenges, changing expectations, developing capabilities both within

11

and outside the health sector, and pre-eminently finite resources. There is an increasing responsibility with the public to participate so far as possible with politicians, health planners and providers in decisions regarding financing, organising, managing and evaluating all aspects of health care. Thus the primary health care concept is as relevant for Europe as for other regions of the world. Targets 26 to 31 deal with priorities for primary health care and the quality of health services.

Health Development Support

The attainment of the targets set out in the preceding paragraphs will require a fundamental change of attitudes and working practices among politicians, health authorities, health personnel, people in other sectors, and the general public. The targets, 32-38, in this section will have to be reached much earlier than the other targets since the support measures with which they are concerned are in themselves pre-requisites for a successful health development process. Health policy formulation, the managerial process, human resource development and health technology assessment will comprise the content of the targets for health development support. In some member states health legislation may need to be strengthened, and decisive action taken to ensure that national policies are in line with community needs and are in accordance with the country's political and administrative setting.

Irrespective of the scale and type of approach which a country considers appropriate, increasing emphasis will be laid on continuous and thorough evaluation and, wherever necessary, re-programming will be undertaken according to the evidence forth-coming from the health information system and the indicators of target achievement.

CONCLUSION

Health for all is a challenging goal for every country in the European Region. The setting of targets provides a framework for initiating the actions necessary, stressing as they do the improvements needed in the health of the people, if they are to lead socially and economically productive lives. The Regional targets outline the contents of a European health policy which should stimulate the member states in the development of health for all policies and programmes.

The 'Health for All' movement is for the people, with the people and, above all, a movement by the people. The first task of governments is to launch the Health for All movement within their own bounds, and health authorities will have to take responsibility for leading the development necessary. Health professionals, too, have a very important role to play in health development in all countries of the Region. Their expert knowledge and the influence they have with politicians and the general public alike make them an important force in mobilising support and initiating change.

The importance of sectors other than health has been stressed throughout, and again targeting of the movement gives additional emphasis to their important and sometimes new responsibilities. Many of the major health problems facing countries today have their roots and their solutions outside national boundaries, and for that reason international co-operation is needed more than ever before. United Nations agencies and other inter-governmental organisations have an important role to play, but it is WHO that bears special responsibility in this respect. The European Region has the people, the knowledge and the resources necessary to attain health for all; the greatest need is the will to bring all those forces more effectively to bear on prevailing problems. A joint commitment to the regional policy and the setting of clear targets has created a broad movement that will foster better understanding and leave a legacy of value beyond our time.

Chapter Three

THE RELEVANCE OF PSYCHOLOGY AND PSYCHOLOGISTS TO
HEALTH FOR ALL 2000

Rene F.W. Diekstra

SUMMARY

In this paper those characteristics of the
World Health Organisation's (WHO) programme Health
for All by the Year 2000 (HFA 2000) that are of
particular relevance for the field of psychology
will be outlined. In relation to that two basic
questions will be addressed, namely (1) is it
justifiable to claim that psychology comprises
specific knowledge that is relevant and essential
for the HFA/2000 programme and (2) are psychologists, both nationally and internationally,
organised in such a way that they can participate in
a structurally solid way in WHO's work?

INTRODUCTION

The role of psychologists with regard to health
and mental health is rather different in different
parts of the world and so is the organisational
status and nature of psychology as an academic and
professional discipline. At the one extreme we have
countries like the United States with over 100,000
psychologists who often have prestige and influence
comparable to that of medical doctors. At the other
extreme, there is the People's Republic of China
with a much bigger population, but only about 2000
psychologists.

It is not only on a global scale, but also in
Europe that international differences are considerable. Greece, for example, has very few
psychologists and no university provides a Master's
or Ph.D. programme in psychology, while countries
like Holland, United Kingdom and Sweden count
themselves among the most densely psych-populated
nations in the world with a considerable number of

14

universities providing Ph.D. curricula and carrying out extensive research programmes. But even in these latter countries the status and role of psychologists in the health field is often subordinate to that of medical doctors and their organisation is weaker and more diffuse.

This situation co-determines the involvement of psychologists in WHO programmes, because that involvement is decided upon by national governments and authorities, to whom the comparative status of relevant professional organisations plays an important role, despite the quality and relevance of the knowledge they have to offer.

Psychological aspects of HFA/2000

When the Thirtieth World Health Assembly in May (1977) accepted HFA/2000, it decided upon a fundamental change in member states' health policies and in international cooperation in health.

This becomes clear from the major themes that the European region of WHO has adopted in her strategy for attaining HFA/2000. These themes are:

   i. equal opportunities to health and health care;
  ii. health promotion and prevention of ill-health or disease;
 iii. community participation;
  iv. multisectorial cooperation;
   v. primary health care;
  vi. international cooperation.

The major categories of change that are supposed to bring about such improvements in health care are:

   i. changes in lifestyle;
  ii. changes in the environment;
 iii. changes in the care system.

The General Programme of Work (GPW) for the present period (1984-1989) cites four major activities in which psychologists can play a central role:

1. The development of mental health policies and the promotion, coordination, evaluation and support of programmes throughout the world.
2. The improved understanding and utilisation of psychosocial factors in the promotion of health and human development.
3. Prevention of alcohol and drug abuse.
4. Prevention and treatment of mental and

neurological disorders (WHO, 1983).

The World Health Assembly recently voted for a resolution that underlines the importance of this part of the GPW by stating that: "use of mental health knowledge and skills can improve health care in general" (WHO, 1984).

Consequently the target document on HFA/2000 of WHO/EURO speaks for the necessity of application of "psychological and biobehavioural principles in preventing, managing and controlling mental health problems and promoting mental health" (WHO, 1983).

In this document 38 specific targets in support of the Regional Strategy for Health for All are stated. A working group of the European Federation of Professional Psychologists Associations (EFPPA) recently concluded that psychology and psychologists have a substantial bearing on at least twenty of these targets (see Table 1).

From the target descriptions it becomes clear that the knowledge needed to implement HFA/2000 includes:-

   i. description of indicators of health in all its facets;

  ii. methods of reliably and validly measuring/ monitoring these indicators;

 iii. determination of the ways in which physical and social factors influence health and health (risk) behaviour of individuals and populations;

  iv. determination of the separate and combined effects of specific types of (covert and/or overt) behaviour on health and of the factors determining each type;

   v. methods of intervention and of evaluation of interventions at individual as well as population level.

Psychologists, especially those working in the subspecialties designated as clinical and health psychology, will readily recognise these desiderata as precisely those that traditionally have been considered as characteristic of their own field and can point to a vast body of knowledge accumulated in these areas. In the following some examples will be presented to illustrate this claim.

Accident prevention

Target 11 refers to the field of accident prevention in which considerable progress has already been made, but in which further progress can be made as the results of psychological research have shown. Consider the case of accidents involving motor vehicles and child pedestrians (McPherson, 1984).

The peak incidence of these accidents is between the ages of 5 and 7 years, and the generally accepted explanation, even by the children themselves, is that children of this age tend to be inattentive to oncoming traffic and attempt to cross streets at inappropriate times and places, giving drivers insufficient opportunity to take effective avoiding action. Preventive methods have therefore concentrated on the children themselves, e.g. by educating them in the dangers of traffic, in the 'stop and look' procedure before crossing, and by providing protected crossing places. However, when behavioural analyses were carried out, based on systematic observations of children among traffic, it was shown that whereas children were clearly anticipating the possibility of an accident, and were taking appropriate avoiding action, drivers were not. Drivers did not appear to anticipate the possibility that a child might step on to the road. For example, when they saw children at the kerb, they did not slacken speed or move further from the kerb, and when an accident did threaten, they usually took action too late to have avoided it, had not the child done so. In other words, the entire responsibility for avoiding such accidents was being taken by the child of 5 or 7 years, and not by the driver. These observations thus suggest that further reductions in this type of accident will occur only if the focus of intervention shifts from the child to the driver. This approach to the investigation of accidents is typical of the 'applied behavioural analysis' approach which is widely used in contemporary applied psychology.

Suicide prevention
Target 12 refers to the field of suicide prevention. Over the past two decades psychologists have extensively investigated the causes of suicidal acts and of the rising trends in these acts. The influence of psychological and social factors on suicidal behaviour is well documented (Diekstra, 1981). However, despite intensive efforts the results of suicide prevention programmes in general have been disappointing. This has led to the conclusion that it is unlikely that further significant improvement will result from merely applying existing methods more extensively or

vigorously. Instead, a reconceptualisation of the problem is required. To illustrate this point, the case of suicide prevention in schools can be considered. Both in the United States and in Holland so-called Adolescent Suicide Awareness Programmes (ASAP) have recently been set up (Diekstra and Hawton, 1987). Such programmes are carried out and coordinated by staff of community mental health centres.

ASAP is directed at influencing the attitudes and behaviours of three target groups, namely pupils, parents and teachers, by holding meetings and mini-workshops for each of these groups on a regular basis. Information on suicidal behaviour, the extent of the problem, its causes, signals and how to react in case one is confronted with a severely depressed or suicidal youngster, is provided. Listening and communication skills and adequate methods for motivating such youngsters to accept required help and for referring them appropriately are also learned.

Although the effect of these programmes on rates of suicide and attempted suicide among the young has not yet been established, due to the fact that they are of such recent date, it has already been shown in two centres that the rate of referrals of high risk adolescents, by teachers, parents and fellow students, has gone up dramatically.

Coined in WHO terminology, programmes like ASAP are community-based, preventive of ill-health or disability, a form of primary mental health care and multi-sectorial.

Developing and supporting health lifestyles

The HFA/2000 target document clarifies this target, by stating that "The skills that enable people to control and direct their lives, and thus to live in a healthy way, include the capacity to formulate problems, find solutions, communicate effectively and question and intervene actively on their own behalf when necessary. These skills are more easily learned in childhood and youth."

What the target document does not say is that developmental psychologists in different parts of the world have found in longitudinal studies that early parent-child interactions are highly consistent over time and situations and that some well-defined patterns of interactions are closely related to behaviour problems and coping styles of children in puberty and adolescence (no longitudinal studies are available yet that have followed children for more that 14 years (ISSBD, 1982)).

Home based intervention (parent centred) may therefore produce substantial initial and continuing gains in the child's development. Studies suggest that the effects tend to be maintained for years after intervention is terminated. The critical activity promoted is parent-, especially mother-child interaction around common activities. Para-professional workers, suitably trained, can act very effectively as home visitors/parent educators.

The emergence of health psychology

From the three examples described above, to which a legion of others can easily be added, it becomes clear that it is not just clinical or medical psychology but psychology in general, including social, developmental, industrial and personality psychology, that is of utmost relevance to present WHO programmes. All the subdivisions or sub-disciplines of psychology have produced and will produce knowledge that is applicable to health and health care. The growing awareness of this fact both among psychologists and in other disciplines in the health field is probably one of the main reasons for the emergence of a new specialty of psychological research and professional practice presently called health psychology.

The designation signifies the broadening of psychology to include the general health of the individual in a social, community and ecological setting. More than ever before psychologists are becoming involved in health promotion, in the relationship between health and environment, in prevention and control of chronic illnesses, and in questions of use of and access to health care by different social groups. They are rapidly accumulating knowledge that is of high relevance in these areas.

Other examples worth mentioning are: the development of procedures for systematic citizen input into decision making with regard to health care; the development of methods of evaluation and procedures for promoting change in community settings, as well as instruments to measure aspects of city readiness for social action (Moos, 1984). A beautiful example of this is the work of Levine (1982) in organising the citizens of Love Canal, a neighbourhood near a toxic waste dump, to take appropriate social action for improving public health.

The dissemination of psychological knowledge

Clearly there is a great deal of knowledge within psychology that awaits broader application. One of the reasons why the available knowledge is not translated into action is that applied psychologists themselves are often not fully aware of what their own field has to offer. Improving training standards, one of the main functions that EFPPA in cooperation with WHO could fulfil, is an important tool in amending this situation. There are, however, other reasons why the public has not benefited enough from what psychology has to offer.

Important political, social, economic and organisational constraints on the application of available knowledge are present. For example, vested interest groups may gain social, inter-political and economic benefits from the status quo and may lobby against the application of new knowledge.

Another reason is that there is still, in many countries, very little systematic review by policy-makers of new knowledge arising from research projects - knowledge which could influence health policies and programmes. This lack of coordination is often the result of weak organisational links between the research community and policy makers both within and among countries. Such links are, however, better established by some academic disciplines, such as the medical sciences, than by others.

Therefore, it is relevant to point out that the expanding of the number of points on which the substantial corpus of psychological knowledge and techniques is brought to bear on human health problems depends on how much better psychologists learn to work with policy makers and community leaders as consultants and participants in the design, implementation and evaluation of health and health care programmes (Holtzmann, in preparation).

Recommendations

What psychology as a body should strive for in relationship with WHO, in particular with WHO/EURO, is:

i. The recognition of organisations like EFPPA as non-governmental organisations collaborating with WHO;

ii. The establishment within the WHO/EURO organisation of an advisory committee on health psychology;

iii. Membership of programme advisory committees where health psychologists could make a significant contribution;

iv. Use of (health) psychologists in designing and evaluating research programmes, studies and applications;

v. The establishment of a clearing house through which (a) names, interests and specialist skills of health psychologists working in the region and (b) the nature of relevant projects being carried out in countries of the region, specifying topic, design, methods, staff and timetable, could be made known to WHO;

vi. The establishment of WHO-collaborating centres for health psychology throughout the region.

Finally, it would be desirable if WHO/EURO would agree to reserve a special issue of Public Health in Europe for a directory and review of European health psychology.

REFERENCES

Diekstra, R.F.W. (1981). Over Suicide.
    Samson: Alphen.
Diekstra, R.F.W., Hawton, K. (Eds) (1987).
    Suicide in Adolescence.
    Nijhoff Int. Publishers: Boston/Dordrecht.
Holtzmann, W.H. (Ed) (In preparation). Psychology
    and Health. A document prepared especially for
    the World Health Organisation. International
    Union of Psychological Science.
International Society for the Study of Behavioural
    Development (1982). Relevance of Developmental
    Psychology and the ISSBD for WHO Mental Health
    Programmes.
Levine, A. (1982). Love Canal: Science, Policies
    and People. Lexington Books: Mass.
McPherson, F.M. (1984). Report of the Consultation
    of WHO and EFPPA. McPherson: Dundee.
Moos, R.H. (1984). Context and coping: towards a
    unified conceptual framework of community.
    American Journal of Community Psychology,
    12, 5-25.
WHO (1983). Global medium-term programme:
    protection and promotion of mental health
    (programme 10). WHO: Geneva.

WHO (1984). Targets in support of the regional strategy towards Health for All by the year 2000. WHO: Copenhagen.

Table 1:   Targets in support of the regional
strategy HFA/2000 of special relevance to
psychology

Target 3   By the year 2000, disabled persons
should have the physical, social and
economic opportunities that allow at least for
a socially and economically fulfilling and
mentally creative life.

Target 4   By the year 2000, the average number of
years that people live free from major disease
and disability should be increased by at least
10%.

Target 9   By the year 2000, mortality in the region
from diseases of the circulatory system in
people under 65 should be reduced by at least
15%.

Target 10   By the year 2000, mortality in the
region from cancer in people under 65 should be
reduced by at least 15%.

Target 11   By the year 2000, deaths from accidents
in the region should be reduced by at least 25%
through an intensified effort to reduce
traffic, home and occupational accidents.

Target 12   By the year 2000, the current rising
trend in suicides and attempted suicides in the
region should be reversed.

Target 13   By 1990, national policies in all member
states should ensure that legislative,
administrative and economic mechanisms provide
broad intersectoral support and resources for
the promotion of health lifestyles and ensure
effective participation of the people at all
levels of such policy-making.

Target 14   By 1990, all member states should have
specific programmes which enhance the major
roles of the family and other social groups
developing and supporting healthy lifestyles.

Target 15   By 1990, educational programmes in all
member states should enhance the knowledge,
motivation and skills of people to acquire
and maintain health.

Target 16   By 1995, in all member states, there
should be significant increase in positive
health behaviour, such as balanced nutrition,
nonsmoking, appropriate physical activity and
good stress management.

Target 17   By 1995, in all member states, there

should be significant decreases in health-damaging behaviour, such as overuse of alcohol and pharmaceutical products, use of illicit drugs and dangerous chemical substances, dangerous driving and violent social behaviour.

Target 24 By the year 2000, all people of the region should have a better opportunity of living in houses and settlements which provide a healthy and safe environment.

Target 25 By the year 1995, people of the region should be effectively protected against work-related health risks.

Target 28 By 1990, the primary health care system of all member states should provide a wide range of health-promotive, curative, rehabilitative and supportive services to meet the needs of vulnerable and under-served individuals and groups.

Target 29 By 1990, in all member states, primary health care systems should be based on cooperation and teamwork between health care personnel, individuals, families and community groups.

Target 31 By 1990, all member states should have built effective mechanisms for ensuring quality of patient care within their health care systems.

Target 32 Before 1990, all member states should have formulated research strategies to stimulate investigations which improve the application and expansion of knowledge needed to support their health for all developments.

Target 36 Before 1990, in all member states, the planning, training and use of health personnel should be in accordance with health for all policies, with emphasis on the primary health care approach.

Target 37 Before 1990, in all member states, education should provide personnel in sections related to health with adequate information on the country's health for all policies and programmes and their practical application to their own sectors.

Target 38 Before 1990, all member states should have established a formal mechanism for the systematic assessment of the appropriate use of health technologies and of their effectiveness, efficiency, safety and acceptability, as well as reflecting national health policies and economic restraints.

Chapter Four

DEVELOPING A PSYCHOLOGICAL CONTRIBUTION TO
HFA 2000: SMOKING PREVENTION

Roger Paxton

This paper begins with a brief review of previous actions against smoking before suggesting contributions that psychologists should make.

What have clinical psychologists done about smoking?

The main contribution of clinical psychologists to action against smoking has been developing, providing and evaluating treatments to help people stop smoking (Bernstein & Glasgow, 1979). These treatments have mainly been offered to groups rather than individuals. Most have been intensive, time-consuming and therefore expensive. Associated with them has been research evaluating and comparing their outcomes. This research has shown a concern with percentage success rates. There has been little attention to the applicability of the methods evaluated and scant concern with the absolute numbers rather than percentages of people who might be helped. A third characteristic has been the isolation of our work from that of other agencies.

Much less work has concerned preventing the onset of smoking (Botvin, 1982). Recent work may be summarised as teaching "lifeskills". It involves teaching young people decision-making, resisting social pessure, and developing awareness of other influences, such as advertising, which tend to promote smoking.

What else has been done?

Psychologists sometimes seem unaware that many groups helping people to stop smoking have been run by professionals other than ourselves. Raw and Heller (1984) reported that only 9% of smoking clinics in the UK were run by clinical psychologists. Sixty two percent were run by Health Education Officers, 13% by medical staff, 11% by Health Visitors and 5% by others.

A second, and very widespread, activity has been health education about smoking.

Thirdly, most District Health Authorities in the UK have or are developing policies against smoking. Most involve increased restrictions on smoking in Health Authority premises, publicity about the policy, offering help in the form of support groups for employees who wish to stop smoking and advice or suggestions to local employers and other organisations that they too should develop policies against smoking.

A fourth kind of action concerns cigarette advertising. Cigarettes may not now be advertised on television in the UK. However, this is a ban in name only. Sponsorship of sporting events by tobacco companies results in massive television exposure of cigarette brand names. Later we shall see that taxation is another powerful but underused means of influencing cigarette consumption.

What have we learned about smoking and its prevention?

We have learned that there is no single reason why people smoke (Ashton & Stepney, 1982). Smoking may serve a range of different functions at different times and under different circumstances. Similarly, we no longer expect that a single form of help will be effective for everybody (Lichtenstein, 1982). However, in contrast to the pessimism of some reviewers in the 1970s we now know that some methods are more effective than others. So far as psychological help is concerned we know that skill-based methods are better than, say, educational or aversive techniques.

We also know that very brief interventions can help some people to stop smoking (Russell et al, 1979). These workers showed a small but significant percentage increase in people stopping smoking after brief advice and information were provided routinely by General Practitioners (GPs). The importance of this finding is that it could be repeated on a very large scale.

We are more aware and accepting of smokers' motives. We know that smoking cannot be dismissed simply as nicotine addiction, but that it is maintained by a number of factors. Related to this it seems that giving up smoking is not one change but the end result of a series of stages and processes (Prochaska & DiClemente, 1983).

We know that most help is unsuccessful. Twenty per cent is often spoken of as an average long-term success rate for a smoking treatment service, but this may be an overestimate. Hunt et al (1971), reviewing a large number of American smoking clinics, reported that around 20% of people who stopped smoking originally were still abstinent at one year. Bradshaw (1973), however, also reviewing the results of a large number of clinics, reported a median end of treatment success rate of 37%. If these two results are taken as representative, putting them together we could expect only around 8% of people entering treatment to be abstinent a year after the end of treatment.

Against this pessimism it is helpful to remember that there are currently estimated to be 10 million former smokers in Britain. We may not be good at helping people stop smoking but many smokers themselves know how it is done.

Finally, we know that increasing taxation on tobacco is effective in helping some smokers to give up the habit. Russell (1973) plotted consumption of cigarettes against real price for the years 1946 to 1971, and showed a striking inverse correlation. Substantial price increases led to marked reductions in consumption.

What has been achieved?

Although the percentage of smokers in the population is falling, successive Chancellors of the Exchequer have failed to seize the opportunity to accelerate this downward trend by increasing taxation markedly. Similarly, the failure to regulate sponsorship of the sports and arts by tobacco companies has meant that there is still a vast amount of cigarette advertising.

Furthermore, there is an inconsistency between the government's initiation, coordination, and funding of action against illicit drugs, tranquillisers and solvent misuse, and the shortage of such actions against smoking.

It is difficult to evaluate the success of Health Authority policies against smoking as most are very new. However, I am pessimistic. I do not know of any British Health Authority which included actions and achievements concerning smoking in the objectives against which the performances of its General Managers will be evaluated. The climate of opinion within Health Authorities does not seem to me to be against smoking. In this context, climate of opinion is not a woolly notion. A General Manager who makes no secret of his view that the anti-smoking lobby is making a fuss about nothing is unlikely to promote or support action against smoking. In short, Health Authority policies against smoking are unlikely to achieve their intended effects because they are not well incorporated within the current management arrangements, and in many cases are not supported by the General Managers whose job it is to implement them.

Clinical psychologists have made little progress in reducing the number of people smoking. Moreover, the work we have done has been less in response to perceived health care needs than to our own professional interests and priorities. We have run and evaluated relatively small treatment groups. There are many other actions we could have taken. How many of us assessed the options before embarking on treatment groups? How many of us asked smokers whether they wished to join treatment groups, or perhaps receive some other sort of help? In addition to all this, our work has usually shown little coordination with other action.

The health costs of smoking

To put this lack of achievement into perspective, consider the health costs of smoking. Around one smoker in four eventually dies from his or her smoking. This amounts to about 100,000 deaths each year in the UK, or about 700 deaths in an average District Health Authority. Smoking is the largest single preventable cause of death in Britain (Royal College of Physicians, 1983). Action against smoking should therefore be central to some of the main aims of Health For All 2000 - promoting lifestyles conducive to health and reducing preventable conditions.

Towards a psychological contribution

If psychologists are to be more responsive and effective in smoking prevention we must first shift the current emphasis in our work from helping people to stop smoking towards preventing young people from starting. Research on skill-based methods of primary prevention was mentioned earlier and some of it is used in schools. We should use our clinical and evaluation skills to promote, improve and evaluate this work, and we should do so in a planned and coordinated way with the other professionals concerned.

Secondly, the study referred to earlier (Russell et al, 1979) showing the effectiveness of General Practitioners' advice against smoking is often cited but rarely applied. We should draw the attention of Health Authority managers and GPs to the method and its implications, and help to implement and evaluate work of the same kind in many localities.

Thirdly, although there are difficulties (Kozlowski et al, 1980), there are also many needs and opportunities for consumer research in smoking prevention. Reports of smokers themselves being asked what help they would like or find useful are rare.

Fourth, and most important, we should take action on a wider scale, and at different levels. A logical place to start is with and within the Health Authorities by whom most of us are employed. It is helpful and right that Health Authorities should serve as exemplars to their consumers and to other organisations and employers.

Our results have been disappointing so far but negative results may be used positively. So far, psychologists, as well as most Health Authorities in Britain and the British Government, have done little more than tinker with smoking prevention. Tinkering has not been effective. We should use the evidence of past failures to argue for wider and more effective action.

One kind of wider action could be pressure within the Health Authorities to include smoking prevention targets in the objectives given to General Managers. Another step would be to propose particular smoking prevention objectives. In doing this we must learn from past mistakes by listening to the people we wish to influence in order to suggest a programme of actions which will be acceptable and achievable. With this in mind a suggested first task for General Managers might be to involve Health Authority staff and managers in proposing actions designed to get people thinking about smoking as a problem about which something should be done. The same wide range of people could be asked to propose restrictions on smoking, and to state how adherence to the restrictions is to be monitored and maintained. Actions of this kind should be the first in a progressive series

formulated by us in cooperation and consultation
with other colleagues.   Again we can learn from past
mistakes.   Most   action against smoking in the past
has been one-off.

Lastly, an important part of our contribution
is that all proposals should include plans for
evaluation and opportunities to modify the action
subsequently.

Conclusions

The proposals here contain little detail, but
that is inevitable.   One of the main lessons to draw
from previous work on smoking is not to assume that
we know what is needed, but to ask the consumers and
look closely at the problems we wish to help with.
A second general point is that future actions should
be better coordinated with other agencies' plans and
not carried out in isolation.   Thirdly, we should
think more of absolute numbers of people and their
needs, and less of maximising percentage success
rates.

If these conclusions sound familiar I suggest
it is because the failings of much of our previous
work on smoking have characterised a good deal of
our work with other problems and client groups.   As
a profession I believe we are beginning to
acknowledge and respond to these mistakes.

Acknowledgement

I am grateful to Stella Dickinson for typing
the manuscript.

REFERENCES

Ashton, H. & Stepney, R. (1982).   Smoking:
    Psychology and Pharmacology.
    Tavistock: London.
Bernstein, D.A. & Glasgow, R.E. (1979).   Smoking.
    In O.F. Pomerleau & D.P. Brady (Eds)
    Behavioural Medicine: Theory and Practice.
    Williams & Wilkins: Baltimore.
Botvin, G.J. (1982).   Broadening the Focus of
    Smoking Prevention Strategies.   In T.J.
    Coates, A.C. Patterson & C. Perry (Eds)
    Promoting Adolescent Health: a Dialogue on
    Research and Practice.   Academic Press:
    New York.
Bradshaw, P.W. (1973).   The problem of cigarette
    smoking and its control.   International Journal

of the Addictions, 8, 353-371.
Hunt, W.A., Barnett, L.W. & Branch, L.G. (1971).
Relapse rates in addiction programs.
Journal of Clinical Psychology, 27, 455-456.
Kozlowski, L.T., Herman, C.P. & Frecker, R.C.
(1980). What researchers make of what
cigarette smokers say: filtering smokers'
hot air. Lancet, 1, 699-700.
Lichtenstein, E. (1982). The smoking problem: a
behavioural perspective. Journal of Consulting
and Clinical Psychology, 50, 804-819.
Prochaska, J. & DiClemente, C.C. (1983). Stages
and processes of self-change of smoking:
toward an integrative model of change.
Journal of Consulting and Clinical Psychology,
51, 390-395.
Raw, M. & Heller, J. (1984). Helping People to Stop
Smoking: the Development, Role and Potential
of Support Services in the U.K.
Health Education Council, London.
Royal College of Physicians (1983). Health or
Smoking. Pitman Medical: London.
Russell, M.A.H. (1973). Changes in cigarette price
and consumption by men in Britain, 1946-71:
a preliminary analysis. British Journal of
Preventive and Social Medicine, 27, 1-7.
Russell, M.A.H., Wilson C., Taylor, C. & Baker,
C.D. (1979). Effect of general practitioners'
advice against smoking. British Medical
Journal, 2, 231-235.

PART TWO: HEALTH PSYCHOLOGY
              WHO/HFA 2000 Target Four:

              By the year 2000 the average
              number of years that people
              live free from major disease
              and disability should be
              increased by at least 10%.

              1.   General Health Psychology
              2.   Mental Health of Ethnic
                     Minorities
              3.   Focus on Therapists
              4.   Focus on Therapy:
                     Cognitive Aspects

Chapter Five

DO HEALTH BELIEFS PREDICT HEALTH BEHAVIOUR?
A FURTHER ANALYSIS OF BREAST SELF-EXAMINATION

D.R. Rutter and Michael Calnan

INTRODUCTION

The purpose of this paper is to explore the relationships between health beliefs and health behaviour. The behaviour in question is breast self-examination (BSE) and the framework for our analysis is the Health Belief Model of Becker and his colleagues (Becker, 1974; Becker et al, 1977). According to the most recent formulation of the model, by Janz & Becker (1984), preventive health behaviour can be predicted from three sets of beliefs: perceived susceptibility to the disorder; perceived severity of the disorder; and the perceived benefits and barriers of doing the particular behaviour. In the case of BSE, women most likely to carry out the behaviour are those who believe they are especially vulnerable to breast cancer, that breast cancer is a severe disorder, and that the benefits of the behaviour outweigh the costs. The purpose of our analysis is to test those predictions.

The study from which the data are taken (Calnan & Rutter, 1986a) was part of an extensive British investigation into BSE (UK Trial of the Early Detection of Breast Cancer Group, 1981). The data were collected prospectively over twelve months, from two cities, and the subjects were selected at random from all women aged 45-64 who were registered with general practitioners in the two locations. In the first, the "BSE city", subjects were invited to attend a BSE class, and those who accepted (278) were compared with those who declined (262). In the second city, there was no such invitation, and subjects acted as controls (594). Beliefs were measured at the beginning of the year and again at the end for all three groups of subjects, and self-reports of BSE were collected at the same time. Since the severity of breast cancer is doubted by few (Stillman, 1977) the second of Becker's dimensions was omitted and just two sets of beliefs were tapped: perceived vulnerability to breast cancer (PVC), and perceived value of BSE (BSEVAL). The measures of behaviour were Frequency and Technique.

METHOD

The first stage of data collection consisted of a home interview, during which questions about many health issues were asked, including the following: PVC (5-point scale); BSEVAL (5 points); frequency of self-examination (10 points, from less than yearly to daily); and techniques of self-examination (6 points), where a score of six denoted full compliance with the "ideal" techniques which were to be recommended in the class. One month after the interview, every woman in the BSE district received a postal invitation to attend a class on BSE at her local city hospital. The class was to consist of a short instructional film and a talk by a nurse, followed by a group discussion. The invitation had not been mentioned by the interviewer, and there was, of course, no provision for classes in the control city. One year after the first interview, the interviewer returned, and the same four measures were taken. The design thus allowed a comparison of three groups - attenders, non-attenders and controls - on two occasions, before the classes began and a year later.

RESULTS

The main findings from our preliminary analyses were as follows. First, there were small but significant differences between attenders' and non-attenders' beliefs at Time 1, in that, for both PVC and BSEVAL, attenders had slightly higher scores. In part, perhaps, that is why they accepted the invitation to attend the class in the first place, and our analyses bear that out. Sixty-four per cent of attenders and 52% of non-attenders were correctly assigned to their group by a discriminant analysis using just PVC and BSEVAL at Time 1. PVC was the more important of the two.

The second finding was that there were marked changes in both beliefs and behaviour from Time 1 to

Time 2. They were strongest for the attenders and they were more noticeable for behaviour than beliefs. Non-attenders and controls, however, also made significant changes, and at least part of the apparent success of the campaign, therefore, was probably due to the publicity it received and to the "cueing" effect of the initial interview. Finally, in all three groups of subjects, there were reliable positive relationships between beliefs and behaviour. The women most likely to do BSE frequently and well were those with high scores on both PVC and BSEVAL, and those most likely to do it infrequently and badly were those with low scores on both measures. "High" and "low" were defined by the median. Together, however, BSEVAL and PVC accounted for no more than 25% of the variance in any of the multiple regression analyses we conducted. BSEVAL was consistently the more powerful predictor of the two, for Frequency and Technique alike.

Those, then, were our preliminary findings, but there remains one final result, which, for the purpose of the present paper, is the most revealing. In the literature on beliefs and behaviour in general - that is, outside health - one of the most valuable contributions of late has been the Theory of Reasoned Action of Fishbein (Fishbein & Ajzen, 1975; Ajzen & Fishbein, 1980). Behaviour, Fishbein argues, is predicted by two measures: the subject's "private" beliefs about the consequences of doing the behaviour; and her perceptions of how those who are important to her believe she should act. Recently, however, it has been suggested that a third predictor might be added to the model, namely how the subject has behaved in the past (Bentler & Speckart, 1979; Fredericks & Dassett, 1983). Since our design was prospective, we had an ideal opportunity to examine the suggestion ourselves, and we did so in a further series of multiple regression analyses.

The results are given in Table 1. For all three groups, it emerged, behaviour at Time 1 did predict behaviour at Time 2, and it was a much stronger predictor than either BSEVAL or PVC. The most marked effects were for the control group - where there had been relatively little change in either beliefs or behaviour from Time 1 to Time 2 - and the proportion of variance explained by the three measures was now around 50%, against 25% before behaviour at Time 1 was included. Beliefs, in other words, did predict behaviour, but behaviour predicted behaviour even better.

Do Health Beliefs Predict Health Behaviour?

Table 1. Beliefs at Times 1 and 2 and Behaviour at Time 1 as Predictors of Behaviour at Time 2

			CUM.MR^2	BETA	r
ATTENDERS (N=278)					
FREQ 2 Step 1		FREQ$_1$	0.11	0.22**	0.34***
Step 2		BSEVAL$_2$	0.18	0.28***	0.34***
TECH 2 Step 1		TECH$_1$	0.15	0.34***	0.38***
Step 2		BSEVAL$_2$	0.19	0.22***	0.31***
Step 3		PVC$_2$	0.20	0.16*	0.21***
NON-ATTENDERS (N=262)					
FREQ 2 Step 1		FREQ$_1$	0.30	0.36***	0.55***
Step 2		BSEVAL$_2$	0.35	0.21***	0.40***
TECH 2 Step 1		TECH$_1$	0.35	0.49***	0.59***
Step 2		BSEVAL$_2$	0.38	0.14*	0.35***
CONTROLS (N=594)					
FREQ 2 Step 1		FREQ$_1$	0.46	0.57***	0.68***
Step 2		BSEVAL$_2$	0.51	0.26***	0.47***
TECH 2 Step 1		TECH$_1$	0.41	0.50***	0.64***
Step 2		BSEVAL$_2$	0.46	0.25***	0.45***
Step 3		PVC$_2$	0.46	0.12**	0.30***

Note: The subscripts 1 and 2 indicate the times at which the measures are taken.

*p $<$ 0.05   **p $<$ 0.01   ***p $<$ 0.001

DISCUSSION

Taken together, our findings lead to perhaps three main questions, and the first is whether the Health Belief Model is supported. The data confirm that beliefs do predict behaviour, for both perceived benefits/barriers and perceived susceptibility made significant contributions to the belief-behaviour equations and the relationships were generally highly reliable statistically. To that extent the model was supported. However, the evidence also suggests that the relationship between behaviour and the dimensions of belief which the model stresses was neither strong nor linear.

There were two pieces of evidence in particular. First, only a small proportion of the variance was explained in the analyses, a common-place finding in studies using the Health Belief Model (Langlie, 1977). The figure was never more than 25%, and it was generally much lower. It was also noticeable that the greatest variance was explained in the control group, where the least behaviour change was found. Second, the strongest predictor of all was prior behaviour. Prior behaviour plays no part, apparently, in the Health Belief Model - or, indeed, in rival models such as Fishbein's - but from now on, we suggest, it should.

The second issue to discuss is how to improve upon the Health Belief Model. The modest relationship between beliefs and behaviour suggests at least two directions for future research. First, it might be worthwhile to incorporate other belief dimensions. In addition to specific beliefs, more general beliefs might be introduced, such as the value placed on health (where health is often only one of many competing values), the way health is defined, beliefs about the extent to which the individual feels responsible for her health and in control of it, and beliefs about the value of disease prevention and health promotion.

Alternatively, it may be even more useful to focus on the dimensions of belief included in Fishbein's Theory of Reasoned Action. According to this model, as we have seen, behaviour which is under conscious control is predicted by our "private" beliefs about the consequences of performing the behaviour and our "normative" beliefs about the behaviour, which are the perceptions we have of how people who are salient for us believe we should behave. Private beliefs about the consequences of performing the behaviour are exactly what BSEVAL measures - and it is important to note that BSEVAL was consistently a better predictor than PVC. But, and this is the crucial point, normative beliefs play no part in the Health Belief Model, even though it is known that they may sometimes be more important than private beliefs (Ajzen & Fishbein, 1980). Fishbein's model, in other words, already includes the most powerful predictor from the Health Belief Model - the perceived value of the behaviour - and we still have normative beliefs to add to the equation. The Theory of Reasoned Action, we suggest, will be well worth pursuing.

A further direction for research might be to move away from beliefs and to concentrate instead on the structural factors which modify beliefs, and the circumstantial factors which enable or constrain intended or preferred courses of action. In a recent analysis, for example, marked social class differences emerged in a variety of health behaviours among middle-aged women (Calnan, 1985, Calnan & Rutter, 1986b), and the differences remained even when a range of other measures, including beliefs, had been taken into account. What matters now is to find out the mechanisms by which social class - and structural factors in general - have their effects. Do they shape beliefs from the outset, or do they merely influence the ways in which beliefs are translated into intentions and behaviour?

The third and final issue raised by our findings is the practical implications for people who plan programmes for the early detection of breast cancer - and for health education in general. The evidence from our study shows tht even a single class on self-examination is valuable, particularly for improving technique, though further evidence is needed on how long the effects last and what, if anything, is needed to maintain the improvement. The results also indicate that health education might be more effective in encouraging women to practise self-examination if it focused on changing beliefs about the value of the behaviour rather than beliefs about susceptibility to breast cancer. The latter is the more important for the decision to attend the class in the first place - and it is gaining that attendance which probably matters more than anything else - but BSEVAL then takes over as the underpinning for BSE itself. The first stage in any campaign must therefore be to find out the targets' salient beliefs - and then to persuade them to take notice of the campaign, to attend the classes which are offered, and to carry out and maintain the behaviour which is recommended. If those beliefs are not discovered, and they are not attacked, the campaign will fail.

REFERENCES

Ajzen, I. & Fishbein, M. (1980). Understanding Attitudes and Predicting Social Behavior. Prentice-Hall, Englewood Cliffs, New Jersey.

Becker, M.H. (Ed) (1974). The Health Belief Model and Personal Health Behaviour. Slack: New Jersey.

Becker, M.H., Haefner, P.D., Kasl, S.V., Kirscht, J.P., Maiman, L.A. & Rosenstock, I.M. (1977).

Do Health Beliefs Predict Health Behaviour?

Selected psycho-social models and correlates of individual health-related behaviors.
Medical Care, 15, Supplement, 27-46.

Bentler, P.M. & Speckart, G. (1979). Models of attitude-behavior relations.
Psychological Review, 86, 452-464.

Calnan, M.W. (1985). Patterns in preventive behaviour: a study of women in middle age.
Social Science & Medicine, 20, 263-268.

Calnan, M.W. & Rutter, D.R. (1986a). Do health beliefs predict health behaviour? An analysis of breast self-examination.
Social Science and Medicine, 22, 673-678.

Calnan, M.W. & Rutter D.R. (1986b). Preventive health practices and their relationship with socio-demographic characteristics.
Health Education Research, 1, 247-253.

Fishbein, M. & Ajzen, I. (1975). *Belief, Attitude, Intention and Behavior.*
Addison-Wesley, Reading, Mass.

Fredericks, A.J. & Dassett, D.L. (1983). Attitude-behaviour relations: a comparison of the Fishbein-Ajzen and the Bentler-Speckart models.
Journal of Personality and Social Psychology, 45, 501-512.

Janz, N.K. & Becker, M.H. (1984). The health belief model: a decade later.
Health Education Quarterly, 11, 1-47.

Langlie, J.K. (1977). Social networks, health beliefs and preventive health behavior.
Journal of Health and Social Behavior, 18, 244-260.

Stillman, M.J. (1977). Women's health beliefs about breast cancer and self-examination.
Nursing Research, 26, 121-127.

UK Trial of the Early Detection of Breast Cancer Group (1981). Trial of early detection of breast cancer: a description of method.
British Journal of Cancer, 44, 618-627.

Chapter Six

LOCUS OF CONTROL, QUALITY OF LIFE AND TREATMENT
STRESS AMONG RENAL DIALYSIS PATIENTS: INTER-
RELATIONSHIPS AND IMPLICATIONS FOR CLINICAL CARE

J. Kincey, V. Hillier, R. Gokal, J. Stout, J. Auer,
G. Simon, D. Oliver and H. Yu

INTRODUCTION

This paper examines the relationship between
several psychosocial variables and the processes and
outcomes involved in the management of patients in
renal failure.   There is considerable recognition
now that the onset of renal failure and its
treatment are stressful phenomena (Kaplan de Nour,
1983;   Nichols and Springford, 1984;   Hardiker et
al, 1986).   The psychosocial aims of renal care can
therefore perhaps be summarised as the attempts to
help patients cope with these stresses and to
maximise the quality of life for them.   It is also
equally important to maximise the likelihood of
informed compliance with the requirements of therapy
in order to achieve the first two aims.

Patients in end-stage renal failure lose the
function of their own kidneys.   This, if they are to
survive, has to be replaced.   The current available
therapies are dialysis and transplantation.   Some
patients may undergo dialysis while awaiting a
suitable matching transplant.   Others may not be
medically suited for transplantation and for them
dialysis is the only option.   There are two major
types of renal dialysis.   Haemodialysis (HD)
necessitates the use of an "artificial kidney
machine" to which the patient is physically attached
in either the hospital or home setting, usually for
three 4-6 hour sessions in a week.   Strict dietary
and fluid restrictions are necessary to control
blood biochemistry between dialyses.   Considerable
amounts of new learning and comprehension of the
processes involved are required for home based
dialysis.   The more recent Continuous Ambulatory
Peritoneal Dialysis (CAPD) presents a seemingly
different physical and psychologial set of

42

experiences for the patient. Fluid is drained into the peritoneum via a catheter from an attached bag which is worn under the patient's clothing. Waste products pass into the fluid which is subsequently drained into the same bag 4-6 hours later. The old bag is then disconnected and a new bag drained in. This procedure is undertaken 3-4 times daily. No external machine is required. This exchange procedure is a cognitively simpler task for the patient than is haemodialysis. Hygiene is essential to reduce the risk of peritonitis but there are less stringent dietary and fluid restrictions.

A number of psychosocial variables have been identified as relevant to coping with the above processes. The present study examined several of these in relation to each other and a number of clinical parameters, particularly the existence of physical or psychosocial "risk factors" among patients.

METHOD

A sample of 159 adult renal dialysis patients, all on treatment for at least six months, were studied using a structured self-report interview and questionnaire approach. Patients came from two renal units in England. Mean age was 50 years (range 18-73 years). Fifty-five were aged over 60 and 104 were aged under 60 years; 94 were male and 65 female; with 81 CAPD and 78 HD patients.

Measures on which data are reported in this paper were as follows:-

1. The Multi-Dimensional Health Locus of Control Scale (MHLC) devised by Wallston et al (1978).
2. A renal care quality of life semantic differential adapted from Johnson et al (1982).
3. The Life Satisfaction Self-Anchoring Ladder Scale of Cantril (1965).
4. A scale to assess perceived renal treatment stresses adapted from Conley et al (1981).

RESULTS

Mean scores for the three dimensions of the MHLC for the current sample were compared with the composite data from Wallston and Wallston (1981) for varied samples of healthy adults or patients. These data are presented in Table 1a.

Table 1a: Comparison of MHLC mean scores with those from other populations (Wallston and Wallston, 1981)

Combined Samples	N	Internal	Chance	Powerful Others
Chronic patients	609	25.78	17.64	22.54
College students	749	26.68	16.72	17.87
Healthy adults	1287	25.55	16.21	19.16
Persons engaged in preventative health behaviours	720	27.38	15.52	18.44
Current study	159	25.43	20.47	26.88

From Table 1a it can be seen that the mean Internal score was very similar to that of the various Wallston samples. The mean Chance score for the sample was higher than all of the Wallston samples, including the "chronic patients". Most notably the Powerful Others score was considerably higher than those of each of the Wallston groups. In the absence of reported standard deviations for the Wallstons' data formal comparisons of statistical significance could not be undertaken but the above does suggest that, particularly for the Powerful Others dimension, the renal patients scored significantly differently from other clinical populations.

The three MHLC dimensions were examined in relation to a number of clinical variables. Results were interestingly predominantly negative. None of the MHLC dimensions were significantly related to type of treatment (HD versus CAPD), or to length of time on treatment, to Treatment Unit in which care was provided or to presence or absence of "risk factors" such as medical risks, e.g. diabetes, cardiovascular disease, or social risks. The only significant relationship with clinical variables was that the over 60 group showed higher scores on the Powerful Others dimension than patients under 60.

The inter-relationships between the various psychosocial parameters were, however, statistically and theoretically significant in several ways. These data are presented in summary in Table 1b.

Table 1b: Relationships between life satisfaction, treatment stress, renal semantic differential and MHLC dimensions (Spearman)

	Life Satisfaction	Renal Semantic Differential	Treatment Stress	MHLC Internal	MHLC Chance	MHLC Powerful Others
Life Satisfaction	–	.660**	-.451**	.201*	-.072	.194*
Renal Semantic Differential			-.517**	.178*	-.105	.049
Treatment Stress			–	-.143	.119	-.078

* p<0.05
** p<0.01

From Table 1b it can be seen that level of Life Satisfaction correlated positively with high Internal and with high Powerful Others scores on the MHLC. Positive quality of life as assessed by the Renal SD was significantly related to high Internal scores but, surprisingly, high Treatment Stress was not significantly related to any of the MHLC dimensions. The Chance dimension was unrelated to any of these three other variables. Not surprisingly the Life Satisfaction and Renal SD correlated significantly and positively (.660). The extent of perceived Treatment Stress correlated significantly negatively with both Life Satisfaction (-.451) and the Renal SD (-.517).

The strategy adopted in the study was to use the three previously established MHLC dimensions in the above analyses. As a check on the relevance of this factor structure in the renal dialysis patient sample the three dimensions were inter-correlated and a factor analysis from the raw data of the MHLC undertaken. The Internal dimension did not correlate significantly with Chance (-.019) but showed a small significant positive correlation with Powerful Others (.209). The Chance and Powerful Others dimensions intercorrelated positively more significantly (.348). The factor analysis based on an oblique factor structure after rotation with Kaiser normalisation produced three factors accounting for a total of 70.7% of the variance. Factor 1 accounted for 31.2% with its three highest loading items all being Powerful Other items from the original scale. Factor 2 accounted for 25.1% of the variance with the three highest loading items all being Internal. Factor 3 accounted for 14.4% of the variance with highest loadings from three Chance items from the scale. Although statistically rather crude these checks suggest that the multi-dimensional nature of the MHLC is confirmed, at least in general terms, for this sample.

The mean score for the population on the Life Satisfaction Ladder scale was 6.62 (SD = 2.35), a score virtually identical to the Cantril general population USA normative data. The distribution was not completely normal and other specific satisfaction and happiness questions not reported here showed some differences from general population norms. Interestingly and importantly this result suggests that the renal dialysis patients' level of life satisfaction was not overall significantly lower than that of the general polulation. Closer examination of subgroups of the sample reported in Stout et al (1987a) suggests that male patients aged under 60 with risk factors have the lowest life satisfaction but that older dialysis patients do not intrinsically have lower life satisfaction on dialysis than younger patients.

DISCUSSION

In summary the above data seem to confirm the factor structure of the MHLC dimension among this sample. They show that although these dimensions are not related in a simple way to the type of treatment, despite seeming differences in the degree of control perceptions under haemodialysis and CAPD, the MHLC is related in a non-random way to other psychosocial variables. Of particular importance perhaps is the finding that life satisfaction is positively related not only to high Internal control but also to high Powerful Other control scores. Given the importance of adequate treatment self-care behaviours for physical survival as well as psychological well-being, the relationship between Internal control and life satisfaction is understandable. It is unclear whether the more satisfied patients had high Powerful Other scores prior to illness and treatment or whether, as is perhaps more likely, these scores reflect the dependency of patients in this situation and the fact that they value the expert support of the renal care team looking after them such that in a causal way this increases life satisfaction. The absence of a relationship between treatment stress and control dimensions is surprising and might be a function of either the measuring instruments used or the failure to identify the subtleties of treatment stress perception among patients, if such a relationship does really exist.

It seems likely that there are complex relationships in several directions of causality between MHLC, measures of quality of life, compliance behaviours, and mood state variables, an issue also addressed in a different setting by Wright (1985). These latter two classes of data were not examined in the present study. It is also important to remember that allocation to treatment type was non-random and the absence of differences between the treatment types therefore must be interpreted with caution. Treatment decisions and physical health outcome could both be causes and effects of locus of control characteristics of patients. Finally, from other data obtained by the team undertaking this research, it seems likely that the patients' perceptions of sexual and marital satisfaction (Stout et al, 1987) and of dependency (Simon et al, 1984) are also related in quite complex ways to the various social and medical aspects of renal care.

It is suggested, therefore, that closer examination of the locus of control dimension is warranted, both at the level of individual patient treatment decisions and in terms of group comparisons as in the present study.

Acknowledgements

We would like to thank Central Manchester Health Authority Research Grants Committee and the Renal Unit, Churchill Hospital, Oxford, for their financial support and Ms. M. Klose, Department of Clinical Psychology CMHA, for typing the manuscript.

REFERENCES

Cantril, A.H. (1965). The Pattern of Human Concerns. Rutgers University Press: New Jersey.

Conley, J.A., Burton, H.J., Kaplan De-Nour, A. & Wells, G.A. (1981). Support systems for patients and spouses on home dialysis. International Journal of Family Psychiatry, 2, 45-55.

Hardiker, P., Pedley, J., Littlewood, J. & Olley, D. (1986). Coping with chronic renal failure. British Journal of Social Work, 16, 203-222.

Johnson, J.P., McCauley, C.R. & Copley, J.B. (1982). The quality of life of haemodialysis and transplant patients. Kidney International, 22, 286-291.

Kaplan de Nour, A. (1983). An overview of psychological problems in haemodialysis patients. In Levey, N. (Ed) Psychophrenology Vol 2. Plenum Press: New York.

Nichols, K. & Springford, V. (1984). The psychosocial stresses associated with survival by dialysis. Behaviour Research and Therapy, 22, No. 5, 563-574.

Simon, G., Kincey, J., Stout, J.P., Gokal, R. & Mallick, N.P. (1984). Quality of life for a group of high risk male continuous ambulatory peritoneal dialysis patients dependent upon a helper for carrying out their treatment. Proc.

of European Dialysis and Transplant Nurses Association, 13, 100-103.

Stout, J.P., Auer, J., Kincey, J., Simon, J., Hillier, V.F., Oliver, D. & Gokal, R. (1987a in press). Sexual and marital relationships and dialysis - the patient's viewpoint. Peritoneal Dialysis Bulletin.

Stout, J.P. Gokal, R., Hillier, V.F., Kincey, J., Oliver, D. & Simon, L.G. (1987b in press). The quality of life of high risk and elderly dialysis patients. Dialysis & Transplantation.

Wallston, K.A. & Wallston, B.S. (1981). Health Locus of Control Scales. In Lefcourt, H.M. (Ed) Research with the Locus of Control Construct. Vol. 1, Assessment Methods. Academic Press: New York.

Wallston, K.A., Wallston, B.S. & Devellis, R. (1978). Development of the Multidimensional Health Locus of Control (MHLC) Scales. Health Education Monographs, Vol. 6, 2, 160-171.

Wright, S.J. (1985). Multidimensional health locus of control and negative life events: their relationships with sociodemographic variables and health status measures and their effects on health self-ratings. Submitted to International Journal of Health Psychology.

Chapter Seven

CHANGING HEALTH BEHAVIOUR OUTCOMES IN ASTHMATIC
PATIENTS: A PILOT INTERVENTION STUDY

S. Maes and M. Schlosser

INTRODUCTION

Together, asthma, chronic bronchitis and lung-
emphysema constitute a group of lung diseases called
Chronic Obstructive Pulmonary Diseases or COPD.
Asthma is less destructive to the lung tissue than
both the other diseases, for, between attacks, the
asthmatic's respiration is normal and the patient
has a normal life expectancy. Bronchial hyper-
reactivity and immunological over-sensitivity play
an important role in the pathogenesis of asthma, and
attacks can be variably elicited by exogenous and
psychological factors. In addition to the fact that
COPD is still responsible for a considerable part of
the mortality in western countries, a notable degree
of morbidity exists, as these diseases are
essentially incurable. According to the Dutch
Asthma Fund, twenty per cent of the total absence
from work and thirteen per cent of the total
invalidity can be ascribed to COPD.
The true cause of asthma is unknown. On the
one hand we find authors who claim that asthma is
only an allergy; and on the other are those who
believe that psychological disturbances are at the
base of the illness. What is established, however,
is that the way patients deal with their chronic
illness influences both the course of the illness
and the medical outcome. It is this which provides
the focus for the present paper.
In a first study we investigated the relationship between coping with asthma and health behaviour
outcomes. In order to do this, we developed a
research model for coping with asthma on the basis
of the stress appraisal theory of Lazarus and his
colleagues (Lazarus & Folkman, 1984). The central
idea of the model is that coping fulfils a mediating

role in the relationship between anxiety and health behaviour outcomes, and that both disease characteristics and cognitions stored in long-term memory play a crucial role in the experience of emotions, in coping, and in health behaviour outcomes in asthmatic patients (Maes & Schlosser, 1987a). The main research question derived from the model was "What is the influence of objective aspects of asthma (such as number of attacks and lung function), cognitive attitudes (such as optimism, locus of control and shame), anxiety and coping on: (a) well-being, (b) use of medical resources (such as the amount of medication taken daily and the number of hospital admissions during the last year), and (c) absence from work?" The results showed that coping variables such as reacting emotionally during attacks, focusing on asthma in everyday life, and maintaining a restrictive life-style explained considerable parts of the variance in the well-being of asthmatic patients, in the number of hospital admissions, and in the number of days absent from work because of asthma (Maes & Schlosser, 1987a). These findings were considered a solid starting-point for an intervention study, which aimed at altering coping behaviour in asthmatic patients in order to influence emotional distress and use of medical resources. The nature of the intervention and a pilot study to test it are described below.

METHOD

In order to change cognitions and coping in asthmatic patients, we chose Ellis's Rational Emotive Therapy as the basis for our intervention (Ellis, 1962; Ellis & Grieger, 1977). The programme itself consisted of eight two- to three-hour group sessions, in which ten asthmatic patients and their partners took part. During the first session, Ellis's scheme was introduced to the patients by a health psychologist. The following sessions were devoted to a specific topic related to asthma. The topics were selected on the basis of prior need assessment, and concerned medical issues, physiotherapy and breathing exercises, use and consequences of medication, working situation and social security, sanitation, emotional distress, and professional and leisure activities. With the exception of the initial meeting, the standard course for each session was that, first, a health professional (depending on the topic, a lung specialist, physiotherapist, pharmacist, social worker, nurse or health psychologist) gave relevant information about the topic. The format was less a lecture than answers to questions which had emerged from the prior need assessment. Next, patients and their partners divided into three small groups and tried (under the supervision of a health psychologist and with the help of a list of specific questions) to discover irrational beliefs and inadequate coping strategies related to the topic. Finally, using the Ellis scheme, the results of the small group work were discussed in the larger group with a health psychologist. At the end of each meeting, the session was evaluated and homework was given. The effects of the intervention on cognitive attitudes towards asthma, emotional distress (anxiety, anger and depression), and medication consumption were determined by means of a pre-test post-test control group design which is described below.

Nineteen patients (9 females and 10 males) were referred to us by two lung specialists. They had a confirmed medical diagnosis of bronchial asthma and a forced expiratory volume in one second (FEV) of at least 80% of the predicted value either with or without use of a bronchodilator, to exclude patients with emphysema. All patients were characterised by a high consumption of medication in proportion to more objective measurements of severity, but were not in hospital at the time of the study. The patients were matched for sex and age in order to obtain a comparable experimental (n=10) and control group (n=9). The experimental group received our programme in addition to standard medical care, whereas the control group received standard medical care only.

In order to measure the effects of the programme, the following instruments were administered to both groups of subjects before and immediately after the completion of the programme: the Respiratory Illness Opinion Survey of Kinsman et al (1976); the Asthma Coping Questionnaire of Maes et al (1986); the Dutch version of Spielberger's State-Trait Anxiety Inventory (Ploeg et al, 1980); the Dutch version of Spielberger's State-Trait Anger Scale (Ploeg et al, 1982); the Depression Scale of van Rooijen (Rooijen, 1977); and the General Questionnaire for Asthmatic Patients, developed by the present authors (Maes et al, 1986).

RESULTS

Table 1 shows the results of analyses of covariance, using the pre-test scores as covariates. For the medication variables, the number of attacks was used as a second covariate. The table shows that there were significant effects for the coping variable "focusing on asthma in daily life" and for state depression, state and trait anger, and trait anxiety. In addition, there was a significant decrease in the number of cortiscosteroids taken in daily life.

Table 1: Results of analyses of covariance with pre-test scores as covariate on post-test scores in the experimental group compared to the control group.

Variables	EXPERIMENTAL GROUP MEANS pre	post	CONTROL GROUP MEANS pre	post	F value
Optimism	16.10	16.50	17.33	18.56	3.25
Locus of control	13.50	13.40	9.66	10.89	0.70
Shame	11.00	11.00	8.44	10.22	0.39
Minimising seriousness of attack	41.56	39.67	39.13	35.22	2.07
Rational action	22.60	21.70	21.57	20.89	0.35
Reacting emotionally	13.10	13.33	11.63	12.50	0.28
Maintaining a restrictive life-style	18.60	17.50	16.13	17.89	1.72
Focusing on asthma	16.50	15.78	15.13	16.67	3.25*
Hiding asthma	10.10	10.50	11.00	9.22	2.99
State depression	10.00	8.33	7.33	10.33	3.13*
Trait depression	10.80	10.00	7.22	9.56	0.41*
State anger	15.00	14.70	12.78	18.22	3.58*
Trait anger	19.10	17.30	19.22	21.44	6.24*
State anxiety	54.50	52.80	50.89	50.00	0.38
Trait anxiety	47.80	40.50	41.22	52.13	44.52*
Oral corticosteroids	0.9	0.7	0.6	1.3	5.27*
Inhaled corticosteroids	0.9	0.5	0.8	0.8	1.58

* $p < 0.05$

DISCUSSION

The results show that there was no significant effect of our intervention on cognitive attitude variables, perhaps because they are relatively stable personality characteristics, which cannot be changed in eight three-hour sessions. There were also no effects for the way patients coped with attacks. This time the explanation may well be that our programme focused on coping with <u>asthma</u> in everyday life rather than coping with <u>attacks</u>. In addition, it may be difficult to induce changes in the way patients cope with attacks by means of a cognitive intervention, for the anxiety during attacks is so overwhelming that patients can hardly gain rational control over their behaviour. The programme did, however, have a significant reducing effect on "focusing on asthma in everyday life". In other words, when compared to the control group, patients who had received the programme were less preoccupied with their asthma in everyday life afterwards than before. Thus, the programme appears effective in altering one of the variables which may mediate reduction of emotional distress and use of medical resources.

As for emotional distress, the programme seems to be effective in reducing attack-related depression and anger but not attack-related anxiety. The intervention also had a significant effect on the experience of anxiety and anger in everyday life, but not the experience of depression. Although depression is a known form of emotional distress in asthmatic patients, anxiety may be considered a more important variable, since it predicts the use of medical resources (Fix et al., 1981; Creer, 1982, Steptoe, 1984; Maes & Schlosser, 1987b). The reduction of trait anxiety must, therefore, be considered an impressive result, especially since the effect is paralleled by the already mentioned change in coping with asthma in everyday life. Trait anger too was significantly reduced by the programme, perhaps suggesting that anger is another important measure, which the programme taught patients to control.

The intervention also led to a decrease in the number of oral corticosteroids taken in daily life – an important achievement, since the patients referred to us were generally taking large amounts of medication, which were disproportionate to their objective measures of severity. One possible explanation comes from Kinsman et al (1977), who demonstrated in a large group of asthmatic patients that people reporting high panic and fear were likely to be prescribed more intense doses of corticosteroids and to be maintained on steroid treatment for longer than similar patients who reported lower levels of anxiety. As there seems to be a linear relationship between anxiety and the prescription and use of cortiscosteroids, it is most likely that a decrease in anxiety is what brings about changes in the number of corticosteroids taken in daily life.

Finally, there was no significant effect on the number of inhaled corticosteroids during attacks - which was only to be expected since the intervention was not designed to change the way patients coped with attacks. In future interventions, more attention should be paid to attack-related behaviour, and at least part of the programme should deal directly with attack-related coping patterns. In a second post-test one year after the intervention, we shall also be measuring the number of attacks, hospital re-admissions, visits to the physician and days absent from work because of asthma. The post-test will also inform us about the stability of the effects.

In summary, our programme has been found to have impressive effects. Patients who received the intervention were less preoccupied with their asthma in daily life; they experienced less emotional distress, both in attacks and in daily life; and they needed less maintenance medication. There is still, however, a long way to go; the effects must be demonstrated in a larger group of patients; and they must prove to be stable over time.

REFERENCES

Creer, T.L. (1982). Asthma. Journal of Consulting and Clinical Psychology, 50, 912-921.

Ellis, A. (1962). Reason and Emotion in Psychotherapy. Lyle Stuart: New York.

Ellis, A. & Grieger, R. (1977). Handbook of Rational-Emotive Therapy. Springer: New York.

Fix, A.J., Daughton, D. & Kass, J. (1981). Behavioural sciences in pulmonary rehabilitation. In C.J. Golden, S.S. Alcaparras, F.D. Strider & B. Graber (eds) Applied Techniques in Behavioural Medicine. Grune & Stratton: New York.

Kinsman, R.A., Jones, N.F., Matus, I. & Schum, R.A.
(1976). Patients' variables supporting chronic
diseases. Journal of Nervous and Mental
Disease, 163, 159-165.
Kinsman, R.A., Dahlem, N.W., Spector, S. &
Staudenmayer, H. (1977). Observations on
subjective symptomatology, coping behaviour
and medical decisions in asthma.
Psychosomatic Medicine, 39, 102-119.
Lazarus, R.S. & Folkman, S. (1984). Stress Appraisal
and Coping. Springer: New York.
Maes, S. & Schlosser, M. (1987a). The role of
cognition and coping in health behaviour
outcomes of asthmatic patients. Current
Psychological Research and Reviews (in press).
Maes, S. & Schlosser, M. (1987b). The cognitive
management of health behaviour outcomes in
asthmatic patients. In S. Maes,
C.D. Spielberger, P. Defares, & I. Sarason
(eds) Health Psychology: An International
Perspective. Wiley: New York (forthcoming).
Maes, S., Schlosser, M. & Vromans, I. (1986).
Asthma, coping en medische consumptie. In
P. Schreurs & R. Rombouts (eds) Omgaan met
ernstige ziekten. Swets & Zeitlinger: Lisse,
78-115.
Ploeg, H.M. van der, Defares, P.B. & Spielberger,
C.D. (1980). Handleiding bij de Zelf-
Beoorelings Vragenlijst (ZBV). Een
Nederlandstalige bewerking van de Spielberger
State-Trait Anxiety Inventory (STAI).
Swets & Zeitlinger: Lisse.
Ploeg, H.M. van der, Defares, P.B. & Spielberger,
C.D. (1982). Handleiding bij de Zelf-Analyse
Vragenlijst (ZAV). Een Nederlandstalige
bewerking van de Spielberger State-Trait Anger
Scale. Swets & Zeitlinger: Lisse.
Rooijen, L. van (1977). Enige gegevens over de
VROPSOM-lijsten voor de bepaling van depressie
gevoelens. Onderzoeksmemorandum RN-PS 77-01.
Vrije Universiteit Amsterdam: Amsterdam.
Steptoe, A. (1984). Psychological aspects of
bronchial asthma. In S. Rachman (ed)
Contributions to Medical Psychology, Volume 3,
Pergamon Press: Oxford.

Chapter Eight

PSYCHOLOGICAL PROBLEMS AND SUPPORT IN AN ENGLISH
BURNS UNIT

Louise M. Wallace, Jacqueline Lees and
Norman R. Bernstein

INTRODUCTION

Advances in medical care since the Second World
War have enabled previously unsaveable patients with
serious burns to be saved, but there has been
relatively little study of the quality of life for
these survivors, nor developments in professional
services geared to improving the psychosocial
outcomes for these survivors.

The present study was initiated in
collaboration with Professor Norman Bernstein whose
work at the Shriner's Burns Institute of Boston has
stimulated interest in the immediate and long term
psychological impact of burns. This study
investigates the psychological disturbance of
patients in an English burns unit as the first step
in planning a comprehensive professional and self-
help support service.

DESIGN

As the study was conducted by a psychology
student Jackie Lees, on placement with the Principal
Clinical Psychologist (Physical Health), Louise
Wallace, standard screening questionnaires were
employed to measure mood state, adjustment to
illness and self esteem. The questionnaires
selected were appropriate to the age range of
patients from a few months to the very elderly.
The Mood and Adjustment scales were: Hospital
Anxiety and Depression Scale (Zigmond and Snaith,
1983); Psychosocial Adjustment to Illness Scale
(Derogatis and Lopez, 1983) and the Burn Specific
Health Scale (Blades et al, 1982), for adults aged
16 years or over. Parents were interviewed for
children aged 3½-16 years using the Child Behaviour

Checklist (Achenbach and Edelbrock, 1983) and the Behaviour Checklist of Richman and Graham (1971) for toddlers aged 2½-3½ years. Self-esteem measures were completed by the patient. These were the scales developed by Rosenberg (1965) for adults, Piers (1972) for those aged 8-16 years and an adapted version of the Coopersmith Self-Esteem Inventory (Coopersmith, 1967).

It must be recognised that these methods may only produce minimum estimates of disturbance since more skilled questioning is often needed to elicit problems such as alcoholism.

PROCEDURE

Every effort was made to obtain a complete sample of patients discharged from the unit within a six week period. However, patients with little English (3) or major communication problems such as senile dementia (2) were excluded, although where possible information was obtained from relatives. Patients were seen in the clinic or at home, but a significant number (7) refused to be inter- viewed, and a small proportion (6) were untraceable, leaving 85 out of 99 patients who were interviewed at least once, 45 in the first sample and 40 in the two year follow-up sample.

RESULTS

It was expected that the sample would reflect the high degree of psychosocial problems typical of major burns injury. Table 1 shows the levels of psychological disturbance of patients in comparison to the norms available for the measure. As the sample contained patients across the whole age range, inevitably there are relatively small numbers represented in some of the age groups. For the adult patients at discharge from hospital, 31% showed clinically significant levels of anxiety, and 12.5% showed clinically significant levels of depression. The rates of depression were similar to those of a mixed medical sample, but the rates of anxiety were twice as great (Zigmond and Snaith, 1983). There was evidence of a slight decrease by six months follow-up, but the sample at two years showed no overall reduction in symptomatology. It is also interesting to note that 47% of patients at six months were experiencing significant problems of psychosocial adjustment on the Burns Specific Health Scale, that is, they were showing 22% or above

Table 1: No. of burn patients with "abnormal adjustment" in comparison to norms for the measure

	Time of Assessment					
	Discharge		6 Months		2 Years	
Age/Measure	Total N	% of age sample	Total N	% of age sample	Total N	% of age sample
ADULT						
Mood:						
Anxiety	5/16	31.25	3/16	18.7	4/15	26.6
Depression	2/16	12.5	3/16	18.7	3/15	20.0
Psychosocial Adjustment:						
B.S.H.S.	–	–	8/17	47.1	5/15	33.0
P.A.I.S.	–	–	6/15	40.0	5/14	35.7
Self-Esteem:						
Rosenberg	2/19	10.5	4/16	25.0	2/15	13.3
ADOLESCENTS						
Behavioural Adjustment: Achenbach* C.B.C.L.						
1. Behaviour	0/3	0	1/8	12.5	2/12	16.7
2. Social Competence	2/3	66.7	5/8	62.5	3/12	25.0
Self-Esteem:						
Coopersmith	0/1	0	0/2	0	2/6	33.0
CHILDREN 3½+yrs Behavioural Adjustment: Achenbach* C.B.C.L.						
Self-Esteem:						
Coopersmith	1/1	100	1/2	50.0	3/6	50.0
CHILDREN 2½-3½ yrs Behavioural Adjustment: Richman						
Graham B.C.L.	2/2	100	0/1	0	9/12	75.0

*Data combined for adolescents and children

levels of disability. Also in the two year sample, 33.3% of patients were showing above the 38% mean level of the normative sample. Using the Psychological Adjustment to Illness Scale, which is standardised on healthy people, psychiatric and burn patients, the estimates of "psychiatric caseness" were 40% at 6 months and 35.7% at 2 years. The small samples of child and adolescent patients made interpretation difficult, but there was evidence that, while few patients showed behavioural problems at discharge, 1 out of 8 and 2 out of 12 patients at six months and two years were showing behavioural problems typical of a clinical population. Approximately two thirds of patients at discharge and six months, and a quarter of patients at two years were showing problems of social competence. Children less than 2½ years were not assessed for behavioural disturbance. Of the eligible children assessed at two years after injury, 75% were showing problems of significant behavioural disturbance.

The responses to specific questions asked of parents of children at six months and at two years revealed that they believed that all 24 children were significantly more withdrawn as a result of their burn injury at six months but only 1 out of 26 (4%) of the sample at two years believed their child was significantly withdrawn. Problems of sleep, toileting, aggression, overactivity, eating and bed-wetting were reported by not less than two and not more than seven out of 24 parents at six months and between one and five out of 26 at two years. Parents reported they had received no special professional help for these problems at either time period.

T-test comparisons were made between scores at six months and two years on all measures with sufficient data, and there were no significant differences. This may indicate pre-existing differences between the two samples, or alternatively it may disprove the commonsense hypothesis that psychological problems diminish once the major medical treatment has been completed.

CONCLUSIONS

As discussed, the methods are only likely to produce minimum estimates of psychological disturbance. The psychosocial adjustment results confirm that clinically significant levels of mood disturbance are manifest in between 20% and 40% of adults and, although a number of the children were showing levels of behavioural disturbance equivalent to those of clinic populations, none of the patients were receiving professional help for their problems. Although the samples at discharge and six months and the sample at two years were different, there was no evidence that the majority of problems diminish by two years post injury. There is therefore evidence of a continuing need for psychosocial care for extended periods after a major burn injury for at least 20%-40% of patients. Further analyses are required to delineate those patients most at risk for adverse effects; likely factors include specific age groups, the visibility of injury and the availability of familial support.

Evidence from a survey of U.K. burn units to be reported shows that the problems of this particular unit are by no means unique, and that the psychosocial problems of burn injured patients are typically neglected. There are, however, models of some forms of both professional and self-help initiated supports which may go some way to ameliorate the psychological problems experienced by burn injured patients and their families which persist well beyond the time that the physical aspect of the burn injuries are healed, reconstructed and rehabilitated. Future studies will compare the samples with American samples studied by Professor Bernstein. In particular, in depth studies will be made of survivors who have completed all physical treatment in order to determine how well people cope with the residual permanent physical disability and disfigurement, and how they can best be helped.

REFERENCES

Achenbach, T.M. and Edelbrock, C. (1983). Manual for the Child Behaviour Checklist and Revised Child Behaviour Profile. University of Vermont: Burlington.

Blades, B., Mellis, N. & Munster, A.M. (1982). A Burn Specific Health Scale. The Journal of Trauma, 22, 10, 872-875.

Coopersmith, S. (1967). The Antecedents of Self-Esteem. W.H. Freeman and Company: San Francisco.

Derogatis, L.R. and Lopez, M.C. (1983). PAIS and PAIS SR: Administration, Scoring and Procedure Manual - 1. John Hopkins University: Baltimore.

Piers, E.V. (1972). Parents' prediction of
    children's self concepts. Journal of
    Consulting and Clinical Psychology,
    38, 3, 428-433.
Richman, N. & Graham, P.J. (1971). A behavioural
    screening questionnaire for use with 3 year
    old children: preliminary findings.
    Journal of Child Psychology and Psychiatry,
    12, 5-33.
Rosenberg, M. (1965). Society and the Adolescent
    Self-Image.
    Princeton University Press: Princeton.
Zigmond, A.S. & Snaith, R.P. (1983). The Hospital
    Anxiety and Depression Scale.
    Acta Psychiatrica Scandinavica, 67, 361-370.

Chapter Nine

IN VITRO FERTILISATION: A PSYCHOSOCIAL AND
DEVELOPMENTAL STUDY

Maria Barreda-Hanson, David Mushin and John Spensley

INTRODUCTION

In vitro fertilisation (IVF), management of
frozen embryos and embryo transfer have progressed
from science fiction to scientific medical reality,
outstripping legal and moral frameworks. New
directions have arisen for infertile couples
bringing with them various physical and
psychological questions regarding the development of
children conceived by these means.

There have also been concerns regarding ethical
and moral issues. Yet there has been no scientific
follow-up of a significant group of such children.
This study is particularly concerned with the
following factors:
Biological issues querying increased congenital
abnormalities including mental retardation.
Parent issues exploring positive and negative
factors such as parental reasons to have children,
unsuccessful resolution of marital problems or
psychological conflicts including infertility that
may resurface at certain stressful periods and
influence the couple's relationship and/or
parenting capacity. These issues can be further
confounded if donor sperm or ova are used and if
this is kept a secret.
Issues of the child, looking at the possibility of
these children being seen as special in many ways
other than those related to their manner of conception and made vulnerable to unreal concerns or
expectations, affecting the parent/ child relationship and later the child's interactions with peers
and teachers. Failed parental expectations and the
child's internalizations of parental issues can
greatly affect the child's self-esteem and self-
control.

Family Issues are concerned with possible stressful effects that fertility, the desire to have children and the intrusive nature of the infertility management, particularly the IVF management, may place on the marital and sexual relationships of the couples as well as disrupting their socio-familial life. If unresolved these conflicts may be displaced on to the children and inhibit parent/child communication regarding IVF origins. These issues can be enhanced by the exploitation, demands and expectations as a result of publicity.

More general issues are concerned with the importance of a better understanding by medical practitioners of the couples, the consequences of intervention and procedures, in order that adequate counselling and intervention can be provided from the beginning of the programme. It is important to determine whether there is a significant risk of physical pathology or psycho-pathology pertinent to children and their families.

With these concerns in mind, we felt it important that we see these families. As an initial step we studied the first group of children to be conceived through the Monash University IVF Programme. While recognising the need for a more extensive study, this group was clinically evaluated in order to determine whether or not they presented clinical concerns which might call into question the clinical justification for IVF conception.

METHOD

The first 52 children born from the Monash IVF Programme received paediatric evaluation at 6 weeks and after 10 months of age. One child died at $4\frac{1}{2}$ months and one family with twins refused follow-up. Thirty-three of these children were seen by a psychologist and a child psychiatrist and had psychosocial and developmental assessments between 1 and 3 years of age - the majority between 12 and 20 months. These children were basically selected in order of presentation to the paediatrician, with any bias going towards those about whom he was concerned. Because of various logistic reasons some of the 49 children were not seen for psychosocial evaluations. A review of these cases by the paediatrician revealed no current concerns about developmental problems at the 12 month evaluation and he did not consider any of them to be at risk for such problems (see Spensley et al, 1986, for information on paediatric assessments). The psychosocial evaluation consisted of:

A parent interview regarding their child, themselves, their marriage and their experience of the
IVF Programme. This included parental perceptions
of problem issues concerning the child, parental
assessment of their child's developmental status,
history of current and past psychiatric problems and
contacts with psychiatric facilities (see Mushin et
al, 1985 and 1986, for more details).
Administration of the Bayley Scales of Infant
Development to the children. This instrument was
chosen as it is well researched and
standardised and commonly used in Australia for
developmental evaluation of children in the age
range seen. In one child the McCarthy Scales of
Development were administered because the Bayley
only goes up to 30 months of age.
Observations of family functioning and interactions
in the interview setting. Evaluators also noted
congruency between their observations and parental
perceptions.

Population Studied

Children - Nineteen boys and fourteen girls,
including six sets of twins, with a mean age of 17
months were included in the study.
Parents - The age of the parents was, as expected,
above average. The mean age of mothers was 33 and
of fathers 36. The cause of infertility was
idiopathic in 26%; and 18% were due to factors in
the male partners, this being the percentage of
children conceived with donor sperm. The remainder
of cases had medically diagnosed factors in the
female partner. Sixty percent conceived at the
first IVF cycle and 8% required four or five
attempts. All couples were married.
Method of delivery - Nine births were normal vaginal
delivery, nine were forceps, one was breech, one was
vacuum and thirteen were caesarian sections.

RESULTS

Five children were considered by their parents
to have significant problems with behaviour. In all
of these families, problems could be related to
parent/child interactional difficulties where
parents had adaptational problems. No significant
marital problems were reported. Two mothers
described significant depression following child

65

birth but depression had spontaneously resolved by the time they were seen. There were no cases of child neglect or abuse and none of severe disturbance in the child's ability to relate to others.

Twelve of the 33 couples seen for psychosocial evaluations reported issues concerning the IVF programme. Five had concerns regarding staff communication and support and four had concerns over collection of sperm. Other issues, such as difficulty with travel, were reported. Three couples felt that IVF had altered their perception of the child. Despite the concerns, none of the couples reported strong negative feelings towards the programme. It will be important to follow up couples who were unsuccessful in conceiving in order to ascertain their perception of the programme.

Factors relating to the birth

There was a high rate of caesarian section (37%). This is greater than twice the expected rate. In addition, the incidence of pre-term children was approximately four times the expected rate and that of very low birthweight children, below 1500 gm, was greater than ten times that expected in the population at large. The incidence of twin births was twenty times that found in the general population. These factors, particularly those relating to prematurity, seem to be the main ones influencing IVF children at this early stage in their development.

Severe Physical and Psychosocial Problems

If both physical and psychosocial findings are considered together, four families were noted to have issues of significant clinical magnitude. In three of these families the children had a significant physical problem. One had severe congenital heart disease requiring surgical correction and periods of hospitalisation. Two children had significant neurological problems acquired in the perinatal period. These last two children were in the very low birthweight group. In the fourth family, there were significant mother/child interactional problems, with the mother having difficulties in adapting to her parenting role and interfering with the child's attempts to explore the environment. These four children showed significant developmental delays on the Bayley Scales.

Less Severe Clinical Conditions

Apart from the three children with physical problems, ten were reported to have physical features of a less severe nature. These included colic (30%) and asthma (12%). A number of mild conditions, such as eating and sleeping problems, occurred in less than 10% of the children seen. Two of the families reported some mild problems of adaptation to parenthood. These findings are in line with the occurrence of such conditions in the general population (Thomas, 1981; Williams and Phelan, 1975). Forty eight percent of the children had neonatal jaundice. If the pre-term group is discounted, 23% are left in this group, a percentage comparable with figures for the general population of new born children (Maisels, 1982). On follow-up one child was found to have an asymptomatic congenital defect. This was not considered to be of clinical concern.

Psychosocial Development

The Bayley Scales of Infant Development were administered to 32 of the 33 children seen for psychosocial assessment. The means were well within the expected normal range. Only one child had significantly low Mental Development Index (MDI) and and three other children had low Physical Development Indices (PDI). The child with the very low MDI also had a very low PDI. These four children were the ones referred to in the section on severe conditions. Paediatric follow-up of these children some months later showed that the child with congenital heart disease was making good progress and the child with the interactional problems had significantly improved. As can be seen, most developmental delays were in the physical-motor areas. Given the low birthweight, the high number of twins, and some bias towards seeing children over whom the paediatrician had expressed some concern, the range of findings do not indicate reasons for concern. Most of the children, 31 out of 32, showed social development within the accepted range. The child given the McCarthy Scales of Intelligence also scored well within the expected range in both intellectual and social skills.

DISCUSSION

While the study did not have a control group it is considered that the above findings are consistent with what might be expected of a group of 33 children and their parents. Studies such as that of MacFarlane and co-authors (1971) point to figures of 33% for sleep and feed disorders and 58% and 44% for "bad temper attacks" in boys and girls respectively.

Colic is reported in about one third of the children. Thus there is no data at present to indicate an increased incidence of minor behavioural problems in the children at this stage in their development. This is supported by positive results in the assessment of social skills on the Bayley. It is thus considered that, given a sample bias towards problem families and high incidence of premature birth and twins the findings do not support the hypothesis postulating an increase in physical and psychosocial problems in children born by IVF conception. It is recognised, however, that longitudinal controlled studies will be necessary to address many of the issues raised. Issues of identity and sexuality will not be evident until the children are older, nor will the nature of their relations with teachers and peers.

Future Issues

The present study employed a small sample population without a control group and was undertaken at an early stage of development. In order to understand fully the effects of IVF on children and families, it will be necessary to undertake a longitudinal study with a variety of relevant control groups. The population needs to be studied at various stages of development. The focus should be at two levels - the evaluation of significant pathology and the study of particular differences in developmental, interactive and family parameters. Focus should be placed on the children, their needs and their rights. Such investigations may also add to the understanding of infertility and its significance, by evaluating how infertile couples manage as parents and how these children develop. From a management point of view, such findings may indicate whether or not it is important for these couples to have resolved conflicts about their infertility prior to having children. Thus the question of screening prospective parents should be reviewed.

Such investigations would also clarify whether or not these families have greater difficulties in resolving problem issues should they occur, and if so, whether undue focus on IVF issues serves to inhibit problem resolution. Another important area is that of the child's perception of IVF conception, i.e. what it means to the child to be told of such origins. As the children develop, social, peer and sexual issues (including their own fertility or

infertility) will become more prominent, as will the
effects on the family of community anxieties.

REFERENCES

Macfarlane, J.W., Allen, L. & Honzik, M.P. (1971).
A developmental study of the behaviour
problems of normal children between 21 months
and 14 years. In M.C. Jones, N. Bayley,
J.W. McFarlane & M.P. Honzik (Eds) The
Course of Human Development. Zerox College
Publications: Waltham, Mass.
Maisels, M.J. (1982) Jaundice in the newborn.
Paediatrics in Review, 3, 305-319.
Mushin, D.N., Barreda-Hanson, M. & Spensley, J.,
(1986) In vitro fertilization children: early
psychosocial development. Journal of In-Vitro
Fertilization and Embryo Transfer (in press).
Mushin, D.N., Spensley, J. & Barreda-Hanson, M.
(1985). Children of in vitro fertilization.
Clinics in Obstetrics and Gynaecology, 12,
December.
Spensley, John C., Mushin, D. & Barreda-Hanson,
Maria (1986). The children of IVF pregnancies:
a cohort study. The Australian Paediatric
Journal, 22, 285-289.
Thomas, D.B. (1981). Aetiological association in
infantile colic - an hypothesis. The
Australian Paediatric Journal, 17, 292-295
Williams, H.E. & Phelan,P.D. (1975). Respiratory
Illness in Children. Blackwell Scientific
Publications, Melbourne: Australia.

Chapter Ten

SPONTANEOUS REGRESSION OF CANCER: A SEARCH FOR
PSYCHOLOGICAL FACTORS

Martin A. van Kalmthout and Marina B. Kuyper

INTRODUCTION

The phenomenon of spontaneous regression of
cancer (SRC) has attracted the attention of medical-
biological researchers as well as of psychologists
and psychiatrists, the first being interested in the
understanding of the biological mechanisms involved,
the latter in the role of psychological factors.
For both, the importance of this research is that
the understanding of this phenomenon will eventually
be of significance to the therapy of the cancer-
process.
Researchers of psychotherapy are familiar with
the phenomenon of spontaneous remission of
psychoneurotic disorders: in research on the
effects of psychotherapy the spontaneous remission
group represents the control group for the
estimation of the degree of natural recovery from
these disorders, independent of the formal psychotherapeutic treatment. This type of research is
directed exclusively however to the calculation of
the quantity of natural recovery and not, of course,
at the exploration of the psychological change
processes involved in it. There is, on the other
hand, very interesting research on the phenomenon of
spontaneous remission which is directed exclusively
at the process of spontaneous remission itself. An
excellent example is the research on spontaneous
remission in alcoholics (Tuchfeld, 1981). In this
paper we consider the possibility that psychological
change processes are also involved in the phenomenon
of SRC. It is clear however that, in comparison to
psychoneurotic disorders and addictions, SRC poses a
special problem, because the role of psychological
factors in cancer remains controversial (Cassileth
et al, 1985). Research on SRC is therefore also

directed at the question of whether and how psychological processes influence the course of the somatic cancer process.

We start our paper by discussing some problems of definition. Then follows a review of the medical and psychological research on SRC and some theoretical explanations are discussed. Next, our own experience with psychological research on SRC is described and we conclude by discussing briefly the practical and theoretical relevance of this type of research.

DEFINITION

In popular literature and alternative thinking SRC is considered an example of a so-called "miracle cure". This indicates that the phenomenon is widely known in medical and lay experience. We need not follow, however, the popular (often occult or religious) thinking about it, but can approach the phenomenon in a strictly scientific way (van Kalmthout, 1985). This means that it should be defined in clear operational terms, and that explanations should be given by natural psychological and/or medical-biological theories. In this paper we will try to approach the phenomenon of SRC in this manner.

Everson and Cole (1966, p.4) give the following definition of SRC:

> "..... the partial or complete disappearance of a malignant tumor in the absence of all treatment or in the presence of therapy which is considered inadequate to exert a significant influence on neoplastic disease. It is not implied that spontaneous regression need progress to complete disappearance of tumor nor that spontaneous regression is synonymous with cure; ...It is our feeling that the factors responsible for temporary regression of cancer in some patients may be the same factors which are responsible for permanent regression of cancer in other patients."

This definition implies not only that partial regression of the cancer-process is included, but also prolonged arrest and delay of metastasis or recurrence of cancer-growth. The latter assumes that reliable knowledge is available as to normal expected survival time, which is not always the case. The more extreme the arrest or delay the more reason there is to consider it a case of SRC according to the above definition.

In the reliable assessment of SRC it is important that no medical misdiagnosis is present. For that reason histologic confirmation of the primary tumour and/or metastasis is a prerequisite. Besides that, strong decay in general health (a manifest in loss of gut and weight) is an important indication of the seriousness of the illness, as is the opposite of SRC.

It should be noted also that the presence of medical or other therapies does not necessarily mean that SRC is excluded. If it can be reasonably assumed that the regression is not due to these therapies, SRC can be a possible explanation.

Although there are many pitfalls here (even histologic misdiagnosis is possible), careful examination of each case certainly makes the material trustworthy regarding the question of the real existence of SRC. For our own research purposes we use the following criteria for including the case in our SRC-group:

1. There should be no doubt about the diagnosis of cancer. Most of the time this means that histologic confirmation is necessary.
2. In the cancer process there must be a remarkable turning point, which is unlikely to be the result of a recognised adequate medical therapy. This turning point must manifest itself as a clear improvement of the somatic condition of the patient and in regression of tumour and/or metastasis.
3. Remarkable cases of arrest of the cancer-process are also included as possible cases of SRC. The longer the duration of the arrest (as manifest in prolonged survival-time, arrest of tumor-growth and delay of metastasis and/or recurrence of cancer growth) the greater the probability of SRC.

REVIEW OF RESEARCH

The most extensive medical documentation of SRC has been given by two surgeons, Everson and Cole, in their 1966 book (Everson & Cole, 1966). They collected 176 cases of SRC (according to their own definition as cited in this paper) from the published world medical literature during the period 1900 to 1965. In fact they studied many more cases, but a large number of cases were rejected by them

because of absent, inaccurate, or controversial
histological diagnoses. The same scientific rigour
was present in a conference on SRC, organised in
1976 by the National Cancer Institute of America
(National Cancer Institute, 1976). Most notable
from the present authors' perspective is the
complete absence in these studies of any reference
to the role of psychological factors. The medical
explanations mentioned are, amongst others, misdiagnosis, false estimation of the effectiveness of
medical treatment used, endocrine influences, and
allergic or immune reaction. The latter two factors
are certainly not incompatible with psychological
explanations, since it is generally accepted that if
psychological factors influence the cancer process
this will be via the immune system (The Lancet,
1985).

Psychosomatic studies of SRC are much rarer
than medical studies. As far as we know only three
groups have published data on this topic, the
psychosomatic cancer study group in New York, headed
by psychiatrist Weinstock (1977), a Japanese group
of the department of Psychosomatic Medicine of
Kyushu University (Ikemi et al, 1975) and a Dutch
group headed by the pathologist De Vries (Vries,
1986). Weinstock (1977) mentions twelve cases of
SRC. On psychosocial aspects he stresses a
favourable change in the situation just preceding
the cancer shrinkage, the supportive role of the
family, the placebo effect, and ".. the favourable
inner change that occurs upon facing death (and
deciding to live differently and more
constructively)".

The 1975 Japanese study (Ikemi et al, 1975) is
a carefully documented psychosomatic study of five
cases of SRC. Besides the clinical history and
course of illness a well documented life history is
presented for each case. Among the psychosocial
factors mentioned by these researchers are:
accepting the responsibility for resolving an
existential crisis in their life, the absence of
anxious and depressive reactions and a dramatic
change of outlook on life.

De Vries (1986) reports seven cases of SRC,
selected from fifteen cases referred to his team.
All seven cases could be demonstrated to obey the
strict criteria of SRC. This study used semi-
structured interviews to elicit psychosocial
correlates of SRC and concluded that a relatively
sudden increase in autonomous behaviour and/or
a sudden change in attitude towards the illness,

treatment or environment, are among the most important psychological correlates of SRC.

The studies certainly represent interesting pioneering efforts on the eventual role of psychological factors in SRC which deserve more extensive research in the future.

ONE YEAR OF RESEARCH ON SRC

Research in this field is directed at exceptional cases rather than at statistically determined group means. Therefore research methodology must be adapted to this end. As far as the medical diagnosis is concerned the most rigorous approach is necessary. In our research project we have ensured this by collecting the written documents from the medical specialists. After studying them carefully we make a precise summary of the crucial elements and ask the opinion of one external pathologist and one external oncologist. The search for psychological factors is conducted in an exploratory manner using semi-structured interviews. The specific questions asked concern medical history, reaction to diagnosis, changes during SRC and life history. The more data we collect the more specific our questions become. The same is true for our theorising. We consider it premature to make use of one limited theory, but little by little, our insight into this complex phenomenon is increasing, making it possible to formulate useful explanatory concepts. In the first year of our project we studied eight cases. In addition, two cases were referred that could not be interviewed because they did not know their diagnosis and their family physician, quite rightly, did not want to cause them worry. One other patient refused to cooperate because she denied her diagnosis. After extensive study two further cases had to be eliminated because medical intervention could not be excluded as the reason for the cure. One other case had to be excluded because of the lack of a histologically confirmed diagnosis, although the patient was known in her town as being a "miracle cure". So, five cases were left. One of these five cases could not be interviewed because the patient had died many years before (not because of cancer). We included this case in our project however, because the medical evidence was very convincing and the interview with the family physician gave us some information on the psychological factors.

All interviews were audiotaped and later transcribed. We are currently analysing this material and as more patients are interviewed we hope to find some general characteristics of this group of "survivors of expected death".

DISCUSSION

In this paper we have briefly discussed the phenomenon of SRC, reviewed the relevant literature and summarised our own one year experience with research on SRC. In concluding we would like to emphasise that this research seems to us of great importance both for psychosomatic medicine and psychotherapy in general. In cases of SRC a fundamental change process seems at work which may be crucial and common in all forms of psychotherapy and mental healing (Kalmthout et al, 1985).

REFERENCES

Cassileth, B.R., Lusk, E.J., Miller, D.S., Brown, L.L. & Miller, C. (1985). Psychosocial correlates of survival in advanced malignant disease. The New England Journal of Medicine, 312, 1551-1555.

Everson, T.C. & Cole, W.H. (1966). Spontaneous Regression of Cancer. W.B. Saunders: Philadelphia.

Ikemi, Y., Nakagawa, S., Nakagawa, T., & Mineyasu, S. (1975). Psychosomatic consideration on cancer patients who have made a narrow escape from death. Dynamische Psychiatrie, 2, 77-92.

Kalmthout, M.A. van (1985). The scientific study of so-called miracle cures. Paper presented at the Second European Conference on Psychotherapy Research, Louvain-la-Neuve, Belgium, September 3-7.

Kalmthout, M.A. van, Schaap, C.P., & Wojciechowski, F. (eds) (1985). Common Factors in Psychotherapy. Swets & Zeitlinger: Lisse.

The Lancet Editorial (1985). Emotion and immunity. The Lancet, July 20.

National Cancer Institute (1976). National Cancer Institute Monograph, 44.

Tuchfeld, B.S. (1981). Spontaneous remission in alcoholics. Empirical observations and theoretical implications. Journal of Studies on Alcohol, 42, 626-641.

Vries, M.J. de (1986).   Crisis en transformatie:
     Lessen van wonderbaarlijke patienten.
     Medisch Contact, 24, 751-756.
Weinstock, Ch. (1977).   Notes on spontaneous
     regression of cancer.   Journal of the
     American Society of Psychosomatic Dentistry
     and Medicine, Vol. 24 (4), 106-110.

Chapter Eleven

CROSS-CULTURAL EPIDEMIOLOGY OF PSYCHOSOMATIC
DISORDERS: WHAT CAN ACCOUNT FOR THEIR VARYING
PREVALENCE ACROSS DIFFERENT COUNTRIES AND SOCIETIES?

Thomas Koehler

This paper is intended to be a critical review
of studies on cross-cultural epidemiology of some
so-called psychosomatic disorders and of their over-
hasty conclusions. There is a widely held view that
migraine, essential hypertension, coronary heart
disease (CHD), asthma, peptic ulcer and ulcerative
colitis are rare and do not occur at all in many
non-European countries or in "untouched" societies.
Furthermore, this is often regarded as proof that
such disorders are caused by western civilisation
and emerge from industrial stress and the decay of
families or other intact communities.
This is only true to some extent. Differences
in prevalence of the disorders listed above
certainly do exist, but they are mostly
overestimated. Some of the differing prevalence
rates can easily be explained by less subtle
diagnostic means in non-European countries, for
example by the lack of sophisticated X-ray
examination, colonoscopy or electrocardiography.
In addition it is a well established fact that even
in European cities many people with migraine,
essential hypertension and CHD will not seek a
doctor's help, because they do not suffer from pain
or decide secretly to endure it. For instance, a
large epidemiological study on migraine in Wales
yielded the results that approximately 50% of the
persons suffering from migraine have never been
seen by a doctor (Waters and O'Connor, 1975). A
psychological investigation at the University of
Hamburg found that even among students the
percentage of migraine sufferers who never seek a
doctor's help was nearly 45% (Koehler, to be
published). On screening more than one million
Americans it was detected that 27.7% of persons with
high blood pressure (diastolic of 95mm Hg or above)

were not previously diagnosed as hypertensives; the percentage of undiagnosed hypertensives was 49.2% for persons under 40 years of age (Stamler et al, 1976). In West Germany six million people have been diagnosed as hypertensive by medical examination; it is estimated that another three million hypertensives go unnoticed (for references see Koehler, 1985). Thus prevalence figures as assessed by clinical statistics are greatly underestimated which suggests that this effect is even more pronounced in rural societies, especially in isolated communities of the Third World. This general remark should be kept in mind since it applies to the remainder of this paper.

As for migraine, to my knowledge, no large-scale epidemiological investigations have yet been carried out in countries outside Europe or North America. Nevertheless it is a well established fact that attacks of typical migraine headache were observed in Mesopotamia 3000 years ago and Roman, Byzantine and Arabian physicians have tried to describe, explain and treat migraine attacks (for references see Koehler, 1985). In a very undisturbed part of Madagascar, I have diagnosed a case of severe classical migraine in a young man and in Bali I observed a young woman suffering from an acute attack of common migraine. These arguments are not very convincing, of course, and they don't tell us anything about the real rate of prevalence. However, they should refute the widely held view that migraine is strictly limited to countries of western civilisation and emerged only some decades decades ago.

According to Groen (1970, p. 202) "ulcerative colitis is a disease of western culture, it is very rare in underdeveloped countries of Asia and Africa". No exact figures were communicated in Groen's acticle; however, cases of ulcerative colitis have been observed in India, Thailand, Turkey and some African countries (for references see Koehler, 1985). Furthermore one should bear in mind that diarrhoea is very common in underdeveloped countries, and that most of these patients are not examined properly to establish the cause of their disease. Thus I think we should not jump to the conclusion too early that western civilisation is the major cause of ulcerative colitis.

As for peptic ulcer, the assumption can definitely be refuted that prevalence rates are notably higher in western countries (for a thorough overview of empirical data see Pflanz, 1971). In

spite of some difficulties in comparing data about
prevalence rates we still have sufficient information that the incidence of peptic ulcer is not
remarkably lower in at least some African or Asian
countries. For example, in post-mortem
examinations, peptic ulcers and scars were found
more often in Uganda (14.5% in 1958) than Germany
(11.4% on average between 1953 and 1962). Furthermore some studies yielded the result that the
percentage of patients with duodenal ulcers amongst
patients in hospitals was greater in India, Peru,
Uganda and Senegal than Italy, Greece or the
Netherlands (see Pflanz, 1971, p.127 f.). I shall
not go further into details, but I quite agree with
Pflanz who states: "nor can the psychosomatic claim
be supported that duodenal ulcer is a 'disease of
civilisation', in other words that 'civilisation' is
conducive to certain kinds of psychological
conflicts not found in persons who live in 'underdeveloped' countries" (p.123).

To my knowledge, no large-scale epidemiological
investigations on prevalence of asthma have been
carried out in any part of the world (cf. Clark &
Godfrey, 1977). Thus all figures communicated so
far are based on clinical estimations, therefore not
many conclusions can be drawn from these statistics.
There are some interesting hints, however, that
prevalence of asthmatic symptoms grows with the
degree of industrialisation and adaption to western
civilisation. For instance, it has been shown that
asthma is very uncommon in the inhabitants of the
Tokeleau Islands in Polynesia, whereas people from
these islands who shift to New Zealand are much more
likely to develop the disorder. The relative risk
of asthma was found to be about 19 times greater in
Tokeleau males and about 4.5 times greater in
Tokeleau females in New Zealand compared with those
in the Tokeleau Islands (Prior, 1977). It is
questionable, however, what accounts for this. It
must be left open for discussion whether the absence
of industrial pollutants and chemicals in the home
islands or the limited availability of daily
products (the consumption of which can lead to
allergic reactions) may be sufficient to explain the
difference in prevalence rates. Similar data were
communicated by Japanese authors (Ikemi et al,
1974). The incidence of child asthma, for instance,
has increased twice as much in Japan since the war.
It was discovered that incidence is considerably
greater in industrial areas with a high degree of
air pollution; furthermore the percentage of adult

asthmatics has been shown to be higher in smokers than non-smokers. So one should be careful in drawing the conclusion that the psychological impacts of sociocultural changes account mainly for the growing prevalence of asthma in some countries.

There is ample evidence that hypertension is much less frequent in untouched isolated societies and rural populations of the Third World (for reviews see Prior, 1977; Ostfeld & D'Atri, 1977; Murphy, 1982, Koehler, 1985)). Though, to my knowledge, no epidemiological studies have been carried out in underdeveloped countries, it is fairly obvious that the prevalence of coronary heart disease (CHD) is much lower in less industrialised parts of the world. This statement should still be valid even if we take into account the fact that, due to less subtle diagnostic means figures concerning prevalence of CHD are certainly underestimated. In post-mortem examinations in Nigeria, for instance, myocardial infarctions were seldom found (Williams, 1971). It seems at first sight that lower prevalence rates of hypertension and CHD can be attributed to fewer stress factors in untouched societies, but this conclusion is certainly drawn too rapidly.

First, it should be kept in mind that essential hypertension and CHD develop on a larger scale only in individuals over 40-50 years of age. In the above mentioned screening study it was found that, based on the 95mm Hg cutoff, the rate per 1000 people with elevated diastolic blood pressure rose from 39.9 for the age group under 20 years (and 112.2 in the age group between 20 and 29) to 348.8 for those 60 to 64 years old (Stamler et al, 1976). Thus in populations where life expectancy is reduced, prevalence of these disorders is necessarily lower. In addition, nutritional factors play an eminent role in the pathogenesis of essential hypertension and CHD. It is a well established fact that excessive salt intake raises blood pressure, and that heightened fat intake and obesity increase the risk of hypertension and CHD. After a thorough review of data concerning epidemiology of high blood pressure, Ostfeld & D'Atri (1977, p.31) come to the conclusion: "Our view is that rapid sociocultural change does, indeed, lead to a higher prevalence of high blood pressure and a greater rise in pressures with age. The intermediary mechanism is a change in diet that causes gain in weight. There is no need to assume that breakdown of traditional social roles and conflict about them directly affect blood pressure."

Finally it should be kept in mind that smoking habits also play an important part in the patho-genesis of arteriosclerosis. The influence of these variables must be eliminated before assumptions are made about different prevalence rates in European industrial countries and non-European rural societies and about the potential causal role of psychological factors.

Taking all this into account we cannot rule out that there are still differences in prevalence rates which cannot be attributed to statistical or biological factors, but they are certainly much smaller than figures published so far seem to suggest.

There is no doubt that the onset and course of somatic illnesses can be influenced by psychological variables, and that cross-cultural epidemiology can reflect their influence. This paper does not intend to demonstrate that cross-cultural epidemiological studies in psychosomatic medicine have yielded no or at best trivial results, and should thus be given up entirely. On the contrary, cross-cultural epidemiological research is a very sophisticated way of deriving hypotheses about psychological variables that may have some bearing on the development or maintenance of somatic diseases. Therefore, these should be carried out on a much larger scale than at present, but we should endeavour to keep the errors previously mentioned to a minimum. We must be sure that what we attribute to hypothetical psychological factors cannot simply be explained by organic variables we did not think of.

REFERENCES

Aoki, H., Ikemi, Y. & Ikemi, A. (1982). Some psychosomatic disorders in Japan from a cultural perspective.
Psychosomatics, 23, 1171-1184.
Clark, T.J.H. & Godfrey, S. (Eds) (1977). Asthma Chapman & Hall: London.
Groen, J.J. (1970). Influence of social and cultural patterns on psychosomatic diseases. Psycho-ther., Psychosom., 18, 189-215.
Ikemi, Y., Ago, Y., Nakagawa, Sh., Mori, Sh., Takahashi, N., Suematsu, H., Sugita, M. & Matsubara, H. (1974). Psychosomatic mechanism under social changes in Japan. J.Psychosom. Res., 18, 15-24.

Koehler, Th. (1985). Psychosomatische Krankheiten.
    Kohlhammer: Stuttgart.
Murphy, H.B.M. (1982). Blood pressure and culture.
    The contribution of cross-cultural comparisons
    to psychosomatics. Psychother. Psychosom., 38
    244-255.
Ostfeld, A.M. & D'Atri, D.A. (1977). Rapid
    sociocultural change and high blood pressure.
    In Kasl, S. & Reichsman, F. (Eds),
    Epidemiological studies in psychosomatic
    medicine. Advanced Psychosomatic Medicine,
    9, 20-47.
Pflanz, M. (1971). Epidemiological and socio-
    cultural factors in the aetiology of
    duodenal ulcer. Advanced Psychosomatic
    Medicine, 6, 121-151.
Prior, J. (1977). Migration and physical illness.
    In S. Kasl & F. Reichman (Eds),
    Epidemiological studies in psychosomatic
    medicine. Advanced Psychosomatic Medicine,
    9, 105-131.
Stamler, J., Stamler, R., Riedlinger, W.F.,
    Algera, G. & Roberts, R.H. (1976).
    Hypertension screening of 1 million Americans.
    Journal of Americal Medical Association, 235,
    2299-2306.
Waters, W.E. & O'Connor, P.J. (1975). Prevalence of
    Migraine. Journal of Neurology, Neurosurgery,
    and Psychiatry, 38, 613-615.
Williams, A.O. (1971). Coronary arteriosclerosis in
    Nigeria. Br.Heart J., 33, 95-100.

Chapter Twelve

BULIMIA: RESEARCH AND TREATMENT IN FRANCE

J. Bullerwell-Ravar

        Interest   in   Bulimia   (repeated   binges   followed
by self-induced vomiting   or   some   other   stringent
strategy to avoid weight gain) has only received the
serious attention of the French medical and scientific
community   since   1983.   The   aim of this paper is to
report   briefly   on   research   already   carried out or
under way.

First Study : Epidemiology

        The   first   research   study   carried   out   was   a
replica of the Fairburn and Cooper (1982)pilot study.
The   aim of the study was to ascertain the presence of
Bulimia in France.

Results
        An   analysis   of   500   questionnaires returned by
women corresponding   to   DSMIII   criteria   yielded the
following characteristics: The mean age of the sample
was   29   (s.d.   8), and average duration of the eating
disorder   was   10   years   (s.d. 7).   Two thirds of the
population were normal weight (measured by a body mass
index   W/h2).   Half   of   the 500 women (49.3%) binged
once   a   day   or   more.   Among the strategies to avoid
weight   gain,   self-induced vomiting was used by 51.2%
(N=256   cases).   Laxative   abuse   and   medical
complications   (amenorrhoea,   spasmophilia,   dizzy
spells) were also commonly found.
        The   difference   between the mean body index of
the   vomiters   and   that   of   the   non-vomiters was
significant   at   the threshold p$<$0.01, which   tends
to indicate a relative efficacity of the method.
        This   study   confirms the presence of Bulimia in
France,   obtaining   comparable characteristics of the
population to those obtained by Fairburn and Cooper in
their   pilot   study.   The   main   differences [a higher

mean age of the sample, 29 (S.D. 8) versus 23.8 (S.D. 5.5) and greater laxative abuse (38.5% vs 18.8%)] could be due to the different readership of the magazines involved or a real difference between the two populations.

Second study: a preliminary report

In November, 1985, a two-page questionnaire on eating habits was published in another woman's magazine (younger readership, accent on health, exercise and beauty).

One of the aims of the survey was to ascertain how many women considering themselves bulimic actually correspond to the DSM criteria.

Results

The number of women who reported binge-eating and who could not currently be diagnosed as anorexic was 1227.

When the questionnaires were analysed as to conformity with the other four diagnostic criteria required to qualify as bulimic, only 494 subjects (40.3%) could be considered as fulfilling all the DSMIII criteria. Of these, 23.1% were vomiters (N=114) and 76.9% non-vomiters (N=380). Approximately the same percentage of subjects reported three out of the four criteria (40.42%, N=496), but not always the same ones. Finally a group of 247 subjects (20.1%) corresponded to only one or two of the criteria (binge-eating episodes, either alone, or else with one other criterion). These figures confirm that the DSMIII excludes a certain number of cases (in our study 60%) of women who manifestly suffer from binge-eating behaviour and need treatment for this disorder.

The preliminary results of the second study also bring to light a significant difference in the percentage of vomiters among women meeting the DSMIII criteria: in the first study, 51%, in the second 23%. The discrepancy between the vomiting figures obtained is possibly due to the younger, health-orientated readership of the second magazine.

Outcome research

A controlled treatment programme was set up in three medical centres in 1984-85. Clinical and psychological testing was carried out at the beginning and end of each six month period. Two groups of patients started treatment, one in March,

1984, the other six months later.

Of the 34 patients who returned for evaluation after treatment, most had been treated by cognitive behavioural methods, one third individually and two thirds in groups.

Results

Acting as their own controls, the bulimic patients showed definite improvement in bingeing behaviour and in all the personality characteristics assessed at the end of six months of treatment. The

Psychological Assessment of Bulimics before and after Treatment

Comparison of mean scores

	Pretest	s.d.	Posttest	s.d.	Sig.
E.P.I. Neurot.	14.15	4.95	7.85	5.28	.001
E.P.I. Extrav.	11.47	3.93	8.76	3.90	.01
Depression	30.24	14.3	18.24	12.09	.01
Self Esteem	33.26	12.59	42.18	13.89	.001
Assertiveness	101.35	23.26	117.35	16.59	.001
Body Image	21.97	9.71	30.97	10.44	.001

difference in the mean scores of the various tests before and after treatment was significant for all measures, with $p < .01$ for the scales of Depression and Extraversion (E.P.I.) and $p < .001$ for Self Esteem, Self Assertion, Body Image and Interpersonal Sensitivity.

These results correspond to an increase in Self Esteem, Assertiveness and positive Body Image and a decrease in the factors measured by Eysenck's E.P.I. (Extraversion and Interpersonal Sensitivity) as well as a decrease in Depression.

Discussion

Surprisingly, the mean score obtained on the Extraversion scale of the E.P.I. is significantly less after treatment than before (8.76 vs 11.47). However this scale includes a certain number of items related to impulsivity, and most bulimics consider their bingeing to be impulsive and due to lack of control. An improvement in bingeing behaviour is therefore most likely to modify any measure of impulsivity.

It does seem that such variables as poor Self Esteem, lack of Assertiveness, Hypersensitivity, Impulsiveness, poor Body Image and Depression are closely linked to the presence of Bulimia and improve when this condition itself improves.

REFERENCES

Aimez, P. & Michaut, S. (1986).   Bulimia Nervosa in France. In Proceedings of the 15th Conference on Psychosomatic Research, London, Chapter 37, John Libby & Co.

Fairburn, C.G. & Cooper, P.J. (1982). Self-induced vomiting and bulimia nervosa: an undetected problem.
British Medical Journal, 284, 1153-1155.

Chapter Thirteen

THE MENTAL HEALTH OF ETHNIC MINORITIES

Raymond Cochrane

The purpose of this paper is to provide a context for the papers which follow. Some data on the relationship between country of birth and one index of mental illness rates in Britain will be presented and then some questions arising from these data will be posed.

Britain has always been a centre for migration. Many people have left this country to settle elsewhere in the world and fewer, but still substantial numbers of people, have come from elsewhere to live here. Since the second world war, however, there have been some changes in the patterns of immigration to Britain which have affected the way in which immigration is regarded. First, an increased proportion of immigrants are non-white and therefore more visible than the previous waves of Irish, Jewish and European immigrants which occurred earlier in this century. Second, some of the immigrants came from very different religio-cultural backgrounds to those of the host society and, what is more, some groups have shown no desire to abandon their culture of origin and to become homogenized into the dominant Anglo culture. Third, perhaps as a result of the fact that many post world war II immigrants came from societies which had previously been subjected to British imperialism, prejudice, racism and discrimination against them has become widespread.

In the 1970s the liberal establishment became concerned about a number of aspects of this migration, one of which was the mental health of those involved (others were, for example, the progress of children of immigrants in schools, equality of opportunity in employment and housing, "race" relations etc.). Perhaps the most extreme, and in many ways misleading and distorted expression appeared in a booklet published by the Commission for Racial Equality entitled: "Aspects of Mental Health in a Multi-Cultural Society". Based on a few early studies of mental illness rates among West Indian and Asian immigrants which were methodologically weak and which have been discredited (Cochrane, 1983), the CRE perpetuated the myth that ethnic minorities, and immigrants in particular, pay a heavy psychological price in terms of mental illness for living in Britain. This booklet listed the following as being groups at special risk of mental illness: immigrant adolescents, second generation immigrants, Muslim women, Sikh women, Hindu women, West Indian women, West Indian men, Asian men, the elderly - in other words almost everyone who was not native born white British!

The fact of the matter is that rates of mental illness, however these are indexed, are very variable between different ethnic groups, some being higher than those of natives but more often they are lower than those of natives (Cochrane, 1977; 1983).

Take, for example, the most recent figures available from the DHSS. The considerable difficulties involved in defining and analysing these data have been described elsewhere (Cochrane & Bal, in press) but they do provide the most accurate picture of mental hospitalisation rates broken down by country of birth (not ethnic origin) available anywhere.

Table 1: Age adjusted rates of admission to mental hospitals in England, 1981, per 100,000 population aged 16 years and over by country of birth.

Country of birth	No. in population (000s)	No. of admissions[3]	Rates per 100,000	
			Males	Females
England	41,084	157,763	419	583
Scotland	731	5,451	740	847
N. Ireland	202	1,601	793	877
Ireland[1]	567	6,192	1,051	1,102
Caribbean	292	1,590	565	532
India	379	1,210	317	326
Pakistan[2]	227	500	259	233

1 Includes "Ireland - part not stated"
2 Includes Bangladesh
3 Includes those for whom country of birth was
    not stated, redistributed as described in
    Cochrane, 1977.

These data are broadly in line with those resulting from an analysis of 1971 admissions data (Cochrane, 1977). The most obvious differences between the two studies are the lower rates of admission in 1981 compared to 1971 found for those born in India and for Pakistani born females. What is clear however is that the rates of admission for Asian born groups are actually substantially lower than those of the native born. The rates of admission for the Caribbean born are basically similar to those of the English born - the males being slightly higher, the females slightly lower. The rates of admission for the Irish born are particularly high.

The admission data in Table 1 are for all diagnoses combined and this, of course, conceals many interesting variations in diagnostic patterns between the various groups. The most significant of these are the extraordinarily high rates of schizophrenia found among the Irish born and the Caribbean born populations of England. The figures for men (expressed as rates per 100,000) are English born - 81, Irish born - 191, and Caribbean born - 278. Thus, Caribbean born males have a schizophrenia rate approximately three and a half times that of English born males. The rates for those born in India and Pakistan are also higher than the native born rate (with the exception of Pakistani born females). Interestingly, although the Scottish born residents of England have high overall admission rates (Table 1), their rates for schizophrenia are not so exceptional, being 99 per 100,000 for men and 112 per 100,000 for women. These findings for schizophrenia are difficult to explain but a number of hypotheses have been put forward (Cochrane and Bal, in press), and the possibility of misdiagnosis, especially of black patients, cannot be ruled out.

The data in Table 1 raise several other important questions, some of which are addressed in subsequent papers:

1. Mental hospital admission figures refer only to actual migrants, i.e. those born abroad but now living in England - what of the "second generation"? If the patterns of mental illness found in the different groups is associated with the stresses of migration and relocation into a different culture, should we expect the children of immigrants and subsequent generations to show a pattern more similar to that of the native born white English? Dermot

McGovern will consider one aspect of this question with regard to schizophrenia among the Caribbean born and their descendants.

2. The repeated finding that those migrating from India and Pakistan have relatively low rates of mental hospital admissions inevitably raises the question of whether this particular index of mental illness is equally appropriate for all ethnic groups. It has been suggested, for example, that Asian born residents of Britain are likely to take advice from traditional healers and thus possibly avoid coming into contact with formal psychiatric services. It is also possible that some psychologically disturbed immigrants return to their native land rather than seek help here and so again do not appear as a statistic in the mental hospital admission data, even though they may be severely disturbed. Even if Asian people do seek medical help for their problems is it not possible that misunderstandings between doctor and patient are more likely to occur than in the case of an English person consulting a doctor? There are good reasons for thinking that the way in which psychological problems are conceptualised, developed, described and presented, differ considerably between cultures (Marsella and White, 1982; Rack, 1982).

Sukhwant Bal takes up one of these themes when he discusses the hypothesis that Asian patients are more likely to "somaticise" psychiatric problems than are English patients and therefore run the risk that the true nature of their disorder will go undetected by their doctors.

3. Some particularly striking data contained in Table 1 are those showing the exceptionally low rate of admission of Pakistani born females, which is considerably less than half that of their English born equivalents. Again, while this is not a new observation, it has never been satisfactorily explained. One possible reason for their very low rate of in-patient treatment is that Pakistani women shun contact with the medical and psychiatric services, but the evidence to hand indicates that this is unlikely to be the whole story (Cochrane, 1983; Brewin, 1980). It could also be that Pakistani women have more successful ways of dealing with the stresses they encounter in everyday life than do English women and this is one of the

questions addressed by Shamim Mahmud in her paper which reports on a comparison of life stresses and symptoms in Pakistani and English women.

4. So far this paper has dealt exclusively with the mental health of migrants to Britain with no reference to the great deal of work that has been done in other countries. Indeed, there are good reasons for suspecting that the situation of newcomers in those countries which have traditionally received a lot of immigration (such as Canada, Australia and the USA) will be different from those pertaining here. In the USA for example most immigrants typically come to a society used to large scale migrations from many sources and arrive with every intention of settling for good, and of adapting, to some extent at least, to the dominant culture. Neither of these conditions necessarily exist in Britain. Neither is it the case that immigrants to the USA came from societies which have previously experienced colonial subjugation by the society to which they are migrating, as is the case for many migrants to Britain.

If extrapolations from the American (and the white Dominion) situation to Britain are unwise, what about the rest of Europe? Are there more continuities of experience of migration (from both sides) in countries which have a greater geo-policital similarity? Elina Haavio-Mannila presents a detailed analysis of the mental health and social adjustment of Finns and Yugoslavs living in Sweden. It shows that there are some similarities between the way Finns respond to their new environment (and the way in which they are perceived by native Swedes) and the patterns of adaptation of the Irish in England.

There are now sufficient data on the relative mental health statuses of different ethnic groups within societies. It is time to focus more explicitly on explanations for these patterns of differences in adjustment. The four papers which follow are examples of such studies. They take off from what is well established and attempt to show how survey research, epidemiology and statistical studies can be used to provide valuable insights and practical implications for clinical psychology.

REFERENCES

Brewin, C. (1980). Explaining the lower rates of psychiatric treatment among Asian immigrants to the UK. Social Psychiatry, 15, 17-20.

Cochrane, R. (1977). Mental illness in immigrants to England and Wales: an analysis of mental hospital admissions. Social Psychiatry, 12, 25-35.

Cochrane, R. (1983). The Social Creation of Mental Illness. Longmans : London.

Cochrane, R. & Bal, S. (in press). Migration and schizophrenia: an examination of five hypotheses. Social Psychiatry.

Marsella, A.J. & White, G. (Eds) (1982). Cultural Conceptions of Mental Health and Therapy. Reider: Dordrecht, Holland.

Rack, P. (1982). Race, Culture and Mental Disorder. Tavistock: London.

Chapter Fourteen

FIRST ADMISSION RATES AND DIAGNOSES OF FIRST AND
SECOND GENERATION *AFRO-CARIBBEANS IN THE WEST
MIDLANDS

Dermot McGovern

Numerous studies on Afro-Caribbean migrants to
Britain are reported in the psychiatric literature
(Littlewood and Lipsedge, 1981a). Most report
excessive rates of psychiatric illness, particularly
schizophrenia, and excessive psychiatric admission
rates, compared with the native population.
There has, however, been little work on the
British born children of these migrants. These
individuals (often called the second generation) now
comprise almost 50% of the total population of Afro-
Caribbean origin in Britain (OPCS, 1981). Predictions (Cochrane, 1983) have been made that their
psychiatric morbidity would approach that of the
host population. A psychiatric study of the second
generation would not only test this prediction but
also allow further elaboration of the theories
offered to explain higher rates of psychiatric
morbidity in Afro-Caribbean migrants.
Until recently one of the difficulties facing
an epidemiological study was that there was no
indication of the numbers of British born Afro-
Caribbeans in the general population. The 1981
census (OPCS, 1981) gave no direct measure of
ethnicity but it is now clear that indirect measures
available in the census do give a valid estimate.
As described elsewhere (McGovern and Cope, in press)
I have used such measures to calculate population
figures for both Afro-Caribbean migrants and British
born Afro-Caribbeans.

*Footnote: The term Afro-Caribbean has been used
throughout rather than West Indian. It refers to
people of African heritage who themselves or whose
recent ancestors were born in the Caribbean.

93

Although the term second generation is usually limited to those Afro-Caribbeans born in Britain, it is probably useful to consider the second generation as also comprising those individuals who migrated as children and are of a similar age to the British Afro-Caribbeans. My definition of second generation Afro-Caribbean therefore is that the individual is raised in Britain.

METHOD

The present study examines first psychiatric admissions to a Birmingham mental hospital in whose catchment area reside nearly one third of the total Afro-Caribbean population of the West Midland region. Details of age, sex, country of birth, race and final case note diagnosis were recorded for all first admissions from 1st January 1980 to 31st December 1983. An estimate was made of the local catchment area population by age, sex, country of birth and race. All other groups apart from white British and Afro-Caribbean were excluded.

First admission rates were calculated by sex for three groups: White British, Afro-Caribbean migrants and British born Afro-Caribbeans. They were divided into two age groups: 16-29 and 30-pensionable age. This was partly to comply with census data but also to provide a divide for first and second generation Afro-Caribbeans, the first generation being 30 years and over and the second generation under 30 years of age. (There were no British born Afro-Caribbean patients over the age of 30.) Diagnosis was considered in two ways. Firstly the proportion of patients given a psychotic diagnosis was calculated and then rates of first admission for four diagnostic groups were compared.

RESULTS

Table 1 gives the first admission rates for the three groups by age and sex. The rates for whites and Afro-Caribbeans aged 30 years and over (first generation Afro-Caribbeans) do not differ significantly but there are large and significant differences between the younger, second generation Afro-Caribbean groups and similarly aged whites.

When considering diagnosis, for the sake of simplicity, the 16-29 year old British born Afro-Caribbeans will be grouped together with the 16-29 year old migrants to form a second generation Afro-Caribbean group. Each of the Afro-Caribbean groups

Table 1: Total number of first admissions over four years and four year first admission rates by age and sex for Whites, Afro-Caribbean migrants and British born Afro-Caribbeans per 10,000 population.

Age	White		Afro-Caribbean Migrant		British-born Afro-Caribbean	
	n	Rate	n	Rate	n	Rate
MALES						
16-29	71	21.5	17	144.1#	21	98.4#
30-64	193	26.7	18	40.7		
FEMALES						
16-29	96	29.6	21	151.1#	17	69.7#
30-59	251	40.2	16	42.2		

# Denotes significant differences Afro-Caribbean versus White

has a higher proportion of admissions with a diagnosis of psychosis (eg schizophrenia, affective psychosis etc). In the older group (first generation Afro-Caribbean versus Whites) 61% of male Afro-Caribbeans and 69% of females have such a diagnosis compared with 51% and 54% of whites. The differences are larger when comparing second generation Afro-Caribbean and Whites: 88% of male and 82% of female Afro-Caribbeans have a psychotic diagnosis compared with 49% and 44% of Whites.

As to particular diagnoses, four groups were examined: Schizophrenia/paranoid psychoses; affective disorder, Cannabis psychosis and other diagnoses. Because overall first admission rates differed significantly only between second generation Afro-Caribbean and young Whites, the differences in diagnostic rates will be given for these groups only. In all diagnostic categories the second generation Afro-Caribbean first admission rates exceeded those of the Whites. Over 25% of Afro-Caribbean males receive a diagnosis of cannabis psychosis. The male Afro-Caribbean admission rates for cannabis psychosis exceeded the White rate by 100 fold. The diagnosis of schizophrenia/paranoid psychosis was also prominent in Afro-Caribbeans of both sexes, the male rate exceeding the White by nearly seven times and the female by fourteen times. For affective disorder the male Afro-Caribbean rate exceeded the White by four and the female Afro-Caribbean exceeded the White by two.

DISCUSSION

In this study I have used the term second generation Afro-Caribbean to delineate individuals who were raised in Britain. The maximum period of migration to Britain from the Caribbean was between 1955 and 1965 (Ratcliffe, 1981). It is not unreasonable to suppose that those aged 16-29 years during the study (1980-1983) fulfil the criterion of being second generation. The main differences were found between young Whites and this second generation group. Is it appropriate to view this group as a separate cohort from first generation Afro-Caribbeans or is the difference due simply to age differences? For instance, are first generation Afro-Caribbean first admission rates similar to that of older Whites merely because so many Afro-Caribbeans had their first illness at an earlier age? The present study cannot answer this but reference to other studies does not suggest that the incidence of psychiatric illness in Afro-Caribbeans is particularly raised in the young, nor that differences with the native populations are most marked in the young (Littlewood & Lipsedge, 1981a). Clearly, comparisons with other studies should be treated cautiously but it would seem that, contrary to predictions of lower psychiatric morbidity, second generation Afro-Caribbeans may actually be experiencing a higher rate of first psychiatric admission than ever experienced by the first generation.

In the remaining discussion I will examine the findings in relation to the theories which have been put forward to explain the excessive psychiatric morbidity found in Afro-Caribbean migrants (Bebbington, Harvey & Tennant, 1981). These have included suggestions of an increased rate in the country of origin, selection factors pertaining to those who migrate and the stress surrounding migration. More recently, it has been suggested

that differences are more apparent than real and due
to misdiagnosis.

There is no evidence to support the proposition
that rates of mental illness are increased in the
Caribbean but it has been argued by some authors
that migrants may be selectively at greater risk of
developing mental illness (Bebbington, Harvey &
Tennant, 1981). This may be due to incipient
illness or abnormal premorbid personality traits. If
these factors were genetically transmissable, the
second generation might be expected to experience a
similar rate of illness but this would not be good
enough to account for the apparent increase in
illness in the second generation found in this
study. Moreover, when the circumstances of
Caribbean migration and settlement are considered,
it appears less likely that these factors are
relevant. The onset of psychiatric illnesses has
usually been found to occur several years after
migration making it unlikely that incipient illness
was particularly associated with migration
(Littlewood & Lipsedge, 1981b). Pre-morbid personality also seems an unlikely association since
migration became a normative process in the
Caribbean attracting the best adapted members of
society (Ratcliffe, 1981).

The arguments concerning social stress and
increased psychiatric morbidity in Afro-Caribbean
migrants have usually been concerned with the stress
of migration and settlement. The results of the
present study suggest that it is now more relevant
to discuss the stress of being a black person in
Britain rather than being a migrant. The two most
obvious stressors are those of socioeconomic
disadvantage and racism (Brown, 1984). These are
indivisible. Second generation Afro-Caribbeans are
often trapped in cumulative cycles of disadvantage
from birth, escape being limited by racism. Whether
this makes them more vulnerable to developing
mental illness has not yet been investigated.

The main illnesses diagnosed here are psychoses
and the link between psychosis and stress is usually
considered weak (Cochrane, 1983). However, in the
few studies where racism and socioeconomic
disadvantage have been examined, a link has been
established between them and psychosis in general
(Parker & Kleiner, 1966) and schizophrenia in
particular (Bagley, 1971). Bagley found that
schizophrenia in West Indian migrants in London was
associated with attempts to advance in white
society which were frustrated because of racial

discrimination, but which persisted because of a belief in, and expectation of, assimilation. The model demands that discrimination is not recognised as the reason for frustration and failure and the individual blames himself. In fact, it was predicted that this model would be less relevant to the second generation who would recognise the reality of racism and its effect on their lives and rejecting assimilation, forge a separate black identity thus reducing anomie and enhancing self esteem. The results of the present study do not, of course, invalidate the model. It may be too simplistic to assume that the desire for assimilation is an all or none phenomenon. There may be many second generation Afro-Caribbeans who still aspire to assimilation. In addition many of those who reject it may not yet have been able to form the satisfactory mutually supportive groups which Bagley saw as being necessary for mental health.

The importance of a possible organic stressor, cannabis, is suggested by the frequency of diagnosis of cannabis psychosis among second generation Afro-Caribbean males. However, there has been considerable debate (Carney & Lipsedge, 1981) about the validity of the diagnosis. Clearly, there is a need for further research on this issue and also the reason for the diagnosis being given so much more often to Afro-Carribeans than Whites.

The final area I will discuss concerns the possibility of misdiagnosis being the cause of the apparent increase in psychiatric morbidity in the second generation. The proportion of admissions within the broad category of psychosis has been given in an attempt to avoid the difficulty of obtaining precise diagnostic accuracy. However, a much higher proportion of second generation Afro-Caribbean admissions have such a psychotic diagnosis. It has to be asked, therefore, whether neurotic or adjustment difficulties or even normal behaviour is being diagnosed as psychosis and whether this may be occurring more in the second generation Afro-Caribbeans than the first.

I hope that a follow-up study, currently taking place, will clarify this; but, of course, the present study can offer no answer, nor has there been any other work on diagnostic accuracy in the second generation. In a study of West London migrants (first generation) Littlewood and Lipsedge describe how a brief stress related condition was misdiagnosed as schizophrenia. They entitled this

condition 'acute psychotic reaction' and related it
to earlier experiences in a non-industrial society.
One would, therefore, expect it to occur less
frequently or indeed be absent in the second
generation.

Cultural differences between psychiatrist and
patient may lead to less competent diagnoses. One
might expect second generation Afro-Caribbeans to be
less culturally different from the host population
than their immigrant parents. However,
psychiatrists, predominantly white and Asian and
middle class, may be less able to make appropriate
diagnoses in those second generation Afro-Caribbeans
who follow cultural and religious practices such as
Rastafarianism.

Racial differences (Mukherjee et al, 1983) in
themselves may produce less competent diagnosis.
If this were happening on a large scale it could
be seen as one aspect of institutional racism
but by itself would not account for mis-diagnosis
being more frequent in the second generation.

In conclusion, the whole area of diagnosis of
Afro-Caribbeans by psychiatrists requires further
study. As mentioned earlier, there is also a need
for research on the relationship between cannabis
and mental illness and the psychological effects of
the cumulative disadvantages experienced by young
Afro-Carribeans and their relationship to ethnic
identity and group support.

REFERENCES

Bagley, C. (1971). The social aetiology of
    schizophrenia in immigrant groups.
    International Journal of Social Psychiatry,
    17, 292-304.
Bebbington, P.E., Harvey, J. & Tennant, C., (1981).
    Psychiatric disorders in selected immigrant
    groups in Camberwell. Social Psychiatry,
    15, 43-51.
Brown, C. (1984). Black and White Britain. The
    Third PSI Survey. Heineman: London.
Carney, P. & Lipsedge, M. (1984). Letter:
    Psychosis after cannabis abuse. British
    Medical Journal, 288, p1381.
Cochrane, R. (1983) The Social Creation of Mental
    Illness. Longmans: London
Littlewood, R. & Lipsedge, M. (1981a). Some social
    and phenomenological characteristics of
    psychotic immigrants. Psychological

Medicine, 11, 289-302.

Littlewood, R. & Lipsedge, M. (1981b). Acute psychotic reaction in Caribbean-born patients. Psychological Medicine, 11, 303-318.

McGovern, D.A. & Cope, R.V. (in press). The compulsory detention of males of different ethnic groups with special reference to offender patients. British Journal of Psychiatry.

Mukherjee, S., Shukla, S. & Woodle, J., Rosen, A.M., & Olarte, S. (1983). Misdiagnosis of schizophrenia in bipolar patients: a multi-ethnic comparison. American Journal of Psychiatry, 140, 1571-1574.

OPCS Census, 1981. County report West Midlands Part 1. HMSO: London.

Parker, R. & Kleiner, S. (1966). Mental Illness in the Urban Negro Community. Free Press: New York.

Ratcliffe, P. (1981). Racism and Reaction: a Profile of Handsworth. Routledge & Kegan Paul: London.

Chapter Fifteen

PSYCHOLOGICAL SYMPTOMATOLOGY AND HEALTH BELIEFS OF
ASIAN PATIENTS

Sukhwant S. Bal

INTRODUCTION

An individual's cultural and ethnic background
are of importance in the clinical setting in the
sense that how illness is perceived, experienced and
coped with is based on how sickness is understood in
that culture. The cultural interpretations
individuals place on their symptoms have been shown
to influence the perceived intensity and expression
of pain (Diller, 1980); the way symptoms are
presented (White, 1982); the attributions placed on
the illness (Abrahamson et al, 1961) and subsequent
help-seeking behaviour (Carstairs & Kapur, 1976).
Cultural influences on symptomatology are
epitomised in the form of culture-bound syndromes
which are very specific, localised interpretations
and manifestations of illness. There are also more
general national differences of culturally
appropriate expressions of distress encoded in
symptoms that have symbolic meanings within their
cultural context: the French are said, for example,
to place great emphasis on the liver (Herzlich,
1973), American Blacks on the blood and Iranians on
the heart and blood (Helman, 1985).
It has already been illustrated that many
ethnic communities present differential symptom
patterns, but does the same apply to 'psycho-atric'
patients (patients presenting with psychological
problems or a psychiatric illness)? To be more
specific, do Asian 'psycho-atric' patients in
Britain present symptoms differentially from
indigenous patients? The evidence from China and
Taiwan, for example, would strongly suggest that
'psycho-atric' patients present with somatic
symptoms more often than Western patients (Kleinman
and Good, 1985). There is also evidence, however,

to suggest that 'psycho-atric' patients generally present with many somatic complaints (Bridges and Goldberg, 1985); though it is believed that developing countries have a higher rate of somatic presentation (Lloyd, 1986).

What is meant by somatisation is essentially a coded message, whereby the individual having problems in various areas of life chooses consciously or unconsciously to convey these in bodily terms. The aim is presumably to obtain relief both from the physical complaints and from the underlying difficulty.

This paper describes a preliminary study carried out by the author comparing the symptoms of 50 Asians (25 Punjabi Sikhs; 25 Pakistanis) and 50 English born patients at four General Practitioner clinics in Birmingham. The study aimed to assess if Asian patients presented a psychological problem with physical symptoms more often than did English patients and, if this was the case, whether GPs were making a diagnosis of the patients' physical illness more often than of the psychological distress.

Four family practitioners in a central area of Birmingham consented to their patients being interviewed by the author. From each of the two English and two Asian GPs, 25 patients were interviewed, matched for sex and ethnic group, as far as possible.

The main part of the interview comprised administering the Langner 22-item questionnaire. With Asian patients, a culturally validated version of the Langner was used either in Punjabi or Urdu (Cochrane et al, 1977). Patients were further asked about their presenting symptoms and how many visits they had made to their G.P. for the same complaint.

Scores from the Langner-22 questionnaire indicated whether the patient had any psychological problems. This was compared with the patients' presenting symptoms to assess if the symptomatology and psychological state were concordant. The GPs were also asked to complete a diagnostic sheet for each patient requesting details of the patients' symptoms, the diagnosis and whether they felt the patient had any psychological problems.

A comparison of the two independent measurements (from patient and doctor) was used to indicate whether ethno-cultural differences existed:

a. Whether Asian patients presented with more somatic and psychosomatic symptoms compared

with English patients;
b. Whether the GP had a differential rate of diagnosing psychological problems in Asian and English patients;
c. Whether there was a relationship between the patients' presenting symptoms, their Langner score and the doctor's diagnosis. In other words, would a doctor diagnose an Asian patient presenting with a somatic (or psychosomatic) symptom but with a high score on the Langner as having a psychological or non-psychological problem any more or less often than an English patient with the same symptoms and the same Langner score?

RESULTS

Before describing the results, it is important to define the interpretations placed on (a) somatic, (b) psychosomatic, and (c) psychological symptoms:

a. Symptoms were classified as 'somatic' when the patient was presenting with physical symptoms with clear bio-physical origins; eg a twisted foot; industrial or domestic burns to the skin; viral infections, etc.
b. A 'psychosomatic' symptom was clasified as one where the patient was complaining of vague physical symptoms which could have either a physical or psychological aetiology: eg skin rashes, headaches, overall muscular-skeletal pains.
c. Symptoms were classified as 'psychological' when the patient described them in purely psychological terms without any physical component: eg anxiety, depression, stress, nervousness, etc.

Results

The data reveal that a comparable number of Asian and English patients presented with somatic symptoms. The results differed markedly, however, for psychosomatic and psychological presentations. Of the 50 Asian born, 20 presented with psycho-somatic symptoms; 28 with somatic and 2 with psychological symptoms. With the English born, the figures are 10 with psychosomatic, 33 with somatic and 7 with psychological symptoms ($\chi^2 = 6.52$, 2 df, $p < 0.05$).

A similar pattern emerges when patients' presenting symptoms are cross-tabulated with GP's diagnoses. Whereas of the 10 English patients presenting psychosomatically, 5 were diagnosed as having a psychological problem, of the 20 Asian patients presenting psychosomatically, only 7 were diagnosed as having a psychological problem.

Figure 1:   Interaction between ethnic group and presenting symptoms on Langner scores

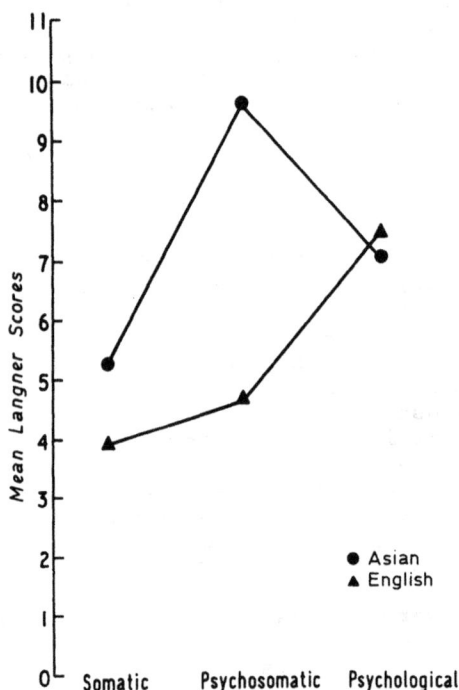

Inconsistencies also arose between the patients' Langner scores and the recognition by the GP of psychological problems when Asian and English patients were compared. There was a good match between Langner non-cases and the GP's recognition of non-psychological problems for both groups of patients. GPs were not, therefore, misdiagnosing non-psychological patients as "cases". With those English patients scoring highly on the Langner, once again GPs are accurately recognising the psychological origins of their problems. Where the GP's recognition of psychological problems comes into question is with those Asian patients who score highly on the Langner. Of the 30 Asian patients classified as cases by the Langner scale, only 9 were recognised as such by the GP ($\chi^2 = 0.212$, 1 df NS), whereas of the 14 English patients scoring 7 and above on the Langner scale, 10 were recognised as having a psychological problem ($\chi^2 = 7.36$, 1 df, $p < 0.01$).

For a more complete analysis of the relationships between Langner scale scores and other variations, a two-way analysis of variance was undertaken using ethnic group and presenting symptoms as the main effect. As a diagrammatical interpretation of the 2-way ANOVA shows (Figure 1) Asian patients scored more highly on the Langner than English patients, except for psychological symptoms, where they scored fractionally lower. An interesting point which the figure reveals quite clearly is the very high Langner score of Asian patients presenting psychosomatically. Certainly, one implication of this is that Asian patients with 'psycho-atric' problems were manifesting them psychosomatically. A more typical trend is shown with English patients and Langner mean scores, with gradual increase in scores from somatic through psychosomatic to psychological symptomatology.

DISCUSSION

The findings of this study can be discussed with reference to ethno-cultural factors pertaining to traditional health beliefs and aetiologies that may explain the greater psychosomatic presentation of psychological problems by Asian patients.

It is important, however, to understand the concepts the Asian patient has concerning the aetiology and attributions of 'psycho-atric' problems before any insight can be gained into symptomatology and health beliefs. On the Asian subcontinent, but in India specifically, mental illness is thought to be caused by one of three main factors (Weiss et al, 1986):

a. Firstly illness can be caused by an imbalance of body humours, a view subscribed to for some 3000 years and forming the basis of the Asian medical system. Illness, according to this theory, can be caused by eating foods with a constitution that might cause an excess of heat or cold in the body. Alternatively, an imbalance can be caused by an exposure to extremes of temperature.

b. Mental illness is also thought to be caused by another person's wish to cause harm through sorcery or magic - a concept, again, that is adhered to by different nationalities (Helman, 1985).

c. Finally, mental illness is believed to be caused by gods who become angry after they are treated irreverently, or by supernatural powers as punishment for breaking a taboo or cultural rule.

Clearly, an individual's health beliefs are culturally determined. Health beliefs are not ad hoc transitory notions of illness and disease, but are part of a rigid, structured, medical system which defines clinical reality. Similarly, the way the individual explains his/her illness (the explanatory model) is strongly related to ethno-cultural health beliefs influencing illness-presentation, illness-behaviour and help-seeking behaviour (Nations et al, 1985).

Turning then, to the cultural influences which may determine the greater psychosomatisation of Asian patients, the first explanation to be considered concerns the concept of locus of controls or the extent to which patients believe they have control over their illness. It can be argued that Asians feel they are, in many instances, responsible for their own illness, through having violated a taboo, angered a god or by having eaten the wrong type of food. As such, they have brought the illness upon themselves. One purpose of soma-tisation, therefore, could be a mechanism for the denial or repression of the existence of a psychological problem.

In contrast, studies on the health beliefs of British working-class women have shown that ill-health is thought to come about either through environmental factors, such as the weather, through heredity, family and individual susceptibility, or by germs, viruses and infections (Helman, 1985).

The point being emphasised here, then, is that these differential interpretations of illness and disease, and the amount of control the individual feels they have, will often result in differences in illness-presentation and help-seeking behaviour. These points may be reflected in the greater numbers of Asian 'psycho-atric' patients presenting psycho-somatically.

Another insight into lay beliefs is the way illness is expressed. In Britain, for example, somewhat over-generalised and vague mechanistic interpretations are often attributed to physical and mental ill-health: "I feel run down", "my batteries need charging", "I had a nervous breakdown", "I'm on the mend". Contrast this with the metaphors likely to be used by Asians: "Mera dil dukh da he" (my heart hurts) for "I am depressed". Although a somatic presention is used, it is not the same as the vague mechanistic interpretations, previously cited as being typical of English patients. Whereas the latter example is a cultural interpretation of depression, the heart being regarded as the seat of the emotions, the former illustration is an example where responsibility is shifted from the individual by analogising illness with mechanical failure.

These expressions of health and ill-health have implications not only for the individual but also for the clinician. Whereas one could say with some certainty that a clinician would not mis-understand an English patient's "I am heart-broken", the same could not be said for an Asian patient's "my heart hurts". There are also practical reasons why Asian patients may present psychological problems somatically. The first, and most obvious, concerns the language barrier. If patients have difficulty in articulating their complaints because they are unable to clearly express themselves, it may be that presenting somatically reduces that difficulty. The responsibility is placed on the clinician to define and ascribe illness. In fact, in the traditional Asian health setting, it is the role of the healer to tell the patient what is wrong with them and not vice versa (Carstairs & Kapur, 1976). Alternatively the Asian patient may present with a somatic symptom, believing the clinician as a bio-medic treats bio-physical ailments only.

Implications

There are several important points to consider for the clinician who is dealing with Asian patients, issues which have a direct bearing on the patients' compliance with treatment regimens and with clinical outcome.

Although language can often be a barrier between the clinician and the patient, it has to be remembered that many Asians have been resident in Britain for ten years or more, so their grasp of English is often better than they care to admit. Holding a dialogue with an Asian patient may be difficult, but not impossible. Given the inter-actional nature of the clinician-patient encounter, it becomes clear how attributions are important to each. For the patient distressed by bodily or psychological feelings, a causal explanation provides some control of them. Furthermore, causal explanations indicate forms of lay and medical consultations that may also be pursued to control the discomfort.

For the clinician, illness attributions are important precisely because they reveal the meanings patients attach to those symptoms or disabilities which they bring to the consultation. It is this meaning of illness that determines, in turn, the patient's illness behaviours, coping responses and clinical outcome. Effective communication requires that the patient's conceptions of illness be explored and differences from the clinician acknowledged, interpreted and, if possible, resolved.

It must be difficult for any practitioner to by-pass conventional medical explanations and treatment programmes for the sake of getting the patient's whole-hearted agreement and compliance. How, for example, would one begin to help an Asian patient who is tense and anxious because he or she feels that a relative in India is making life extremely difficult through actively wishing him or her harm. This belief may be further strengthened in the patient's mind through a series of ill-fates.

Conventional relaxation programmes may help overcome physical symptoms of stress and anxiety but would do little for the underlying problem. To try and convince the patient that there is no evidence that a relative is bearing a grudge might seem a natural step, but one which overlooks a cultural milieu where it is believed that one individual can have a malevolent impact on the life-events of another. A more positive approach would be to accept the patient's explanatory model and to incorporate it in the treatment process.

The suggestion here, then, is that despite these conflicting ideas about illness causation between clinician and patient, successsful treatment may still be accomplished. By eliciting the patient's ethno-cultural, patho-psychological ideas, the clinician and patient can then discuss, negotiate and co-operate for a successful outcome. Questions such as: "What do you feel may be causing your problem?", "How do you feel the illness is affecting you?" and "What do you feel might be of benefit?" are possible ways of gaining insight into the patient's explanatory model.

Acknowledgements

I am indebted to everyone who made this research possible.

My special thanks to Professor Ray Cochrane, who provided invaluable assistance during every stage of this paper; to the General Practitioners of Handsworth who gave of their time; to Dr. Akhter and Dr. Roland Littlewood of All Saints Hospital; to Sue Garvey for her typing and a special, personal thank you to the patients who made this study possible.

REFERENCES

Abrahamson, J.H., Mayett, F.G.H. & Majola, G.C. (1961). What is wrong with me? South African Medical Journal, 19, 690-694.

Bridges, K.W. & Goldberg, D.P. (1985). Somatic presentation of DSM III psychiatric disorders in primary care. Journal of Psychosomatic Research, 29, No. 6, 563-569.

Carstairs, G.M. & Kapur, R.L. (1976). The Great University of Kota: Stress, Change and Mental Disorder in an Indian Village. Hogarth: London.

Cochrane, R., Hashmi, F. & Stopes-Roe, M. (1977). Measuring psychological disturbance in Asian immigrants to Britain. Social Science and Medicine, 11, 157-164.

Diller, A. (1980). Cross-cultural pain semantics. Pain, 9, 9-26.

Helman, C.G. (1985). Culture, Health and Illness. John Wright: Bristol.

Herzlich, C. (1973). Health and Illness: A Social Psychological Analysis. Academic Press: London.

Kleinman, A. & Good, B. (Eds) (1985). Culture and Depression: Studies in the Anthropology and Cross-Cultural Psychiatry of Affect and Disorder. University of California Press: Berkeley.

Lloyd, G.G. (1986). Review article: Psychiatric syndromes with a somatic presentation. Journal of Psychosomtic Research, 30, No. 2, 113-120.

Nations, M.K., Camino, L.A. & Walker, F.B. (1985). "Hidden" popular illnesses in primary care: residents' recognition and clinical implications. Culture, Medicine and

Psychiatry, 9, 223-240.

Weiss, G.M., Sharma, S.D., Gaur, R.K., Sharma, J.S., Desai, A. & Doongaji, D.R. (1986). Traditional concepts of mental disorder among Indian psychiatric patients: preliminary report of work in progress. Social Science and Medicine, 23, No. 4, 379-386.

White, G. (1982). The role of cultural explanations in 'somatization' and 'psychologization'. Social Science and Medicine, 16, 1519-1530.

Chapter Sixteen

LIFE STRESS AND SYMPTOMS: A COMPARATIVE STUDY OF
PAKISTANI AND ENGLISH WOMEN

Shamim Mahmud

INTRODUCTION

Comparisons of the psychological health of
immigrant ethnic groups with that of the native
population in Britain, have yielded ambiguous
results. The rates differ depending on whether
treated morbidity or untreated morbidity figures are
examined. For instance, Pakistani immigrants had
low admission rates to mental hospitals in
comparison to the natives but reported similar
symptom levels in a community study (Cochrane and
Stopes-Roe, 1977).
Two explanatory hypotheses have been put
forward to account for the differential rates found.
It has been suggested that low rates of treated
morbidity could be attributed to differential
selection. That is where migration is difficult and
failure to achieve acceptable living standards is
not due to personal failure, it would be the most
stable and enterprising individuals who succeeded
in migrating. Higher rates of psychological ill-
health have been explained in terms of negative
selection. However, equivalent rates of untreated
morbidity have been attributed to under utilisation
of psychiatric services and the use of lay health
networks. Furthermore, there has been no published
research validation to indicate whether immigrants
are a negatively or positively selected group in
comparison to the non-migrants remaining in their
country of origin.
The other major hypothesis put forward to
explain differential rates of illness between
migrants and natives is that of stress. Although a
number of studies have linked higher rates of
illness among migrants with stress, this has been a
post hoc explanation. With two exceptions most

investigations in the field of migration and mental health have largely ignored the findings of the increasing literature on stress and psychological disorder.

It was against this background that the present work was done. There were two aims: to investigate whether the earlier findings of equivalent rates in a community survey could be repeated, and to determine whether there was a link between stress and illness in a group of Pakistani women.

Women were specifically selected to minimise the effect of self selection. Usually the decision to migrate is made by Pakistani men, with women migrating to join their families later. It is unlikely that mate selection would be operating either, with enterprising men choosing similar spouses, as Pakistani marriages tend to be arranged by families who favour traditionalism rather than enterprise in a prospective wife.

Selection of Sample and Instruments Used

Two groups of women, 39 Pakistani and 40 English, were randomly selected from the general practice records of a Health Centre in Central Birmingham. Details of the criteria for inclusion in the study and specific procedures for selection have been reported previously (Mahmud, 1983).

Initially, potential respondents were contacted by a letter in either Urdu or English, as appropriate, and this was usually followed by a telephone call or visit. The response rate was 87% for the English sample and 82% for the Pakistanis. All women were interviewed in their own homes, in the appropriate language, on at least three occasions. Information was collected about stressful life events and long term difficulties in the year prior to the interview; the presence or absence of symptoms as well as degree of severity; and finally the appropriate general practitioner was contacted for information on the frequency and type of consultation in the previous year for each woman.

Information on stressful life events was collected using a translated and adapted version of the Life Events Interview (LEI) developed by Brown and Harris (1978). This interview had been adapted to include events which would be relevant to the immigrants' experiences in Britain. The adapted and translated interview was piloted in a reliability study in Edinburgh (Mahmud, 1983). The results had indicated a satisfactory degree/ of reliability for use with Pakistani immigrants. Obviously when the English women were interviewed, the English version of the adapted instrument was used, with the exception of items which were only relevant to immigrants.

A scoring system developed by the original authors was used to determine the differences between events and difficulties as well as the degree of threat these held, for the women concerned. The level of threat corresponded to scores for major or minor events and difficulties. Previous work based on the life events interview has indicated that it is the occurrence of major (or severely threatening) events and difficulties which have consequences for the psychological health of the individual.

Symptom level and symptom severity were established using the Comprehensive Psycho-pathological Rating Scale (CPRS). However as the correlation between reported and observed symptoms for both the Pakistani sample (r=0.64, p <.001) and the English sample (r=0.83, p <.001) was high, the decision was made to base later analyses on the dependent variables of reported symptoms and consultation rates only.

Finally information about GP consultations was collected by requesting the G.P. concerned to complete a form giving date of consultation, nature of the problem, whether it was a first or subsequent episode of the problem and, finally, the action taken.

RESULTS

The results will be discussed in two sections. The first section will focus on the difference and similarities between the two groups (see Table 1), while the second will focus on the relationship between the independent and dependent variables for both samples.

The expectation that Pakistani women would have equivalent levels of psychological symptoms to the English women was not substantiated. Pakistani women reported significantly fewer symptoms in com-parison to the English sample. Similarly Pakistani women had significantly fewer consultations with their GP compared to the English women. The mean annual consultation rate was 1.92 for the Pakistani women in comparison to 3.75 for the English women. However no differences were found between the two groups when symptom severity was examined.

Table 1: Differences in scores on measures of stress, symptoms and consultation rates in two samples of women

| Variable | Ethnic Group | | | | t value |
| | Pakistani N=39 | | English N=40 | | |
	X̄	s.d.	X̄	s.d.	
Reported symptoms	8.18	5.45	11.20	5.21	2.52*
Observed symptoms	3.38	2.99	4.03	3.25	0.91
GP visits in year	1.92	1.94	3.75	1.94	3.02*
Total LTD	4.69	1.82	5.78	2.55	2.18*
Major LTD	1.77	1.37	2.23	1.75	1.29
All events	2.64	1.66	6.03	3.38	5.67**
Major events	0.18	0.39	0.35	0.92	1.08

*=p< 0.05;   **=p<0.01

Significant differences were found between the two groups for two measures of stress. English women reported significantly more of both total Long Term Difficulties (LTD) and total number of events, while Pakistani women reported fewer LTDS as well as a smaller total number of events. However, when stress was broken down into separate categories of severe and non-severe stress for both LTDs and events, no differences were found.

Stress was directly related to the dependent variables of psychological symptoms for both samples. For the Pakistanis, major events, major LTD and total LTD were significantly correlated with reported symptoms. For the English women, all measures of stress were significantly correlated with reported symptoms. However, with one exception, stress was not significantly correlated with frequency of consultation. The exception was for the English sample where a significant relationship was found between total LTD and frequency of consultation.

The relationships between the two independent variables and the dependent variables were examined by multiple regression analyses. The rationale for this was to predict the variance in reported symptoms and consultation rates for the two samples respectively using a combination of stress variables. For the Pakistani sample major events and major LTD successfully explained 37.2% of the variance in reported symptoms. For the English sample major LTD on its own explained 27.8% of the variance in reported symptoms. While major events did explain a further proportion of the variance, it was entered later into the regression equation for the English sample, other variables such as social support being entered earlier in the analysis.

Finally, the stress variables were not successful in explaining a significant proportion of the variance in consultation rates for either sample.

DISCUSSION

The results suggest that, though the English women experienced significantly more overall life events and long term difficulties, there were no differences between the groups with respect to major life events and major long term difficulties. The present finding of more overall life stress for the English sample is in agreement with results reported earlier in the literature (Cochrane & Stopes-Roe, 1977); the only point of departure is in the lack of difference between the groups when compared with respect to severe stress.

Similarly comparable results to those reported earlier in the literature (Cochrane & Stopes-Roe, 1977; Roskies et al, 1977) were found when the association between stress and symptoms was examined. Given the different measures used in earlier studies and the present work both in the assessment of psychological symptoms and life stress, the comparability of the results is reassuring.

In contrast to earlier findings, the proportion of variance in psychological symptomatology explained by life events was much higher in this study. Previous work has indicated that life events account for approximately 10% of the variance in psychological well being (Cochrane & Sobol, 1980); however, the proportion of variance accounted for by major events and long term difficulties was higher in the present work.

Although Pakistani women reported less experience of stress, these results do not justify the dismissal of the hypothesis which links migrants' psychological health with the stress encountered. The results of the multiple regression analyses clearly indicate that severe stress accounts for the greatest proportion of variance explained in psychological symptoms among Pakistanis. This lends support to the contention that stress is implicated in migrants' psychological disturbance.

In contrast to earlier work (Cochrane & Stopes-Roe, 1977; 1981) where no differences were found, Pakistani women reported lower levels of symptoms than did native women in this project. There are two probable explanations for this. First, it is possible that the different instruments used in the previous work and the present study elicited different patterns of symptoms. Second, it is possible that when a scale, such as used in previous work, contains a greater number of items concerning physical symptoms, people with physical illness and little or no emotional disorders could show up as false positives (Muller, 1971) since physical illness may or may not reflect psychological distress.

There were no differences between the groups with respect to the severity of symptoms. That is, although Pakistani women had fewer symptoms than did English women on average, the symptoms they had were of equal severity. Pakistani women also had lower rates of consultation in comparison to the English women. This may be due to the use of alternative treatment networks, but it has been suggested (Rack, 1982) that the use of traditional healers or lay networks is a supplement, rather than an alternative, to orthodox medicine. The obvious explanation is that immigrant women in this study consulted less frequently than the English women because they had less illness. However, the consultation rates for the Pakistani women were not significantly associated with the presence of reported psychological symptoms. This would, therefore, suggest that there is not as direct and obvious a relationship between psychological symptoms and going to the doctor for the Pakistani women as there is for English women.

Although the present results suggest that Pakistani women have lower levels of psychological symptoms in comparison to the English women as well as lower consultation rates, the results need to be interpreted with caution. These findings are at variance with the only other two studies which have examined psychological symptoms (Cochrane & Stopes-Roe, 1981) and consultation rates (Brewin, 1980) among Pakistanis using community samples. It may be that the results differ from earlier work on account of either the differing instruments used or the particular social context of the ethnic group studied.

The major findings of the present work would suggest that the differences in the psychological health of a minority ethnic group and of native women are not a consequence of some fundamental differences between the groups, but more a consequence of their life situations. The same psychological processes underlie health and illness irrespective of ethnicity.

REFERENCES

Brewin, C. (1980). Explaining the lower rates of psychiatric treatment among Asian immigrants to the UK. Social Psychiatry, 15, 17-20.

Brown, G. & Harris T. (1978). Social Origin of Depression: A Study of Psychiatric Disorder in Women. Tavistock: London.

Cochrane, R. & Sobol, M. (1980). Life stresses and psychological consequences. In M.P. Feldman & J. Orford (Eds), The Social Psychology of Psychological Problems. Wiley: London.

Cochrane, R. & Stopes-Roe (1977). Psychological and social adjustment of Asian immigrants to Britain: a community survey. Social Psychiatry, 12, 195-207.

Cochrane, R. & Stopes-Roe, M. (1981). Psychological symptom levels in Indian immigrants to England - a comparison with natives. Psychological Medicine, 11, 319-327.

Mahmud, S. (1983). Life stresses, social support and psychological symptoms in Pakistani women in Britain. Doctoral dissertation, University of Birmingham.

Muller D.J. (1971). Discussion of Langner's psychiatric scale: a short screening device. American Journal of Psychiatry, 128, 601-606.

Rack, P. (1982). Race, Culture and Mental Disorder Tavistock: London.

Roskies, E., Iida-Miranda, M.L. & Strobel, M.G. (1977). Life changes as predictors of illness in immigrants. In C.P. Spielberger & I.G. Sarason (Eds), Stress and Anxiety. Hemisphere Publications: London.

Chapter Seventeen

MENTAL HEALTH AND VALUE SIMILARITY AMONG IMMIGRANTS
IN SWEDEN

Elina Haavio-Mannila

INTRODUCTION

The relationship between migration and mental
health has been studied from three points of view
(Stenius, 1983).

1. According to social selection theories,
   migration, particularly emigration, is an act
   which is more predictable in certain (negative)
   living conditions or for certain types of
   people, especially those with a greater dis-
   position for psychic problems.
2. Migration is an upsetting life event which
   produces changes in most aspects of the
   migrants' life and induces special strains in
   the individuals involved.
3. Many immigrants live under social conditions
   which favour the development of psychiatric
   problems.

In this paper the mental health and
utlilisation of health services of immigrants to
Sweden, particularly those from Finland, are
examined. The interpretations are linked more to
life event and social condition theories than to the
social selection theory.

In addition to survey and hospital case data on
psychiatric problems, early retirement and sick
leave statistics also reveal some aspects of
psychological problems and how people cope with
them. Statistics on early retirement of immigrants
collected by Reinans (1986) are combined with
earlier research results (Haavio-Mannila, 1984).
Mental health data are related to the extent of
value similarity and the familiarity of different
immigrant groups to the Swedish host populations

(Westin, 1984). The paper focuses on the specific situation of Finns in Sweden.

Early Retirement as a Consequence of Cultural Distance

In Sweden the official retirement age is 65 years. In 1981-82 about 1% of the 3.9 million people aged between 16 and 64 years working for pay took early retirement. Early retirement was more common among persons born abroad than among native Swedes. While foreign born persons composed 9.5% of the gainfully employed population, as many as 14.5% of persons retiring before the age of 65 years were born abroad (Reinans, 1986).

Early retirement can be looked upon as an indicator of poor adjustment to working life, since early retirement pensions are mainly given for health reasons. Diseases of muscles, skeleton and connective tissues were, in 1981-82, the most common diagnoses of those taking early retirement (38%), with diseases of the circulatory system and mental problems being the next most common causes of early retirement (17% and 17% respectively).

With the exception of Germans, all immigrant groups have higher early retirement rates than native Swedes (Table 1). In addition to Germans, Norwegians and Danes also have low rates of early retirement. Estonians, Poles, Turks, Finns and Hungarians were, in this respect, intermediate while early retirement rates for Yugoslavians and Greeks were very high.

The proportion of persons retiring with a psychiatric diagnosis as the main cause of retirement indicates adjustment problems more directly than does the overall retirement rate. In general this proportion is well correlated with the overall early requirement rate (Table 1). Exceptions are the Poles and the Turks whose proportions of people retiring for mental reasons are high compared to the overall rate for these groups.

In earlier studies, it has been shown that the geographical and cultural distance between the country of origin and destination are good predictors of probability of becoming mentally ill in the new country. For example, according to our studies in the Vesteras psychiatric clinic and Sundby mental hospital there were, in 1971, about 300 psychiatric patients from Denmark, Norway and other Western European countries per 100,000 population; 576 per 100,000 from Finland; 1479

Table 1: Early retirement rate and proportion of retired men and women with psychiatric diagnosis according to country of birth, Sweden 1981-82 (Reinans, 1986); and similarity of values and familiarity with culture of these countries as experienced by Swedes, 1981 (Westin, 1984, 335-337).

Country	Numbers aged 16-64	New early retirements 1981-82		Value simil- arity 1)	Famil- iarity 2)
		Age-weighted rate per 1000 persons in 1980	Percent due to psychiatric diagnosis		
Total Swedish Population	5,221,809	15	17	–	–
Germany	31,232	14	18	94	73
Norway	33,765	18	15	91	73
Denmark	35,571	18	16	46	25
Estonia	9,764	24	9	16	19
Poland	16,561	25	28	2	5
Turkey	10,553	26	27	83	59
Finland	220,412	27	18	–	–
Hungary	11,427	30	21	5	12
Yugoslavia	34,533	48	31	4	14
Greece	13,814	49	33		

1) Proportion (%) of Swedes aged 18-70 years (N=1202) considering that the ethnic groups share similar values with them on issues such as children's education.
2) Proportion (%) of Swedes considering that they are familiar with the ways of life and culture of the group (i.e. they know them very well or quite well).

from Yugoslavia; 1682 from Eastern Europe; and 1870 from Italy (Haavio-Mannila and Stenius, 1977).

The cultural difference between the country of birth of the immigrant and the Swedish culture can be measured on the basis of value similarity and familiarity as experienced by Swedes (Westin, 1984). In general, the more similarity in the values of the the countries of origin and destination, according to the opinion of Swedes, the lower the early retirement rate for the immigrant group. Value similarity may be partly an expression of other similarities with regard to life conditions, standard of living, structure of health service, etc. in the two countries, not just cultural distance.

The most noticeable exception to this generalisation is the Turkish immigrant group, which has a relatively low early retirement rate in spite of a great perceived dissimilarity of values between them and Swedes. This may be due to several factors: Turks live together in certain areas of Sweden and, according to Murphy (1965), it is advantageous to mental health to have one's countrymen nearby in the new environment. It has also been shown that Turks get social support from their family and relatives to a higher degree than, for example, Yugoslavian immigrants (Simila, 1986). Turks are devoted Muslims compared to Greek Orthodox or atheist Greeks and Yugoslavs. Religion may help them in getting along in the new environment. Finally, as a recently arrived group, Turks may not yet be sensitive to hidden discrimination in Swedish society, from which the earlier arrived Greeks and Yugoslavs, with better language skills and higher ambitions, also suffer (Jaakkola, 1983).

Mental problems as a cause for early retirement are most frequent in the culturally distant immigrant groups. Turks have lower proportions than Greeks and Yugoslavs, but differences are not as large as in the total early retirement rates. Immigration into a culturally dissimilar society is a more critical life event than moving to a country in which values are relatively similar. The living conditions in a dissimilar country create more strain than those in a more similar country. The stressfulness of the migration itself and the strain experienced in the remote culture can create psychological problems which lead to early retirement. In some culturally remote ethnic groups there may be some intervening social support mechanisms, which help the immigrants to cope with these strains.

Mental Health and Use of Health Care Services among Southern European and Finnish Immigrants

A group in which the early retirement rate - both overall and due to mental problems - is relatively high, in spite of similarity in values with Swedes, is the Finnish immigrant group. This may be related to an ambivalent image of Finns, which is held in Sweden. They are, seen as both hardworking and rowdy, and this "double bind" may create mental health problems (Haavio-Mannila, 1984).

The Swedish Institute of Social Research conducted three surveys on the standard of living in 1968, 1974 and 1981 (cf. Leinio, 1984) in which Finnish and Yugoslavian immigrants were compared to Swedes matched according to age, sex and occupation. The mental health of both immigrant groups was found to be poorer than that of native Swedes.

Yugoslavian immigrant men in particular were very often registered as sick (Haavio-Mannila, 1984). Jansson and Papastavrou (1984) suggest that being registered as sick with an instruction to rest is considered by many immigrant groups to be a functional form of treatment, but it is not any more regarded as such by Swedes. In the same way early retirement, being registered sick or getting sick leave may be a preventive measure taken in order to avoid a mental or physical breakdown. Accordingly, Southern European immigrants act rationally in the cultural crisis created by the arrival in a strange country when they resort to the opportunity to take sick leave. Finns, on the other hand, have more inhibitions against utilisation of the Swedish welfare system even though they have as many or more illnesses than Yugoslavs. Both immigrant groups are hospitalized as often as comparable Swedes (Haavio-Mannila, 1984).

In connection with a project aimed at giving psychiatric support to immigrants in the Huddinge hospital in Stockholm, Jansson and Papastavrou (1984) compared the duration of periods of sick leave and the duration of hospital stay among Greek and Yugoslavian immigrants and natives. They also investigated whether periods of mental disorder among immigrants were more often disguised as somatic disorders, and whether immigrants were more often given sick leave certificates from physicians in private practice.

The total period of sick leave during the

period in question was longer for immigrants, particularly for Yugoslavian patients. Still more pronounced was the fact that each period was longer for the immigrant groups, especially in the Greek group than among Swedish patients. However, the Greek and Yugoslavian individuals were treated for significantly less time in hospital during the observation period than were Swedish patients. Immigrant patients treated in a hospital were less often diagnosed as psychiatric patients than were the natives. However, data received from the insurance companies revealed that they suffered from psychiatric problems just as often as Swedes. Jansson and Papastavrou point out that South-Europeans, to a higher extent than Swedes, try to avoid being admitted to a psychiatric clinic out of fear of being stigmatised as mentally ill.

These studies show that immigrants have more mental health problems than Swedes even when age, sex and occupation are controlled. Southern European immigrants take advantage of the sick leave and early retirement schemes in Sweden, but they do not rely so heavily on the public health care system, because they may wish to avoid hospitalisation.

Mental Health of Finnish Immigrants

Finnish immigrants appear to have a high rate of mental problems even though the value similarity, and their familiarity, to Swedes is high. This may be related to the special features of Finnish society and language, and the relationship between Finland and Sweden in general. The historical and political position of Finland as a buffer between Eastern and Western Europe may create cross-pressures and doublebinds. Finns, who have an exacting work ethic (Jaakkola, 1983) try to cope by ploughing themselves into work, frequently over-taxing themselves and, as a consequence, falling ill.

The position of Finland is ambivalent in Sweden. On the one hand, it is distant from Sweden due to different language and a different level of economic development. On the other hand Swedes look at Finns as having fairly similar values and are familiar with their way of life and culture (Finland was part of Sweden until 1809). Finns are partly rejected by Swedes because they are not believed to be interesting newcomers, who bring colour and excitement to Swedish society. On the other hand, Finns are more accepted as immigrants than some other groups by those Swedes who are afraid of losing Swedish customs and traditions because of immigration and who want to preserve Swedish culture (Westin, 1984).

Another kind of problem is the closed nature of social networks among Finnish immigrants, which time does not appear to lessen. Even the Swedish-speaking Finns in Sweden are somewhat isolated and their informal social relations were reduced after emigration.

A further ambivalence experienced by Finns in Sweden is the easiness of return migration, thanks to the geographical proximity to the home country. This creates indecision in relation to where to live. Immigrants from distant countries and political refugees have fewer choices.

Finns are seen by Swedes at one and the same time as hardworking and boisterous; close and distant. Finns may feel themselves trapped in a system of conflicting demands and expectations which they cannot satisfy. They may react in three ways: by fighting back, becoming obstreperous in various ways; by developing an inferiority complex and despising themselves and their own countrymen in a compensatory reaction, or yielding to (mental) illness, drugs, alcohol and suicide. Most of them, however, do rely on more socially constructive ways of coping.

REFERENCES

Haavio-Mannila, E. (1984). Social adjustment of Finns in Sweden. Siirtolaisuus-Migration Vol. 11, No. 3, 26-53.

Haavio-Mannila, E. & Stenius, K. (1977). Mental Health of Immigrants in Sweden. Helsinki: Research Reports, University of Helsinki, No. 211.

Jaakkola, M. (1983). Finnish Immigrants in Sweden Networks and Life Styles. Helsinki: Research Reports. Research Group for Comparative Sociology, University of Helsinki, No. 30.

Jansson, B. & Papastavrou, D. (1984). Sjukskrivningsmonster och slutenvardskonsumtion hos greker, jugoslaver och svenskar sett ur psykiatrisk perspektiv. Nordisk Psychiatriatrisk Tidskrift, 385-392.

Leinio, T. (1984). Inte lika men jamlika? Om
   finlandska invandrares levnadsforhallanden
   enligt Levnadsnivandervsokningarna 1968, 1976
   och 1981. Institutet for Social Forskning:
   Stockholm.
Murphy, H.B.M. (1965). Migration and the major
   mental disorders. In Kantor, M.B. (Ed.)
   Mobility and Mental Health. Charles C. Thomas:
   Springfield, Illinois.
Reinans, S. (1986). Fortidspensioneringar bland
   invandrare. Preliminar redovisning
   DEIFO 30/1 Stockholm. (stencil)
Simila, M. (1986). Kulterell identitet hos unga
   invandrare. Centrum for invandrngsforsking.
   Manuscript: University of Stockholm.
Stenius, K. (1983). Invandrarna och den
   psyckiatriska varden. Socialstyrelsen
   redovisar, 3.
Westin, C. (1984). Majoritet om minoritet. En
   studie i etnisk tolerans i 80-talets Sverige.
   Liber: Stockholm.

Chapter Eighteen

THE HEALTH BELIEFS OF THE HEALTH PROFESSIONALS

Marie Johnston and Theresa Marteau

Health Psychology is concerned with all aspects
of behaviour pertaining to health, disease,
prevention and treatment. Many aspects of behaviour
have been studied including uptake of medical
screening, behavioural factors in the aetiology of
coronary heart disease, adherence to medical
regimens, distress caused by medical procedures and
coping with chronic disease. This work has been
applied in a variety of settings, including
hospitals, health centres, schools and worksites and
has resulted in improvements in health outcomes for
patients. A major focus has been the beliefs that
people, including patients, hold about their health,
their symptoms and about their medical treatment
(see for example Johnston & Marteau, 1987 in press).
The behaviour and beliefs of politicians,
planners, administrators, receptionists, doctors,
nurses and therapists may all influence health
outcomes for the individual. However, research to
date has focused on the patient, largely ignoring
these other sources of variance. In this paper, the
beliefs of health professionals, those providing
clinical care directly to patients, are examined.
The relative neglect of the study of health
professionals may be due to an implicit assumption
that their behaviour and beliefs are based directly
and invariantly on medical care, an empirically
derived set of shared beliefs. We have argued that
the invariance assumption is false, there being
numerous published examples of diverse approaches to
identical clinical situations (Marteau & Johnston,
1986b). One explanation put forward to explain
these differences is that they stem from differences
in medical knowledge. However many of the
situations concern events for which there is no
knowledge.

Beliefs can be characterised by their empirical status and by consensus (see Figure 1). Using this categorisation, knowledge refers to those beliefs which have been verified; they may be shared (box a) or unshared (box d). Where knowledge exists, a belief can be categorised as erroneous and labelled as adherence to a myth (box b) or personal ignorance (box e), depending on whether it is shared or unshared.

The majority of clinical situations require decisions based on untested beliefs (boxes c and f), untested either because the evidence has not been collected or because they are untestable. For example, until recently, the treatment of mild hypertension with anti-hypertensive medication was based on a working hypothesis (box c) from the shared generalisation from data on the treatment of severe hypertension. Frequently, patients present with symptoms which resemble but do not exactly fit the textbook descriptions of a disease and the clinician will then prescribe treatment based on a personal belief that the symptoms are compatible with that diagnosis (box f).

Figure 1: Categorisation of Beliefs According to
           Verification and Consensus

Empirical Status of Belief

		tested		untested
		verified	unverified	verifiable or unverifiable
C O N S E N S U S	shared	KNOWLEDGE based on accesible data a	ERROR -myth b	WORKING HYPOTHESIS c
	unshared	KNOWLEDGE based on new or private data d	ERROR -ignorance e	PERSONAL BELIEF f

The Health Beliefs of the Health Professionals

Health professionals spend much of their time dealing with data that are untested, hence decisions are taken on the basis of individual beliefs for which there is no necessary consensus. Thus psychological models that consider beliefs as well as knowledge are more applicable in explaining health professionals' behaviour than models that consider knowledge as the sole determinant of behaviour.

Elsewhere we have demonstrated that various cognitive and behavioural models can explain some of the variance in the behaviour of health professionals (Marteau & Johnston, 1987). In this paper we will review evidence concerning the extent to which the Health Belief Model (HBM), a model of health-related behaviour (Becker et al., 1979), may be applied to the behaviour of health professionals by considering whether the health beliefs of the health professionals vary in accordance with the main parameters of the HBM.

The HBM includes four main dimensions of belief: the individual's perceptions of seriousness, vulnerability, benefits of and costs or barriers to health related behaviours. It also postulates that prior to a health action there is a cue or trigger to act.

Perceived Seriousness of a Condition

Physicians dealing with the same condition (diabetes) have been shown to have quite different perceptions of the disease depending on whether they work with children or with adults (Marteau & Baum, 1984). Paediatricians viewed the condition to be significantly less serious than did general physicians.

There is further evidence of inter-professional differences in seriousness estimates from work on nurses' and physiotherapists' assessments of patients whose care they shared. The nurses rated the patients' pain to be more serious and their disabilities to be more severe than the patients did (Johnston et al., 1987 in press).

Perceived Vulnerability

Marteau & Baum (1984) also found that the paediatricians working with children with diabetes rated the likelihood of a patient with diabetes developing complications of the disease to be lower than did the general physicians, the difference being significant for 7 out of 8 complications.

Physicians' estimates of disease mortality have

been shown to have some of the characteristics of personal beliefs. Deviations from true rates were in part related to the frequency with which the physician had encountered people with that illness and in part related to journal coverage of the disease in the preceding 6 months: the more encounters and the more column inches devoted to an illness in the New England Journal of Medicine, the higher the mortality estimate (Christensen-Szalanski et al, 1983).

Perceived Benefits of a Health Action

Health professionals may vary in their beliefs about the likely effectiveness of treatments they administer. In a recent study of the resuscitation skills of trained nurses, we found widely differing views of the effectiveness of resuscitation; it was rated to be effective in from 2% to 90% of cases, the median being 40% (Wynne et al, 1987).

In the study of physicians' perceptions of diabetes, paediatricians were less likely to believe that reducing blood glucose levels would be beneficial in reducing diabetic complications (Marteau & Baum, 1984). Weinberger et al (1984) found similar differences in belief. Physicians who were successful in achieving glycaemic control in their patients were more likely to perceive glycaemic control to be effective in reducing the likelihood of diabetic complications than were physicians who were unsuccessful.

Perceived Barriers to a Health Action

Health professionals may perceive barriers which prevent them from carrying out appropriate health care actions. Asking the patient's permission to take blood for routine monitoring of diabetes in childhood appeared to act as a barrier to taking the blood. When the barrier was reduced, by sending an advance letter explaining that a blood sample would be required, the rate of sample collection rose from 30% to approximately 70% (Marteau & Johnston, 1986).

Cohen (1983) found that clothing might be a barrier to appropriate patient examination. Physicians looking after patients with diabetes examined the feet of 98% of patients who entered the consultation barefoot but only 52% of those who entered wearing shoes and socks.

Beliefs and Behaviours

Whether these differences in beliefs relate

systematically to differences in how health professionals manage the care and treatment of patients is a further question. There are certainly indications from some of the studies in this area that beliefs are related to behaviours. For example Marteau & Baum (1984) found different beliefs about diabetes associated with different treatment goals; Wynne et al, (1987) found different beliefs about the effectiveness of resuscitation associated with different levels of success in performing the skill; Weinberger et al (1984) found different beliefs about the effectiveness of diabetic control associated with different levels of success in achieving diabetic control.

CONCLUSIONS

In neglecting the systematic study of the beliefs of the health professionals, Health Psychology may ignore an important source of variance in patients' health outcomes. Psychological models which assume knowledge as the basis of beliefs are inadequate to account for the beliefs held by health professionals. Models that consider personal as well as shared beliefs, such as the HBM, illustrate some of the important dimensions of professionals' beliefs in the context of uncertainty, the context in which many health judgements are made. Given that there is some evidence that the beliefs of the health professionals are related to their behaviours which in turn are related to health outcomes for patients, the beliefs of the health professionals may prove to be an appropriate target for interventions.

REFERENCES

Becker, M.H., Maiman, I.A., Kirscht, J.P., Haefner, D.P., Drachman, R.H., & Taylor, D.W. (1979). Patient Perceptions and Compliance; Recent Studies of the Health Belief Model. In R.B. Haynes, D.W. Taylor, & D.L. Sackett (Eds), Compliance in Health Care, pp78-109, John Hopkins University Press: Baltimore.

Christensen-Szalanski I.J.J., Beck, D.E., Christensen-Szalanski, C.M., & Koelsell, T.D. (1983). Effects of expertise and experience on risk judgements. J.Applied Psychology, 68, 278-284.

Cohen, S.J. (1983). Potential barriers to diabetic care. Diabetes Care, 6, 499-500.

The Health Beliefs of the Health Professionals

Johnston, M., Bromley, I., Boothroyd-Brooks, M.,
    Dobbs, W., Ilson, A. & Ridout, K. (1987, in press).
    Behavioural assessments of physically disabled
    patients: agreement between rehabilitation
    therapists and nurses. International Journal
    of Research Rehabilitation.
Johnston, M. & Marteau, T.M. (1987, in press).
    Health Psychology. Special Issue of Current
    Psychological Research and Reviews.
Marteau, T.M., & Baum, J.D. (1984). Doctors' views
    on diabetes. Arch.Dis.Child, 59, 566-570.
Marteau, T.M. & Johnston, M. (1986). Doctors
    taking blood from children: a suitable
    case for treatment?
    Brit.J.Clin.Psychol, 25, 159-160.
Marteau, T.M. & Johnston, M. (1987, Submitted for
    publication). The application of psychological
    models to the behaviour of health
    professionals.
Weinberger, M., Cohen, S.J. & Mazzuca, S.A. (1984).
    The role of physicians' knowledge and
    attitudes in effective diabetes management.
    Soc.Sci.Med., 19, 965-969.
Wynne, G., Marteau, T.M., Johnston, M., Whiteley,
    C.A. & Evans, T.R. (1987). Inability of
    trained nurses to perform basic life support.
    British Medical Journal, 294, 1198-1199.

Chapter Nineteen

DOCTORS' BEHAVIOUR IN THE FACE OF PATIENTS'
NON-COMPLIANCE

Irena Heszen-Niejodek and Gabriela Dlugosz

INTRODUCTION

Patients' non-adherence to a health regimen is
a serious problem, especially in the case of out-
patients who are not under the immediate control of
medical staff. In many studies it was found that
the percentage of persons who follow the regimen
prescribed was far below 100. The compliance of
Polish out-patients suffering from chronic illnesses
was studied by the first author. The results showed
that the numbers taking the doctors' advice varied
from 42% to 93%, depending mainly on the kind of
treatment recommended. When making lifestyle
changes was recommended only about 50% of patients
complied with doctors' advice.

Patient non-compliance is a substantial
obstacle to the achievement of therapeutic goals,
it potentially involves the patient in additional
diagnostic and treatment procedures and is a source
of professional failure for clinicians. Hence the
very important problem arises, how can doctors
improve patients' adherence to the regimen
prescribed? There are a large number of techniques
available for managing non-compliance, depending on
its causes, developed within the areas of medical
psychology and behavioural medicine (Anderson &
Lynne, 1982; Peck & King, 1982; Zisook & Gammon
1980-81). But it would be of interest to know which
forms of non-compliance management are actually
applied in clinical circumstances.

Few empirical findings are available in this
area (Appelbaum & Roth, 1983; Davis, 1966; Hayes-
Bautista, 1976) but from these it may be concluded
that, in dealing with patients' non-compliance,
doctors apply only a small number of the existing
techniques. What are the causes of this limitation?

Doctors' Behaviour and Patient Non-Compliance

It has been stressed that patients' refusal to comply could be the principal cause of doctors' professional frustration (Fedder, 1982, Zisook & Gammon, 1980-81). The authors' assumption is that frustration theory may be a useful frame of reference in studying doctors' behaviour towards non-compliance and its determinants. The aim of the present study was:-

1. To examine this sphere of behaviour and compare its forms in natural clinical settings with those reported by doctors;
2. To explain doctors' attitude towards non-compliance within the framework of frustration theory (Reykowski, 1966).

METHOD

The study consisted of two parts, with two different groups of physicians as subjects. The first part was designed to identify the tactics used by doctors when faced with patients' non-compliance, as observed in the natural setting of polyclinics. The second aimed at describing doctors' behaviours towards non-compliance on the basis of their own reports and ascertaining some determinants of this behaviour by identifying the subjects' habitual way of dealing with frustrating events.

The first study group was selected from among a larger group of 109 doctors on the basis of the content of tape-recorded patient visits and consisted of physicians whose interviews contained evident examples of non-compliance. In all, 30 such events were found and the relevant excerpts from the tape-recordings were transcribed. Both men and women were represented in the group, with different lengths of practice and coming from various specialist medical fields in different out-patient clinics in large Polish towns.

The second group were 60 physicians interviewed by psychologists to learn about their behaviour towards non-compliers. The group was not representative in the statistical sense but, as with the first one, was purposely heterogeneous in order to obtain a broad variety of responses. Immediately after the interview, the Rosezweig Picture-Frustration Study (RPFS) (Dunaj-Kozlowska, 1980) was applied to learn about the subjects' type of habitual behaviour towards frustration.

The doctors' behaviour towards non-compliance was analysed applying the same system of categories in both groups. The system was developed by the authors a posteriori. Altogether 11 different categories of doctors' tactics towards non-compliance were distinguished. These were:-

1. Trying to determine causes of non-compliance;
2. Giving the patient information concerning the treatment to convince him that it is appropriate, explaining the rationale for the regimen;
3. Enlisting family support;
4. Replacing the medicine originally advised with another of similar efficacy but more acceptable to the patient;
5. Tolerant, indulgent dealing with the patient, allowing him to unburden himself, to express his emotions and then carrying the doctor's point;
6. Authoritarian tactics; stressing the doctor's superior position, his professional knowledge and his right to decide;
7. Using medical threat; informing the patient of the dire consequences which will certainly occur if the advice is not followed;
8. Blaming the patient for non-compliance and making him responsible for the eventual consequences;
9. Criticizing, insulting, humiliating the patient;
10. Personal tactics; treating the patient as a personal acquaintance, thus making it difficult for him to refuse the doctor's request;
11. Withdrawal, reducing the doctor's involvement in the case.

To evaluate the doctor's behaviour in the framework of frustration theory, the tactics were then divided into two larger classes, according to the interpreted goal. The tactics numbered above from 1 to 5 were recognised as task-oriented, while the tactics numbered from 6 to 11 as ego-defensive.

RESULTS

The frequency of use of various tactics when a patient failed to follow the doctor's advice is presented in Table 1. The greatest proportion of doctors from both groups applied medical threat. The other tactics reported as most frequently used by the doctors interviewed were:-

i. giving medical information;
ii. stressing the doctor's authority;
iii. reducing his involvement in the case.

The remaining tactics were rarely mentioned. None of the doctors reported applying personal tactics

Table 1: The frequency of application of various tactics towards non-compliance

Kind of tactics	Data observed (I study group)		Data reported (II study group)	
	No. of cases	% of cases	No. of cases	% of cases
Medical threat (7)	8	28	20	34
Carrying the doctor's point in an indulgent atmosphere (5)	5	17	2	3
Authoritarian tactics(6)	4	14	11	18
Medical information (2)	3	11	14	24
Withdrawal (11)	2	7	6	10
Trying to determine causes (1)	2	7	2	3
Personal tactics (10)	2	7	0	0
Altering the regimen (4)	1	3	3	5
Blaming the patient (8)	1	3	0	0
Criticizing, insulting, humiliating the patient (9)	1	3	0	0
Enlisting family support (3)	0	0	2	3
Total	29*	100	60	100

The tactics are ordered according to their frequency in the first study group.
Figures in brackets refer to the description .in the text.
* A single case in the first study group was difficult to classify and not taken into account.

or admitted blaming the patient, criticising, consulting or humiliating him. There were no significant differences between groups as to the tactics used; on the contrary a positive correlation was found between them (Spearman Rank Correlation Coefficient r = 0.62).
Table 2 shows the doctors' reaction to noncompliance grouped into two larger classes as

distinguished within the frustration theory. It is
evident that there were no differences between
observed and reported behaviour from this point of
view. The ego-defensive forms of behaviour toward
non-compliance prevailed in the doctors under study.

Table 2:   The frequency of task-oriented and ego-
           defensive tactics

Kind of tactics	Data observed		Data reported	
	No. of cases	% of cases	No. of cases	% of cases
Task oriented	11	38	23	38
Ego-defensive	18	62	37	62
Total	29	100	60	100

In order to explore the connection between the
habitual way of dealing with frustrating events and
the attitude towards non-compliance, the results of
RPFS were taken into account. For the purpose of
this study only two types of reaction towards
frustrating events were distinguished: task-oriented
and ego-defensive. Of the 60 persons in our second
study group, 10 were finally excluded because their
RPFS results were difficult to classify from this
point of view. Results for the remaining 50 are
presented in Table 3.

Table 3: Type of doctors' reaction in RPFS and
         their behaviour towards non-compliance

The type of reaction in RPFS	The behaviour towards non-compliance		Total
	Task-oriented	Ego-defensive	
Task-oriented	15 (7.22)	4 (11.78)	19 (38%)
Ego-defensive	4 (11.78)	27 (19.22)	31 (62%)
Total	19 (38%)	31 (62%)	50 (100%)

$$\chi^2 = 21.809 \quad df = 1 \quad p < .001 \quad \emptyset = 0.66$$
$$\text{Kendall } Q = 0.92$$

The table contains numbers of persons and
theoretical frequencies (in brackets).

In 42 cases the doctor's own estimate of his reaction to non-complying patients agreed with RPFS results while in 8 cases there was lack of agreement. The statistical indices are high and indicate a strong connection between the attitude towards frustration and the behaviour towards non-compliant patients.

DISCUSSION

The main aim of the study was to describe doctors' behaviour towards non-compliance, either on the basis of observation or of their own reports. Few doctors tried to ascertain the causes of non-compliance, hence the majority of responses were probably unrelated to the specific causes of the patients' poor adherence. The tactic most frequently used was medical threat and authoritarian tactics were applied relatively often. As has been reported (Anderson & Lynne, 1982; Ley, 1977; Zisook & Gammon, 1980-81) both are of doubtful effectiveness, while they also tend to worsen the patients' emotional state. On the other hand many valuable techniques of proved efficacy, elaborated in the field of behavioural medicine (Becker & Maiman, 1980; Peck & King, 1982; Zisook & Gammon, 1980-81) were quite neglected by the doctors.

What are the reasons for the doctors' low efficacy in dealing with non-compliance? One may be a lack of behavioural knowledge or interpersonal skills. However, the psychological mechanisms of the behaviour under study are probably more complex. Frustration theory provides a useful explanatory framework. When the doctors' reactions towards non-compliance were evaluated within the framework of this theory as either ego-defensive or task-oriented, it was found that the first form predominated both in the observed and reported behaviour. Moreover, the kind of tactics towards non-compliance were strongly determined by the subjects' general type of reaction to frustration as measured by RPFS.

We may conclude that patient non-compliance is perceived by the majority of doctors as a frustrating, ego-threatening event, which is accompanied by strong negative emotions. As a result, the doctor's activity is aimed primarily at defending his professional self-esteem and reducing the emotional tension. The original goal of behaviour, i.e. the patient's adherence to the regimen prescribed, is postponed. This emotional arousal   may also limit the doctor's flexibility and his inventiveness in looking for more effective ways of personal influence.

REFERENCES

Anderson, R.J. & Lynne, M.K. (1982). Methods of improving patient compliance in chronic disease states. Arch.Intern.Med., 142, 1673-1675.

Appelbaum, P.S. & Roth, L.H. (1983). Patients who refuse treatment in medical hospitals. Journal of American Medical Association, 250, 1296-1301.

Becker, M.H. & Maiman, L.A. (1980). Strategies for enhancing patient compliance. Journal of Community Health, 6, 113-135.

Davis, M.S. (1966). Variations in patients' compliance with doctors' orders: analysis of congruence between survey responses and results of empirical investigations. Journal of Medical Education, 41, 1037-1048.

Dunaj-Kozlowska, A. (1980). Obrazkowy test frustracji S. Rowenweiga : S. Rosenzweig's picture frustration test. In J.M. Stanik (Ed) Wybrane Techniki Diagnostyczne w Psychologii Klinicznej, Selected Diagnostic Techniques in Clinical Psychology. Uniwersytet Slaski: Katowice.

Fedder, D.O. (1982). Managing medication and compliance: physician-pharmacist-patient interaction. Journal of American Geriatric Society, 30, S113-117

Hayes-Bautista, D.E. (1976). Modifying the treatment: patient compliance, patient control and medical care. Social Science and Medicine, 10, 233-238.

Ley, P. (1977).   Psychological studies of doctor-patient communication. In S. Rachman (Ed) Contributions to Medical Psychology, Vol. 1, Pergamon Press: Oxford.

Peck. C.L. & King, N.J. (1982). Increasing patient compliance with prescription. Journal of American Medical Association, 248, 2874-2877.

Reykowski, J. (1966). Funkcjonowanie Osobosci w Warunkach Stressu Psychologicznego. Functioning of Personality under Psychological Stress, PWN: Warszawa.

Zisook, S. & Gammon, E. (1980-81). Medical noncompliance. Psychiatric Medicine, 10, 291-303.

Chapter Twenty

ENCOUNTERS BETWEEN DOCTORS AND PARENTS: FIRST
DIAGNOSIS OF SEVERE MENTAL HANDICAP

Lyn Quine

Introduction

There is an extensive literature concerned with
informing parents of a child's diagnosis of severe
mental or physical impairment (Ward, 1982). Several
studies have viewed it as a crisis producing grief
followed by stages of shock and disbelief, denial,
anger, adaptation and adjustment similar to the
phases identified in the bereavement literature. It
has been suggested that the way in which parents are
told of a child's impairment may affect both the way
they adjust to the situation and their early
treatment of the child.

There are many ways in which the encounter can
go wrong. The doctor may feel that she or he has
been both sympathetic and informative and may be
dismayed when, at their next meeting, parents seem
to remember little of what they have been told.
Parents may experience severe shock and anger, and
their feelings about how the news was broken may
make them suspicious of professionals in general for
a long time to come. While at one level we are
concerned with an encounter between individuals, at
another level we need to understand the broader
structural context in which the encounter takes
place. In this paper we shall consider some of the
factors which seem to be associated with parents
feeling dissatisfied with how they were told about
their child's impairment.

Methodology

The data presented here were obtained from
interviews with a stratified random sample of two
hundred mothers of severely mentally handicapped
children aged 0 - 16 in two health districts. The

sample was chosen with proportional allocation for age and sex so that it was representative of the population from which it was drawn - the total population of severely mentally handicapped children in the two health districts. The main findings of the study are published elsewhere (Pahl & Quine, 1984; Quine & Pahl, 1986).

For more than one third of the children, the cause of their impairment was unknown: in some of these cases parents attributed their child's problems to a pre-natal injury, to a difficult birth, to vaccine damage or an infection, but for many the lack of a clear diagnosis contributed to their distress. Thirty-three per cent of the children had Down's Syndrome. Fourteen per cent of the children had cerebral palsy. Among the other known conditions (18% of children) were primary genetic or chromosomal abnormalities, metabolic disorders, developmental defects such as spina bifida, and foetal environmental syndromes such as Foetal Rubella Syndrome. Twelve per cent of the sample had siblings who were also mentally handicapped. The children were mostly living at home with their natural mother and father and other children, although a few were fostered and a few were in community homes. The findings are based on the 190 cases where the parent had known the child from birth. Parents were asked a number of questions about the time they first learned about the child's impairment and were asked to give an account of the encounter.

Findings

In our study 29% of parents were told of the impairment at birth or within the first seven days. Thirty-three per cent were told in the first year, 15% in the second and 22% were not told until during or after the child's third year of life. Three quarters of parents were told by a hospital doctor. In some cases the doctor involved was summoned soon after the birth by the midwifery staff who had delivered the baby. In others, it was the paediatrician to whom the child had been referred once developmental delay or other problems had been noted at the clinic.

As other studies have shown, there were high levels of dissatisfaction (Cunningham, 1984). Nearly two thirds (60%) of parents were dissatisfied with the way they were first told about the child's impairment. Why should this be so? One explanation might be that satisfaction is determined by internal factors, by the psychology and personality of the mother, which might lead to a general attitude of dissatisfaction with services. However, there was no correlation between general satisfaction with services and satisfaction with learning about the handicap. Nor was there a significant association between the mother's stress rating, using the Malaise Inventory (Rutter et al, 1970) and satisfaction with learning about the handicap. However, parental satisfaction was found to be significantly related to the time at which the parents were told about the child's handicap. Forty-nine per cent of mothers who were told at the child's birth were dissatisfied compared with 67% of parents who were told during the first year, and 72.5% of parents who were told during the second year or later ($x^2 = 7.57$ df.2 $p < 0.05$), so a greater proportion of parents who had the impairment confirmed early in the child's life were satisfied than were those who found out later.

Next, satisfaction with the first information regarding the handicap was broken down by the presence of an aetiological factor. In conditions where a definite cause could be identified, such as in chromosomal or metabolic disorders or recessive genes, a significantly higher proportion of mothers were satisfied ($x^2 = 4.22$ df.1 $p < 0.05$). The remaining groups are 'non-specific mental handicap' and 'cerebral palsy' for which a cause often cannot be ascribed (Kirman & Bicknell, 1975). Significantly more mothers of children in this group were dissatisfied with the way they were told (70%). It has been suggested that it is much more difficult to come to terms with mental handicap of unknown origin (Hunter, 1980). As one might expect there was an association between the nature of the diagnosis and the age of the child when the parents were first told that the child was mentally handicapped. Nowadays, Down's Syndrome is usually recognised at birth and can be confirmed by a blood test a few days later. Children suffering from non-specific handicap are usually identified much later and parents have often been anxious about the development of their child for a considerable time. Table 1 shows that parents of Down's Syndrome children were more likely to be told of the impairment at birth than were parents of children in other diagnostic groups. Of the Down's Syndrome children, 63% were identified at birth or within the first seven days and 100% had been identified by one

Table 1: Date when parents were first told of impairment by diagnostic category.

	Diagnosis			
	Down's Syndrome	Other known conditions	Cerebral palsy	Cause unknown
	%	%	%	%
Parents were told:				
At birth	63	26	19	5
First year	37	23	52	27
Second year or later	–	51	30	68
Total	100	100	100	100
Number:	62	35	27	66

$\chi^2 = 85.86$; df 6. Highly significant, $p < 0.001$

year. By contrast only 32% of the children with non-specific handicap had been identified by the end of the first year, and only 52% by the end of the second year. About half of the parents in this group had been seriously concerned about their child's development for many months before the diagnosis of severe mental handicap was made. Most noticed developmental delay. Sleeping, feeding and behavioural problems and screaming bouts were also a cause for concern. Some parents were worried when children began to have fits. Many parents in this group were critical of the process by which impairment was identified in their child, and by the lapse of time which occurred between their expression of anxiety and receiving a diagnosis. Parents spoke of long battles with the authorities to get recognition of their child's impairment and of frustration when their anxieties about their child's development appeared to be disregarded by the general practitioner. Thus, it seems that satisfaction may be linked both with early information and with the existence of a possible cause for the impairment. The dissatisfaction may have its roots in the waiting and worrying parents have gone through, and their heart-searching about the cause of the handicap.

Discussion

1. Early Acknowledgement of the Problem

Much of parental dissatisfaction in this study stemmed from the timing of the first identification and diagnosis of mental handicap. In the Down's Syndrome group the parents who were dissatisfied had often faced delay, denial and evasion before the diagnosis was made. Babies were taken away immediately after birth with no explanation, and put in special care nurseries. Nursing staff behaved oddly toward the mother. The mother's questions were evaded or ignored. Even though the time between the mother's suspicions being aroused and diagnosis being made was of comparatively short duration, it was sufficient to raise parental anxiety and anger.

The mothers of children identified as suffering from mental impairment of no known cause were generally told even later about the impairment. In addition, there was often a lapse of time between parents becoming seriously concerned about their child's development, and diagnosis of impairment.

It was apparent from the comments of mothers in this study that they would have preferred to have been told that something was wrong as soon as possible, even though doctors might have been uncertain of the exact nature of the impairment. Delay and uncertainty simply led to additional distress for parents, and may have had a lasting effect on the relationship between doctors and parents.

2. The Importance of a Sympathetic Approach

The findings of this study showed that there was a strong relationship between parental satisfaction with information at first identification and the parents' feelings that the person who communicated the information had a sympathetic approach. Sixty-seven per cent of the dissatisfied parents in our study mentioned the unsympathetic manner of the doctor. Korsch et al (1968) reported some similar findings, showing that satisfaction with information at a walk-in Emergency Clinic at a Children's Hospital was positively related to three parental ratings of doctor's behaviour: being friendly rather than business-like, seeming to understand the mother's concern, rather than not understanding, and being a good rather than a poor communicator. These writers believe that if these ingredients are missing from doctor-patient interaction, patients will be dissatified.

3. Sharing Information and Uncertainty

A large number of parents in our study said that they had not received enough information about their child's condition. Overall, 74% of parents said that it had been hard to get information about their child's condition, and, at another point in the interview, 74% said they wanted more information. A number of studies confirm that patients/ parents do want information. Even if the illness is cancer or the patient is dying, the majority of patients want to be told. Surveys of patient satisfaction show high levels of dissatisfaction with information, which is in sharp contrast to the generally high levels of satisfaction with other aspects of health care.

Ley, in a review of theory and experiment in the field of doctor-patient communication, showed that sometimes patients are dissatisfied even when doctors have made special efforts to give them adequate information (Ley, 1977). He advanced a cognitive explanation for this: that for communi-cation to be effective the message it contains must be understood and remembered. The significance of the failure to understand and remember is that if patients do not understand what they are told, they are likely to be dissatisfied. Ley et al (1976) were able to increase patient satisfaction with communication by increasing understanding and recall.

Intervention

As a result of this study of parental satisfaction and consideraion of the literature in the field of doctor-patient communication, we have produced a model of the ingredients which we feel are important in the encounter between doctors and parents when mental handicap is suspected. This 'model procedure' is to be carried out by doctors in one health district when a child is born with a congenital impairment or when developmental delay or other factors make mental handicap a suspected diagnosis. A similar model procedure carried out in Manchester with Down's Syndrome infants has been shown to be extremely successful in improving the way in which parents are told (Cunningham et al, 1984). In particular, we hope to be able to improve levels of satisfaction in parents of children with non-specific mental handicap.

REFERENCES

Chazan, M., Laing, G., Shackleton-Bailey, M. & Jones, G. (1980). Some of our Children. Open Books: London.

Cunningham, C. (1984). Down's Syndrome: disclosure and early family needs. Down's Syndrome: Papers and Abstracts for Professionals, 7, 4, 1-3.

Cunningham, C., Morgan, D.A., & McGucken, R.D. (1984). Down's Syndrome: is dissatisfaction with disclosure of diagnosis inevitable? Developmental Medicine and Child Neurology 26, 33-39.

Hunter, A. (1980) The family and their mentally handicapped child. Barnardo Social Work Papers, 12.

Kirman, B. & Bicknell, J. (1975). Mental Handicap. Churchill Livingstone: Edinburgh, London and New York, p94.

Korsch, B., Gozzi, E. & Francis, V. (1968). Gaps in doctor-patient communication and patient satisfaction. Paediatrics, 42, 855-871.

Ley, P. (1977). Psychological studies of doctor-patient communication. In S. Rachman (Ed) Contributions to Medical Psychology, Vol. 1. Pergamon: Oxford.

Ley, P., Whitworth, M., Skilbeck, C. Woodward, R., Pinsent, R., Pike, L., Clarkson, M.E. & Clark, P. (1976). Improving doctor-patient communication in general practice. Journal of Royal College of General Practitioners, 26, 720-724.

Pahl, J. & Quine, L. (1984). Families with Mentally Handicapped Children: A Study of Stress and of Service Response. Health Services Research Unit, University of Kent at Canterbury.

Quine, L. & Pahl, J. (1986). First diagnosis of severe mental handicap: characteristics of unsatisfactory encounters between doctors and parents. Social Science and Medicine, 22, 1, 53-62.

Rutter, M., Tizard, J. & Whitmore, K. (1970). Education, Health and Behaviour. Longmans: London.

Encounters between Doctors and Parents

Ward, L. (1982). People first: developing
    services in the community for people with
    mental handicap: a review of recent
    literature. <u>Kings Fund Centre</u>, Oct. 1982.
    London.

Chapter Twenty One

A CONSUMER'S ASSESSMENT OF A GENETIC COUNSELLING
SERVICE

Anne-Marie Toase

INTRODUCTION

"Genetic counselling is the process whereby an
individual or family obtains information
about a real or possible genetic problem."
(Hsia and Hirschhorn, 1979).

Originally, the practice of genetic counselling
reflected a predominantly content-oriented approach
with the provision of medical information and
genetic facts (Kessler, 1979). This approach
assumed that the human decision-making process was
inherently rational. However, the development of a
more person-centred approach was prompted through
recognition that genetic information is not received
in an emotionally neutral manner. It also became
accepted that the psychological responses of
counsellees are often necessary steps in
comprehending, integrating and acting upon the
content material of counselling.
    In genetic counselling, susceptibility to
genetic disease is provided via genetic risks given
to counsellees. Interpretation of risks is highly
subjective (Pearn, 1973). Risks can be perceived
differently by different people and also differently
by the same person on different occasions.
Modifying factors such as intelligence, presentation
of risks and nature of outcome play a crucial role.
    Evaluation of genetic counselling services is
difficult when the aims of counselling are not
coherently defined. Several studies examine the
level of knowledge obtained following counselling
and some review options taken, but relatively few
include consumer assessment as part of their
evaluation, particularly in terms of the match
between the service delivered and clients'

expectations. Of those reporting on knowledge gained, the results paint a somewhat poor picture (Shaw, 1977).

The present study attempted to redress the balance by directly assessing counsellee perceptions in a pilot survey as a means of evaluating a genetic counselling service. Counsellees were Duchenne Muscular Dystrophy Carriers who had received a service from the Genetic Counselling Clinic. Duchenne Muscular Dystrophy (DMD) is a severe X-linked, genetically lethal condition that affects boys, usually before the age of 5. It is transmitted by a female who is apparently perfectly normal and shows no sign of the disease, i.e. a female carrier. The son of a known female carrier has a 50% chance of being affected, any daughter has a 50% chance of being a carrier. In two thirds of cases there is a family history of the disorder; the remainder are spontaneous mutations. DMD is the commonest form of Muscular Dystrophy with an incidence approaching 1 in 3000 male births. It is a severe and relentless disease with boys first noticing difficulty in walking culminating in the necessity of a wheelchair at approximately age 8 to 10. Death usually occurs between the ages of 16 and 25 and at present there is no effective treatment. Carrier status is calculated from the combination of genetic risk from family history and from an estimation of biochemical risk. In carriers there is a reported raised level of the enzyme creatine phosphokinase (CPK). However, only 70% of carriers can be defined accurately as the range of CPK activity overlaps with normals. A woman is a definite carrier if she has an affected son and a family history. A possible carrier is a woman who is related to a definite carrier. As yet there is no prenatal diagnosis available, so information regarding carrier status is important in genetic counselling in order to help couples make reproductive decisions. In addition, options open to couples need to be delineated. The understanding of risks to DMD is important as there is no definite test for carrier status or for the disease itself. Results presented are equivocal in terms of understanding gained (e.g. Emery et al, 1972).

Families' responses to DMD are also important if counselling follows the birth of an affected son. Many clients do not remember information given at diagnosis and would like further follow-up. Many workers now feel counselling should broaden to cover counselling and support of families with an affected child (Frith, 1983).

On the basis of a 1975 report, in which Bundey (1981) assessed the incidence of DMD in the West Midlands, a register for high risk women was set up. The aims of the register were to confirm initial diagnosis, assess genetic risks, to present risks in a comprehensible form to counsellees and to present options regarding families' decisions in accordance with clients' own wishes and goals. In order to evaluate these aims, it seemed necessary to obtain clients' own views and perceptions.

METHOD

Genetic Counselling for DMD
Families can be seen at the clinic or at home where they are visited by a field worker. The field worker aims to visit each family on the Register, every 2 to 3 years, and also to visit every female at risk for being a carrier soon after she has reached the age of 16 years.

Objectives
The aims of the study were to compare clients' expectations of the service with the actual service delivered. In addition, it aimed to test differences in these expectations between high and low risk carriers of DMD in order to assess the need for a selective register for high risk carriers. Satisfaction, knowledge of genetic facts, decisions made and clients' own concept of counselling were assessed using a questionnaire designed to encompass these variables. The questionnaire was utilised in a structured interview format, carried out within the clients' own homes, and was designed in liaison with the Genetics Department.

Sample
In view of one of the aims of this study both low and high risk carriers of DMD were included. Specifically, a low risk carrier was defined as having a 1 in 20 or lower risk for carrying DMD. These women were not put on to the Genetic Register. A high risk carrier was defined as 1 in 10 or worse risk for carrying DMD. Women with risks in between were placed in one of the two groups depending on their family history and pedigree, e.g. a woman with a risk of 1 in 15 may be placed on the Register if there is a family history of DMD or she has a son who suffers from the disorder.

Women on the register who were of childbearing

age (not over 45 years) and of independent status (i.e. 18 or above) as known to the Genetics Clinic were to be included in the sample (N=30).

Women defined as low risk who were of child-bearing age and independent status as known to the Genetics Clinic were also included in the sample (N=18).

RESULTS

Twelve women in each group were interviewed. Each group included one woman who reported receiving no genetic counselling. Neither woman was included in the analysis. Thirty women from the Register were contacted initially by the Genetics Clinic. Of this group, 6 did not wish to take part in the study, 6 had moved from the area and 6 were not visited on geographical grounds. Eighteen low risk women were initially written to by the Genetics Clinic and of these 6 were not visited on geographical grounds.

There were only 3 statistically significant differences between the high risk and low risk carrier groups. These were as follows:

> age - high risk women were on average 3 years older than low risk women;
>
> directiveness - high risk women would prefer a less directive approach to counselling than the low risk group;
>
> awareness of religious beliefs - the high risk women felt the counsellor was more aware of their religious beliefs than the low risk group.

For the remainder of the results, the ratings given by both high and low risk carriers are pooled.

Satisfaction

Eighteen out of 22 women were satisfied with when and where counselling took place. A greater degree of satisfaction was noted if counselling took place within the client's own home. Fourteen out of 22 women, however, felt they received too little counselling.

Knowledge

Twelve out of 22 women gave incorrect risk figures for their carrier status. In addition, over half of these women gave incorrect answers for the risk of a future son being affected and the risk of a future

Figure 1:   Concept of counselling

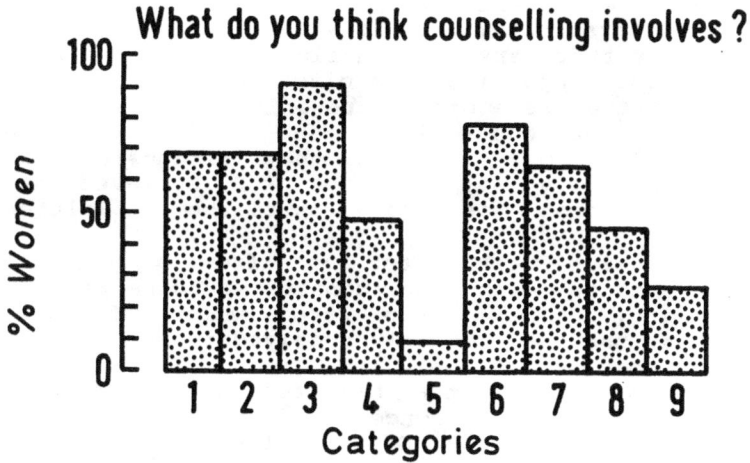

What do you think counselling involves ?

% Women

Categories

Key:

1. Giving information
2. Receiving information
3. Advice
4. Client responsible for decisions
5. Counsellor responsible for decisions

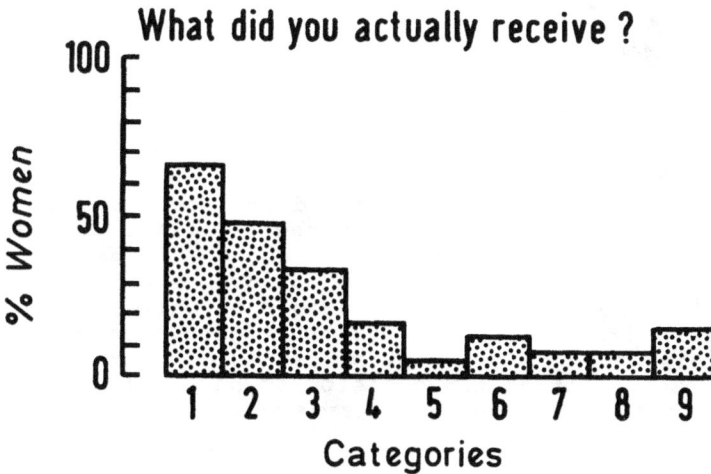

6. Support
7. Accepting emotions
8. Client as part of a family
9. Client as an individual

What did you actually receive ?

% Women

Categories

daughter being a carrier (13/22; 17/22 respectively). Significantly, when asked how women perceived their carrier risk, no woman reported that she saw herself at low risk. Sixteen out of 22 women felt they were at high risk for carrying DMD, despite the objective data given them. When asked how well they remembered the information given to them by the counsellor, the majority rated "averagely". Only 5 felt they remembered the information very well; 17 out of 22 believed that this information was not given to them in written form.

Women were asked to rate from a number of variables those which they considered to be part of counselling. They then rated which of these variables they had actually received in the genetic counselling given to them.

Figure 1 shows the mismatch in some factors between women's own concept of counselling and counselling received. Specifically, 16 out of 22 women rated support as a component of the counselling process, with 13 out of 22 rating accepting emotions as another component. In contrast, only 4 out of 22 and 2 out of 22 women felt they had received support and had emotions acknowledged in the counselling given. Giving and receiving information showed a greater degree of parity between expected and actual counselling. No woman rated the counsellor as being responsible for decisions.

Decision Making

There was a trend, though not statistically significant, for high risk carriers to have had more pregnancies than low risk women. Whilst pregnant women tended to contact the genetics clinic, 17 out of 22 women stated that they would have a termination of pregnancy should they be carrying a male foetus, irrespective of their carrier status. Factors influencing decisions about further procreation most commonly included women's experience of DMD, their age and the number of children they had already. However, decisions regarding children were discussed in only 48% of cases and counselling would only affect the decision to have children in less than half the women interviewed.

Improvements

The majority of women felt a need for more general information plus information specifically related to new research and new procedures. A regular newsletter was a suggestion put forward by several women. Leaflets explaining about genetic risks and about DMD in general were also proposed. One or two women felt the service was lacking in terms of emotional support offered to clients. Those women who have sons with DMD proposed that the clinic should take steps to follow them up more closely. Five women felt they could make no suggestions toward improving the service as they found it completely adequate. These women also felt they had received an adequate amount of counselling.

DISCUSSION

The results presented suggest that several issues need to be addressed by the service offered by the Genetic Counselling Clinic. These include reviewing the actual counselling process itself and what it offers clients through acknowledging the dimensions stated by the clients themselves. Many women count support and accepting emotions as part of counselling but believed they had not received this. Knowledge about carrier status and genetic risk was poor and often confused, with women perceiving their risk differently from the objective risk figure given (see Pearn, 1973).

However, results need to be seen within the context of the assessment carried out. The assessment was a pilot assessment and needs to be validated and tested for reliability. The small sample size and large number of variables employed in this design reduce the power of the study. However, certain significant differences and trends in the data were observed. Moreover, this investigation did not aim to provide a comprehensive evaluation but sought rather to draw attention to some relevant features worthy of further exploration.

Lastly, the study made no attempt to compare the results obtained from DMD families with other groups. This was largely because of the difficulty in finding valid and appropriate controls. Comparing families with a DMD family history who had not been seen by the Genetics Clinic, although useful in terms of information assimilated, allows no comparison of satisfaction with service measures. Practically speaking, access to this group is arduous and problematic. Comparisons with other groups suffering from different genetic disorders also raise impediments as inheritance patterns, risk factors and outcome cannot easily be controlled for.

If it were feasible, however, cross group discriminations would allow some distinction between responses that reflect attitudes to the disease and responses that reflect attitudes to the service. How helpful clients found the service served as one way of attempting to pick up this discrepancy if it arose. Women who found the service unhelpful could be seen to be expressing an opinion that was actually related to the disease itself.

CONCLUSION

Despite some words of caution, several recommendations can be outlined.

Recommendations

1. A low risk register should be compiled in addition to a high risk register since many of the low risk carriers do not feel at low risk and would like further contact with the clinic.
2. When presenting risk figures, terms such as low, moderate and high might be more usefully employed as many women were unable to give accurate responses.
3   To avoid confusion, families should, where appropriate, be given the risk of having an affected son rather than given the risk of carrier status.
4. Families would like written information which could be achieved in the form of a leaflet. As it is unlikely that one leaflet would be sufficient for the needs of all the clients, a number of leaflets may be required. These could range from simple information relating to the genetic counselling service through to more sophisticated and comprehensive literature encompassing modes of inheritance, how to estimate risk and aspects of decision making in connection with the options available. Literature from the clinic should provide space in which to record an individual family's risk of DMD.
5. Content of counselling sessions should include support for decision making and acknowledgement of emotional reactions to the disorder, counselling and information. Many women would like to discuss a range of options during counselling even if they are not immediately relevant to their life situation.
6. A newsletter would be useful to provide infor-

mation about new research and new available procedures. This also allows impressions obtained from television programmes to be substantiated or disconfirmed.

7. The Genetic Counselling Service should aim to keep fuller records of each counselling session so more objective assessments can be carried out and clients' assumptions can then be tested.

8. Involvement of fathers should be included in any genetic counselling. Men should be invited to attend when the field worker makes a domiciliary visit.

REFERENCES

Bundey, S. (1981). A genetic study of Duchenne Muscular Dystrophy in the West Midlands. Journal of Medical Genetics, 18, 1-7.

Emery, A.R.H., Watts, M.S. & Clack, E.R. (1972). The effects of genetic counselling in Duchenne Muscular Dystrophy. Clinical Genetics, 3, 147-150.

Frith, M.A. (1983). Diagnosis of Duchenne Muscular Dystrophy: experiences of parents of sufferers. British Medical Journal, 286, 700-701.

Hsia, Y.E. & Hirschhorn, K. (1979). What is genetic counselling? In Y.E. Hsia, K. Hirschhorn, R.L. Silverberg & L. Godmilow (Eds) Counseling in Genetics. Alan R. Liss Inc.: New York.

Kessler, S. (Ed) (1979). Genetic Counseling: Psychological Dimensions. Academic Press: New York.

Pearn, J.H. (1973). Patients' subjective interpretation of risks offered in genetic counseling. Journal of Medical Genetics, 10, 129-134.

Shaw, M.W. (1977). Review of published studies of genetic counseling: a critique. In H.A. Lubs and F. de la Cruz (Eds) Genetic Counseling. Raven Press: New York.

Chapter Twenty Two

A STRESS-COPING-STRAIN EVALUATION OF A ROUTINE
CLINICAL PSYCHOLOGY SERVICE

Derek Milne

INTRODUCTION

This study assessed two recurring and
alternative explanations for clinical recovery,
transient life stress and improved psychological
coping. The study took place in two 'primary care'
settings, a General Practitioner's (GP) surgery and
a general purpose health clinic. Unlike the
existing studies of clinical psychology in primary
care, the present study considered three variables
that appear to be logically required in an analysis
of clinical improvement in primary care. They are
stressful life events, personal coping strategies
and strain (Cohen & Lazarus, 1979). These terms are
defined by these authors as follows: 'stress'
refers to problematic life experiences that require
action; 'coping' refers to the patient's problem-
solving responses when faced with stress; while
'strain' refers to unpleasant thoughts, feelings or
behaviours (as in anxiety or depression). The
operational definitions provided by the measures
elaborates the meaning of these variables.

These three factors need to be considered in
order to draw valid inferences about therapy
outcome. This kind of analysis has not yet taken
place in primary care because researchers have been
content to infer changes in personal coping from
changes in outcome. One illustration has been the
frequent reliance on medication levels or GP
attendances as an index of 'improvement'. However,
research designs have failed to exclude alternative
explanations for changes in these indices, such as
altered trends in GP's general prescribing habits
(Freeman & Button, 1984).

There is, therefore, a need to investigate
whether the therapy provided by clinical

psychologists affects the patients' coping and thereby their strain; or whether the alternative hypothesis of transient life stress can account for improvements.

METHOD

Measures and Research Design

The patients' stress, coping and strain were measured by means of published self-report questionnaires. Stress was assessed with the 'Schedule of Recent Events', a comprehensive inventory of stressful life events (SRE; Tennant & Andrews, 1976). The 'Coping Responses Questionnaire' of Billings and Moos (CRQ, 1981) gauged three relevant dimensions of coping, namely 'active cognitive', 'active behavioural' and 'avoidance' strategies. Strain was measured by the short form of the 'General Health Questionnaire' (GHQ, Banks et al, 1980).

In addition, patients and referring agents completed outcome ratings based on questions derived from Robson et al (1984). Finally, patients provided 'consumer satisfaction' ratings on a 20 item ad hoc measure.

These measures were administered in a 'waiting-list' control group design, with two baseline measurements prior to therapy and two following therapy. The first set of questionnaires was completed at the time of receiving the referral, the second after the first appointment. On average, the interval between these two baseline assessments was 3.4 months. The immediate effects of therapy were assessed after a further 3 months of appointments by a third administration of the stress, coping and strain measures. The fourth and final assessment, a follow-up, occurred one year after the first appointment when the questionnaires were re-administered and the referring agents were asked to rate the therapy outcome.

This research design, therefore, provided a comparison between equivalent baseline and therapy intervals, allowing an estimate to be made of the relative effects of the two conditions upon the patient's stress, coping and strain. It was predicted that therapy would result in a significant improvement in the patient's coping, leading in turn to reduced strain. This effect would be expected to be absent during the baseline period. As a corollary, stress was not expected to vary with strain.

A Stress-Coping-Strain Evaluation

Subjects

All patients were recruited from a one-year series of consecutive referrals from General Practitioners and Psychiatrists. A total of 47 patients were treated from the 65 who were offered initial appointments. The 18 who did not participate in the study were excluded because they did not attend the first or subsequent appointments (7), because they did not commence therapy (7), or because they were regarded as unsuitable for therapy (4). The mean age of the 47 treated patients was 36.9 years. They reported having had the referral problem for an average of 7.4 years, with professional help for the last 4.3 years preceding this study, mostly from their GPs and psychiatrists. Half of the patients were on psychotropic medication and as a group they consulted their GP on average 7.3 times per year. The problems identified in referral letters were anxiety (40%), depression (24%), specific phobias (24%), obsessional compulsive disorders (8%) and sexual dysfunction (4%).

Therapy Procedure

Each patient was seen individually by the author, a clinical psychologist employed by the National Health Service.

The first appointment was occupied largely with an explanation of the therapy and evaluation procedure, a clarification of the problem and the collection of demographic data. Clients were then seen weekly or fortnightly in order to establish a behavioural analysis of their problems, leading to appropriate behaviour therapy. On average, patients were seen for 11.6 appointments lasting 31.8 minutes over a period of 5.3 months.

The range of techniques employed included progressive muscular relaxation, response prevention, sex therapy, cognitive restructuring methods and anti-depressive activities. Written material and audio-tapes were provided to aid the development of understanding and self-control (eg Milne & Linford, 1984).

More detailed objective specifications of the therapy provided in this study have been reported elsewhere (Milne, 1986a). In short, it was found that the type of therapy corresponded most closely with 'behaviour therapy'; that the therapist's proficiency was 'satisfactory', and that the patients perceived the therapist as high on interpersonal effectiveness.

RESULTS

The main hypothesis of improved personal coping consequent upon behaviour therapy was supported by the data. Table 1 shows the trend for the three scores derived from the coping responses questionnaire (CRQ) to remain stable during the baseline phase, but to increase both immediately following therapy and between then and the follow-up assessment. This statement is true for the two strategies regarded as adaptive by Billings and Moos (1981), 'active cognitive' and 'active behavioural' coping; and untrue, as would be expected, for the maladaptive strategy of 'avoidance'. Statistical analyses, employing the t-test, indicated that the only significant changes occurred in the two 'adaptive' coping strategies, which increased significantly following three months of therapy ($p < 0.05$). These improved scores were maintained at levels significantly higher than baseline figures at the one year follow-up assessment.

In addition to demonstrating the successful impact of behaviour therapy upon personal coping strategies, the data in Table 1 also seem to rule out the alternative hypothesis: no significant change in the patient's stressful life events was obtained during the study. Taken together, these stress and coping data suggest that reductions in strain are mediated by improved coping, rather than by reduced stress. This relationship is indicated by the significant reduction in the General Health Questionnaire (GHQ) score at the same point in time as the CRQ changes.

Expressed in terms of clinical rather than statistical significance, the reduction in strain represented a decline in the proportion of psychiatric 'cases' from 49% and 38% during the initial baseline assessments, to 13% following three months of therapy, and to 2% at the one year follow-up assessment.

The independent ratings made by the referring agents and patients' self-ratings corroborated the impression of real clinical progress apparent from the GHQ and CRQ data. At the one year follow-up assessment 74% of the patients were regarded by the referring agents as requiring no further psychological treatment (with a further 12% stating 'don't know'). Similarly, in the case of 72% of the patients they thought that a 'satisfactory outcome' had been achieved through the patient seeing the psychologist (12% 'don't know'). These figures are

Table 1: Mean scores obtained for the patients' (N=47) stress (SRE), coping (CRQ) and strain (GHQ) during each assessment phase.

MEASURES	ASSESSMENT PHASES							
	FIRST BASELINE		SECOND BASELINE		AFTER 3 MONTHS OF THERAPY		ONE YEAR FOLLOW-UP	
	MEAN	STANDARD DEVIATION	MEAN	STANDARD DEVIATION	MEAN	STANDARD DEVIATION	MEAN	STANDARD DEVIATION
Schedule of Recent Events (SRE)	3·4	2·2	4·0	3·8	4·1	4·3	–	–
Coping Responses Questionnaire (CRQ) a) Active Cognitive	1·7	0·8	1·7	0·8	2·1	0·8	2·5	1·0
b) Active Behavioural	1·6	0·8	1·5	0·7	1·9	0·6	2·1	1·0
c) Avoidance	1·6	0·9	1·5	0·7	1·4	0·7	1·5	0·7
General Health Questionnaire (GHQ) (Likert scoring)	21·5	9·5	17	9·1	10·3	7·9	8·9	6·8

very comparable with the '70% improved' short-term findings of most outcome studies.

Overall, the patients also felt that the therapy had been successful. Their replies to the two questions above were similar to those of the referring agents. Also, on an ad hoc anonymous 'consumer satisfaction' measure, administered after three months of therapy, they highly endorsed the clinical 'outcomes', 'process', 'content' and 'goals' of therapy. These were the four logically derived dimensions of the scale. Mean scores were, respectively, 4.3, 5.3, 4.4 and 5.3, on a bi-polar Likert scale where 0 equalled strong dissatisfaction and 6 represented strong satisfaction. These figures compared very favourably with those achieved on the same measure by a popular local GP, dealing with routine surgery attenders.

DISCUSSION

The principal finding of this study was that behaviour therapy led to significantly improved personal coping and that this, rather than transient life stress, appears to have been the explanation for the reduced strain reported by these patients. This conclusion is a reassuring one for therapists who have always inferred improved coping from reduced strain. However, such inferences can prove invalid, as we know from the use of medication as an outcome measure. This suggests that future studies should investigate the effect of their interventions upon specific and immediate targets, as well as upon the more traditonal outcome measures. A failure to do so appears to lead to at least two difficulties. One of these lies in developing our understanding of the precise mediators of therapeutic change from coarse outome measures. It would seem that in order to produce more efficient interventions we need also to consider mediating variables, such as personal coping strategies, in much greater detail.

The second difficulty lies in the premature abandonment of the 'primary care' approach, on the basis of the inferences drawn from existing studies. These have tended to provide pessimistic conclusions regarding the incremental value of a clinical psychology service and to bolster the view that GPs are dealing adequately with a transient 'worst year' phenomenon (Robson et al, 1984; Freeman & Button, 1984).

The present data dispute these conclusions: baseline data do not suggest a transient period of

161

stress or strain, nor do they indicate the development of better coping strategies. The reason for the unaltered strain in this sample may well be due to the chronic nature of the presenting complaints. In contrast, we found that a randomly selected sample of 40 patients attending the same surgery for the usual range of complaints did fluctuate quite considerably in their level of strain over the same period. These findings suggest that the transient 'worst year' explanation may be adequate for minor, acute episodes of psychological distress, but may be quite inadequate to explain changes in the more chronic sample, as typically referred to psychologists in routine practice.

The implication of the present coping analysis for the role of clinical psychologists working in primary care seems to hold whether or not we accept the above arguments regarding transient episodes or the effectiveness of GPs. This implication is that we need to develop our understanding of personal change if we are to prove optimally successful, either as direct or indirect therapists.

A clear parallel exists in the area of staff training in behaviour therapy, where such an indirect approach to patient care was regarded as unsuccessful by the mid 1970s. However, more systematic investigations subsequently indicated not only that these interventions could prove effective, but that by studying the immediate target of the training more closely (ie skills acquisition) we could learn a lot more about the psychology of change at the organisational level, so developing our analysis and effectiveness (Milne, 1986b). As a consequence of this kind of precedent and the present findings, we may wish to re-appraise our role in primary care. There may yet be benefits in pursuing traditional approaches, provided that these are allied to a more thorough analysis of the effects of our work. In turn, the findings should guide the nature of our future contribution to primary care.

ACKNOWLEDGEMENTS

I am indebted to Eileen Greaves, Trish Harrison, Keith Henshall, Fiona Castle, Julie Sowerby, Sue Candy, Janet Rowntree and Judy Milne for their help in administering, scoring and analysing the measures. My former colleague, Rosemary Jones, participated in the project initially, providing support and encouragement. I am grateful to the referring agents for their ratings, particularly Drs. K.M. Souter, G.D. Slater, P.F. Slater and D.O. Oughtibridge of Southgate Surgery. This study was undertaken in Wakefield while I was employed by the District Health Authority. The manuscript was typed by Stella Dickinson.

REFERENCES

Banks, M.H., Clegg, C.W., Jackson, P.R., Kemp, N.J., Stafford, E.M. & Wall, T.D. (1980). The use of of the General Health Questionnaire as an indicator of mental health in occupational studies. Journal of Occupational Psychology, 53, 187-194.

Billings, A.G. & Moos, R.H. (1981). The role of coping responses and social resources in attenuating the stress of life events. Journal of Behavioural Medicine, 4, 139-157.

Cohen, F. & Lazarus, R.S. (1979) Coping with Stresses of Illness. In G.C. Stone, F. Cohen & N.E. Adler (Eds), Health Psychology: a Handbook. Jossey Bass: London.

Freeman, G.K. & Button, E.J. (1984) The clinical psychologist in general practice: a six year study of consulting patterns for psychosocial problems. Journal of the Royal College of General Practitioners, 34, 377-380.

Milne, D.L. (1986a). Training Behaviour Therapists. Croom Helm: London.

Milne, D.L. (1986b). A process evaluation of a routine clinical psychology service. Paper presented to the annual Conference of the British Association for Behavioural Psychotherapy, Manchester.

Milne, D.L. & Linford, J. (1984). Anxiety: how to understand and control your 'nerves'. MIND: Wakefield.

Robson, M.H., France, R. & Bland, M. (1984). Clinical Psychologist in primary care: controlled clinical and economic evaluation. British Medical Journal, 288, 1805-1808.

Tennant, C. & Andrews, G. (1976). A scale to measure the stress of life events. Australian & New Zealand Journal of Psychiatry, 10, 27-32.

Chapter Twenty Three

USING MIDDLE-RANGE THEORIES & QUALITATIVE TECHNIQUES
TO STUDY STRESS IN PSYCHIATRIC NURSING

Jocelyn Handy

This paper is a critique of traditional models
of organisational stress and outlines an alternative
analysis of stress in psychiatric nursing which is
illustrated with data from an ongoing empirical
study.
Transactional models of organisational stress
have been criticised for failing to develop
satisfactory accounts of the causes of stress within
particular occupational groups. Middle-range
theories which are more closely tied to the
empirical data, more complex and more limited in
scope, are often proposed as a practically useful
alternative (Argyris, 1982). Qualitative methods
are advocated for similar reasons as they provide
more depth and flexibility than positivist
methodologies.
The middle range theory of stress in
psychiatric nursing is derived from the critical
psychiatry literature. The fundamental premise of
this literature is that the functions and structures
of psychiatry are contradictory. Thus whilst the
manifest function of psychiatry is to cure the
mentally ill, its latent function may well be to
control social deviance and deny its social
significance by individualising and medicalising it.
Similarly, whilst the organisational structure of
psychiatric hospitals is superficially aimed at
helping patients, closer inspection often reveals a
structure geared to routine care and control.
One implication of this model is that a
fundamental cause of stress in psychiatric nursing
may be that nurses internalise the official ideology
of psychiatry and identify themselves professionally
as helpers whereas the organisational structure
means that in practice they usually operate as a
cross between room-service and jailers. Since the

Figure 1. <u>Diary Extracts from Second Year Pupil</u>
<u>Nurse</u>

Extract One

Nurse's Description of Events

Nurse's Comments

Admitted an over-active patient. A lady who had delusions of grandeur - Christ reborn. Little insight into her condition. Prior to her admission had been seen over-acting and walking around the streets naked. Admitted as an emergency DV by Dr.

Tried to remain calm throughout admission, took several questions to get this lady to participate with admission forms etc. Frustrated with her as present day happenings are always affecting her - has everybody elses' worries on her mind.

Extract Two

Nurses' Comments

Nurse's Descriptions of Events

Admitted another lady, an old patient who I've known in the past. Hypomanic - also suffers from mood swings. Believes in San Yasin (Orange people). Neglecting hygiene, stopped eating. Varying emotions - crying to laughing, screaming.

Mad at the thought of admitting this lady again as it has only been six weeks since her discharge. Always admitted after her bisexual boyfriend has found another girlfriend. X cannot cope with this - always plays the psychiatric sick role and always warrants admission. Since her arrival has been kissing walls, lifting clothes up in the lounge. Counselled her re this but to little effect. Maintains it is through (boyfriend) she has ended up coming in. Given prescribed injection to calm her.

nurses are unable to articulate the discrepancy between ideology and practice they are unable to take rational action to change the organisation and may therefore become cynical towards patients whilst developing feelings of guilt because they no longer care. In other words, stress in psychiatric nursing may arise because nurses are repeatedly faced with problematic situations brought about by the contra-dictory nature of the psychiatric system. They then interpret and act upon these situations using a contradictory knowledge base derived from their socialisation within the system and by doing so perpetuate the cycle.

The analysis is illustrated with qualitative data from the empirical research. The raw data from a diary kept by a pupil nurse is presented in Figure 1 to show how the inappropriate and inconsistent use of a medical framework generates dysfunctional inter-personal dynamics which help maintain the very acts which the hospital system purports to alleviate. The nurses' comments suggest that the cost in staff stress may be high.

REFERENCE

Argyris, C. (1982). Research as Action. Useable Knowledge for Understanding and Changing the Status Quo. In N. Nicholson & T.D. Wall (Eds) The Theory & Practice of Organizational Psychology. Academic Press: London.

Chapter Twenty Four

COGNITIVE THERAPY: IS IT ALWAYS COGNITIVE, IS IT
ALWAYS THERAPY?

Paul M. Salkovskis

Cognitive Therapy, particularly that described
in detail by Beck et al (1979), has become widely
accepted in clinical research and practice.   A
number of well conducted controlled trials have
demonstrated that cognitive therapy of depression is
as effective as tricyclic antidepressant medication
(e.g. Blackburn et al, 1981). We are awaiting the
completion of further longer term follow up studies,
but there is already some evidence that cognitive
therapy may be more effective in preventing relapse
than pharmacotherapy (Blackburn et al, 1986). Until
recently, cognitive therapy has proved most useful
in areas such as depression where the impact of
psychological treatment had previously been minimal.
However, the last few years have seen the increasing
application of cognitive techniques in a variety of
disorders where <u>limitations</u> in psychological
treatments have become apparent, particularly in
those areas where behaviour therapy has been
generally successful. Notable examples of this
trend are anxiety (Beck, Emery & Greenberg, 1985;
Clark, 1986), panic (Clark, 1986; Salkovskis &
Clark, 1986) and obsessions (Salkovskis & Westbrook,
this volume).

As research into cognitive treatment has
progressed, two important conceptual and
methodological issues have come to the fore:
(i) What is the nature of the link between
experimental cognitive psychology and cognitive
therapy? (ii) What are the necessary and sufficient
criteria for an intervention to be acceptable as
<u>properly conducted</u> cognitive therapy?

There are some interesting parallels between
these issues now being debated in cognitive psychopathology and the situation which arose in behaviour
therapy in the late 1960s. At that point in its

history, behaviour therapy was at a very similar
stage of development. In this paper, an attempt
will be made to draw on this experience.

Is it cognitive?

Those with broadly behavioural orientations have
been especially eager to endorse cognitive therapy;
elsewhere, it has been argued that such ready
acceptance is possible mainly because of the
compatibility of cognitive and behavioural
approaches to therapy and research (Salkovskis,
1986). Despite this, or perhaps because of it, some
cognitive and behavioural psychologists have come
to regard the development of cognitive therapy as
something of a Trojan Horse. In particular, the use
of the term "cognition" as applied to self-report of
mental activity is seen as both a dangerous over-
simplification and over-generalisation. For
instance, the distinction between cognitive
processes (i.e. the mechanisms by which incoming
information is processed) and their products (i.e.
cognitive "events" [thoughts, feelings] identified
by subjects as occurring in consciousness) can be
blurred beyond recognition. This lack of clarity
has undermined the value of much of the research
carried out in this area. The studies which have
been most useful both in research and clinical terms
have been those in which careful operational
definitions have been used, and conclusions have
been derived directly from the measured variables
without undue reliance on inference. In contrast,
an increasing number of studies have appeared in
which the techniques and concepts of cognitive
psychology have been directly applied to
psychological disorders (e.g. MacLeod et al, 1986).
This approach is characterised by careful definition
of concepts, exacting methodology with minimal
reliance on self report and attention to designing
experiments with the minimum of ambiguity. On the
one hand there are therefore cognitive approaches to
therapy and research which rely heavily on
operationalised concepts of cognition easily
applicable to (and well validated in) clinical
populations and treatment settings, but which cannot
easily be regarded as part of the corpus of
cognitive psychology. On the other, we have
paradigms which promise theoretical insights into
cognitive processes involved in psychopathology
consistent with prevailing views in experimental
psychology. Thus far, such work has had no impact
on clinical applications, although it seems likely

that the measures used may be useful as outcome measures. The major strengths of each approach are outlined in table 1.

Table 1: **Strengths of Cognitive Therapy and Cognitive Approaches to Psychopathology**

COGNITIVE THERAPY	Treatment applications; (a) general approach (b) validated good outcome Emphasises operationally defined cognitive events in ways which can be readily applied in clinical work
COGNITIVE PSYCHOPATHOLOGY	Based directly on cognitive psychology Emphasises direct investigation of cognitive processes

Is this as problematic as it appears? These apparently separate clinically based approaches to cognitive phenomena, with little overlap of methodology or theoretical models could be regarded as mutually incompatible because cognitive psychologists are deeply suspicious of self report, whilst clinical psychologists often consider small effects derived from laboratory experimentation as trivial and irrelevant to therapeutic strategies. This seeming conflict of interest requires careful attention if polarisation is to be prevented. It is obvious that both approaches have important elements in common. They have cognitive processes as their ultimate target, both represent attempts to further our understanding of and ability to treat psychological disturbance, and both in fact involve the drawing of inferences about cognitive processes from their products. That a particular approach is more or less direct with respect to these goals may be methodologically important, but does not necessarily carry implications of superiority or inferiority. The same problem is being approached from different directions. An optimal solution should involve a fusion of these two approaches.

In order to show how this division may be more apparent than real, we can examine the split which appeared early in the history of behaviour therapy.

Cognitive Therapy?

Two major schools of behaviourism as applied to abnormal psychology developed; viz. radical behaviourism and methodological behaviourism. The major difference between these approaches lay in the way in which private events (particularly thoughts and emotions) were conceptualised and investigated. Essentially, radical behaviourists followed Skinner's view that detailed, precise microanalysis of behaviour and context was required before it was possible to make any inferences in this respect. On the other hand, methodological behaviourists relied on the use of operational definitions and approximations (e.g. the use of rating scales in the definition of "anxiety", behavioural observation during behaviour tests), whilst at the same time retaining an empirical orientation by drawing on aspects of psychometrics and observational techniques. Both approaches emphasised the importance of proper functional analysis on the basis of data collected in such a way as to maximise reliability and validity, and treatment procedures often did not substantially differ. In the final analysis, the attraction of methodological behaviourism lay in the ease of direct application to clinical settings, and in the inherent flexibility of the type of operational definitions used, which closely corresponded to clinical phenomena. The lesson of time has been that there is no inherent contradiction between these approaches and each has benefited from work carried out in the other.

Perhaps, then, we should consider the situation with respect to cognitive approaches as similar. Radical cognitivism is based on the direct microanalysis of cognitive processes through the delicate exploration of small effects not prone to the problems associated with self report. Methodological cognitivism is based on the analysis of cognitive processes and their correlates, mostly based on data derived from self report and psychophysiological measurement. Such data require careful attention to the methodological and psychometric problems commonly associated with such measurement. In the final analysis, there are a number of assumptions associated with both approaches (e.g. the definition of concepts such as "anxiety" or "neuroticism" have to be operationalised from self report criteria). We can expect to see increasing crossover between these currently different approaches to psychopathology. A good example may be found in a paper by Clark

(1986) who describes a cognitive model of panic which has been derived from systematic clinical and non-clinical studies (dependent on self report data) (Salkovskis & Clark, 1986), but which makes predictions that can be directly evaluated using the methodology of cognitive psychology. This kind of approach is firmly embedded in the tradition of clinical psychology as an applied science, so that therapy and research are both aspects of applying the science of psychology to a clinical setting (Salkovskis, 1984).

Is it therapy?
When is cognitive therapy not cognitive therapy? Since cognitive therapy gained wider acceptance, a number of researchers have employed procedures which they described as cognitive therapy, but which do not conform to some or all of the characteristics considered to distinguish such approaches from "counselling" or other more general psychological procedures. The type of interventions concerned could hardly be more variable. They range from a study in which cognitive therapy lasted for between 1 and 2 minutes, with the intention of identification and modification of idiosyncratic dysfunctional thoughts, through studies in which patients carried cards on which were written positive self statements (e.g. "I feel very calm and relaxed") into anxiety provoking situations. In general, cognitive therapists would emphasise a number of distinctive aspects of therapy; educational, structured, problem oriented, active, collaborative, individually tailored, using specific technical manoeuvres. The definition of the form and content of therapy is carefully described in treatment manuals for these procedures (Beck et al, 1979; Beck et al, 1985). Furthermore, it is possible to assess, using standard criteria, the validity of such interventions by means of a range of psychometrically valid appraisal instruments. The resemblance to behavioural treatments is again striking - frequently, failures to replicate outcome studies in behaviour therapy have been convincingly attributed to faults in treatment administration (for example, not having set proper homework assignments, failure to perform proper functional analyses, using exposure to the wrong stimuli and so on).

Given the characteristic of cognitive therapy, a closely related issue becomes important. To what extent can the effectiveness of cognitive therapy be ascribed to the specific qualities of the treatment set within the context of an active (reciprocal) therapeutic relationship rather than the qualities of that relationship itself independent of the "cognitive" (technical) components. It could be argued that cognitive therapy represents an extreme version of the active, structured therapeutic relationship which may have already progressed as far as is possible with respect to structure, empathy and therapist enthusiasm. Clarification of this issue has crucial implications for the further development of psychological treatments; this is especially important now that the NIMH depression trial results are available (Beck, personal communication). This outcome study showed that cognitive therapy did as well as imipramine – however, so did interpersonal therapy, which shares with cognitive therapy the elements of active and empathic therapeutic style, structure and therapist contact. Two ways of approaching this question are possible. Microanalysis of outcome by therapy characteristics, patient attributes and their interaction is obviously important, and is currently a major line of research in this area (e.g. recently described by Alladin, 1986). Alladin drew attention to the existence of rudimentary computer programmes intended to stimulate "cognitive therapy". At present, these are mostly programmed learning/ educational in content, making the notion of their use to test this issue appear absurd. However, careful consideration reveals real potential, given advances in the technology of <u>intelligent systems</u>. <u>IF</u> it proves possible to construct such a system in a way which would allow it to perform at high levels of competency as objectively assessed by instruments such as the competency checklist for cognitive therapy (Beck et al, 1979), then it should prove possible at least to clarify the contribution of human therapist contact. As ever, it seems most probable that we will discover that "the answer" is actually that technique and contact are both necessary and neither are sufficient for good response. The possibilities in this respect are intriguing; they are also a long way in the future.

In conclusion, it appears that cognitive approaches to psychopathology are proving extremely productive; furthermore, the potential for future development, far from being exhausted, is only just beginning to be realised.

Cognitive Therapy?

Acknowledgements

The author would like to thank Hilary Warwick and Lorna Hogg for helpful comments on an earlier version of this paper.

REFERENCES

Alladin, W.J. (1986). Microcomputers and Cognitive Therapy: Promise or Peril? Paper presented at the annual meeting of the British Association for Behavioural Psychotherapy, Manchester.

Beck, A.T., Rush, A.J., Shaw, B.F., & Emery, G. (1979). Cognitive Therapy of Depression. Guilford Press: New York.

Beck, A.T., Emery, G. & Greenberg, R. (1985). Anxiety Disorders and Phobias: A Cognitive Perspective. Basic Books: New York.

Blackburn, I.M., Bishop, S., Glen, A.I.M., Whalley, L.J. & Christie, J.E. (1981). The efficacy of cognitive therapy in depression: a treatment trial using cognitive therapy and pharmacotherapy, each alone and in combination. British Journal of Psychiatry, 139, 181-189.

Blackburn, I.M., Eunson, K.M., & Bishop, S. (1986). A two year naturalistic follow up of depressed patients treated with cognitive therapy, pharmacotherapy and a combination. Journal of Affective Disorders, 10, 67-75.

Clark, D.M. (1986). A cognitive approach to panic. Behaviour Research and Therapy, 24, 461-470.

MacLeod, C., Mathews, A.M. & Tata, P. (1986). Attentional bias in emotional disorders. Journal of Abnormal Psychology, 95, 15-20.

Salkovskis, P.M. (1984). Psychological research by NHS clinical psychologists: an analysis and some suggestions. Bulletin of the British Psychological Society, 37, 375-377.

Salkovskis, P.M. (1986). The cognitive revolution: new way forward, backward, somersault or full circle? Behavioural Psychotherapy, 14, 278-282.

Salkovskis, P.M. & Clark, D.M. (1986). Cognitive and Physiological Processes in the Maintenance and Treatment of Panic Attacks. In I. Hand and H. Wittgen (Eds) Panic and Phobias. Springer Verlag: Heidelberg.

Simons, A.D., Lustman, P.J., Wetzel, R.D. & Murphy, G.E. (1985). Predicting response to cognitive therapy of depression: the role of learned resourcefulness. Cognitive Therapy and Research, 9, 79-90.

Chapter Twenty Five

COGNITIVE PSYCHOLOGY AND COGNITIVE THERAPY

Colin MacLeod

Most psychologists now agree that our science has indeed undergone a 'cognitive revolution'. For the experimental psychologists this began in the 1950s and involved adopting information processing models of the brain, and developing paradigms capable of testing resulting predictions. The 'revolution' has occurred more recently within clinical psychology, primarily reflecting the recognition that behaviours and feelings may be mediated by thought, and the development of clinical techniques to modify maladaptive thinking patterns. As yet, however, the development of cognitive approaches within each of these two areas has proceeded rather independently. It is the central argument of this paper that a closer integration of theoretical frameworks and experimental methods may represent the most fruitful path for future progress.

While many contemporary issues were addressed by the founders of our discipline more than a century ago, these early researchers were severely limited by their reliance on the introspective method. Two main arguments served to undermine the scientific credibility of the resulting data. First, as it had no objective validity, there was no way of assessing its accuracy. Second, there was a growing realisation that conscious awareness may, at best, be restricted to certain classes of mental event, or at worst may be entirely epiphenomenal. Given its inability to cope with such criticisms, introspection was quickly discredited as a scientific research paradigm, and an important choice point in the development of our discipline was reached. Psychoanalysts largely abandoned the constraints of the scientific method, whereas the behaviourists abandoned the use of subjective reports as data.

The behaviourist movement was powerfully influential in establishing psychology as a rigorous new science, and formed the necessary bedrock for the foundation of clinical psychology. Indeed, the early progress of clinical psychology largely reflects the strong association between the theoretical and applied aspects of the science which characterised this period. Nevertheless, the limitations of behaviourism became apparent when attempting to construct theoretical models to account for such complex human activities as language. Thus it was the experimental psychologist who first became uncomfortable with the constraints of this approach.

With the accelerating development of information processing devices in the post-war years, applied psychologists began to investigate factors influencing the efficiency of man-machine interactions, and came to regard the machine operator as one part of an information processing system. They borrowed many concepts directly from information science, such as the notion of stages of processing, limited capacity systems, serial versus parallel operations, etc., and used these to model the way in which the human operator functioned.

Furthermore, psychologists were now able to develop experimental paradigms capable of objectively testing such models without recourse to subjective report data. Partly this was due to technological advances making possible very precise measurement, particularly of reaction times. Largely, however, the objective testability of these new mentalistic models reflected the precision with which they could be formulated using the modern information processing concepts. Thus the return to mentalism in experimental psychology was made possible due to two factors: the adoption of a rich and powerful theoretical framework for human information processing, and the development of experimental paradigms permitting objective testing of such models without requiring introspection.

It was not until the mid 1970s that the limitations of behaviourism began to disturb many clinicians. Aaron Beck (1976) has been particularly influential in promoting a cognitive model of depression and, more recently, anxiety. Inherent in Beck's account is the notion that such patients show idiosyncratic biases in the way they process information, particularly when this information is of an emotional nature. Ultimately this results in a particular conscious experience, such as a negative thought, and to the aversive emotional state. Clinical psychologists interested in investigating such cognitive accounts of emotional disorders must choose which of two courses to follow. We can rely upon subjective self-report data, thereby restricting research to the unscientific appraisal of a small, and possibly artefactual, class of mental events. Alternatively, we can exploit the rich potential which experimental cognitive psychology offers for the study of human information processing. The potential for a new fusion between academic cognitive psychology and investigation of clinical patients' mental events promises a fruitful partnership, reminiscent of that which existed between academic behavioural research and the development of clinical approaches in the early days of our profession.

However, such clinical research must meet those two requirements which enabled experimental psychologists to scientifically investigate mental processes; the adoption of the information processing framework to formulate precise process models, yielding highly specific predictions, and the development and utilisation of objective experimental paradigms not based upon introspective self-report. Theoretical process models are available for a wide range of cognitive operations, and a multitude of objective paradigms have already been established by the academic scientist. It would be short-sighted indeed if we continue to neglect this immensely valuable source of knowledge.

Let me attempt to briefly illustrate the way in which this approach may illuminate the cognitive factors underlying clinical anxiety. We may entertain Beck's argument that, due to distortions in the way information is processed, such patients experience danger-related thoughts and the emotional state of anxiety. One method of investigating this hypothesis would be to consider self-report data. Indeed Beck himself (Beck, Laude & Bohnert, 1974) employed open-ended questioning and self-completed thought diaries, and concluded that all 32 anxious patients studied did indeed report such thoughts. However the valididy of such data, which may be highly sensitive to demand effects, cannot be assessed. Furthermore, such data cannot illuminate the mechanisms underlying the production of such thoughts. We can only develop the most effective means of modifying information processing in such patients if we directly investigate the way in which

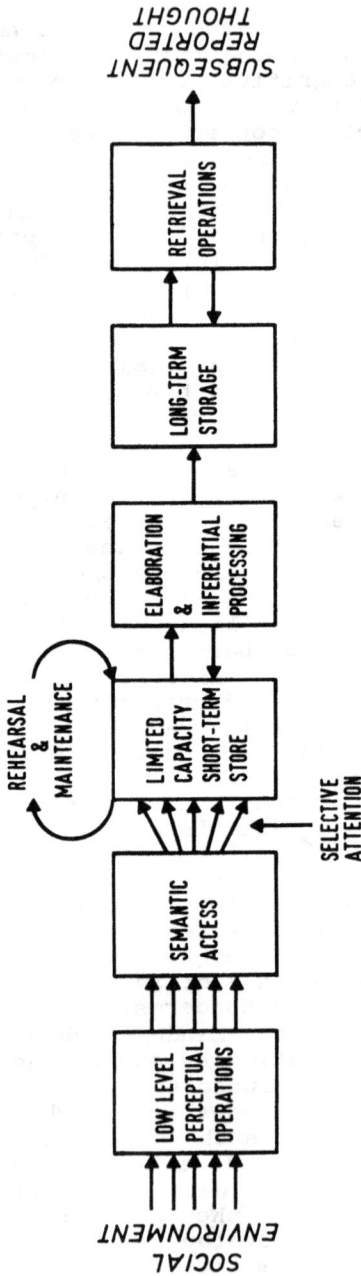

Figure 1: An information processing framework for socially evaluative thinking

they actually do process information.

Now consider the approach favoured by the experimental cognitive psychologist. Let us adopt a simple information processing framework and consider the kind of cognitive operations which may mediate the production of threatening thoughts, such as 'They are critical of me', in certain anxious subjects when they encounter a social situation. Figure 1 provides an extremely simplistic, but nonetheless useful, information processing formulation.

The social environment contains a great mass of information. Certain comments, gestures or expressions may be pleasant, some slightly critical, and many ambiguous – containing both pleasant and critical elements. Perhaps the anxious patient's negative thought results from a bias towards processing the more threatening element from this environment. The adoption of the information processing framework suggests a range of possible cognitive operations where such a bias may occur.

It is perhaps unlikely that low level perceptual processes such as feature extraction will be involved, but consider the next stage – semantic access. Perhaps, the meaning of the more threatening elements from the environment are accessed with disproportionate ease in the anxious subject. Having identified this specific hypothesis we can draw upon the range of paradigms already provided by experimental cognitive psychology to objectively test it. The lexical decision paradigm, for example, can be employed for this purpose. Using this, and other experimental techniques, a number of researchers have failed to find any evidence of such a bias in this particular cognitive operation.

Returning to Figure 1, we see that selective attention must operate to determine the contents of our limited capacity short term store. Perhaps, therefore, anxiety is associated with biases in selective attention, with greater attentional resources being allocated to more threatening inputs. Numerous objective paradigms can be employed to test this hypothesis. For example, are anxious subjects disproportionately disrupted during a dichotic listening task when they must attempt to ignore threatening, rather than neutral, distractors in the unattended ear? Do they show a disproportionate tendency to see the more threatening stimulus in a binocular rivalry paradigm, in which different stimuli are simultaneously presented to each eye? The results of such experiments have provided evidence which clearly support the hypothesis that anxiety is indeed associated with biased selective allocation of attention to more, rather than less, threatening stimuli (Mathews and MacLeod, 1985, 1986; Martin, 1986).

Available space prevents me working through Figure 1 in detail, exhaustively listing hypothetical cognitive biases underlying the observed thoughts and reviewing experimental paradigms capable of testing them. The kind of rehearsal strategies operating on temporary storage systems may or may not play a role, and inferential processing has already been shown to be involved (Eysenck, MacLeod and Mathews, in press). Recognition memory paradigms can be used to measure information storage, and recall paradigms to measure retrieval processes. Recent results from our own laboratory using such paradigms suggest that memory biases may play no role in the maintenance of threatening thinking in anxiety (e.g. Mogg, Mathews and Weinman, in press).

Such investigations have already raised many interesting possibilities. For example, elsewhere it has been suggested, on the basis of available experimental results, that anxiety may predominantly involve biases at the 'front end' of the cognitive system, producing a distorted appraisal of the current environment and preoccupation with future risk. Depression, on the other hand, may be associated with biases involving later stages, particularly memory, which produce a distorted appraisal of past personal experiences and lead to a loss of self-esteem (MacLeod, Mathews and Tata, 1986). We are also currently examining recovered anxious patients, to investigate the hypothesis that recovery may not involve the removal of an existing cognitive bias, but the development of a new compensatory bias at some later stage of processing.

Finally, since cognitive therapy is a clinical intervention procedure, some may argue that our primary concern should be to improve its efficacy, rather than mess around with boxes, arrows and reaction time recorders. However the many different techniques employed by cognitive therapists each assume, at least implicitly, the existence of processing biases in particular types of cognitive operation, and purport to be effective in overcoming those particular biases. Our ultimate ability to refine cognitive treatment approaches, such that they comprise the most useful therapeutic techniques, will therefore depend upon our ability to identify the precise nature of the actual processing biases which underlie any particular disorder, or indeed any specific patient, and our ability to sensitively measure the effectiveness of those techniques in overcoming such biases. The models and paradigms developed by experimental cognitive psychology offer our greatest hope of achieving those goals.

REFERENCES

Beck, A.T. (1976). Cognitive Therapy and the Emotional Disorders. International University Press: New York.

Beck, A.T., Laude, R. & Bohnert, M. (1974). Ideational components of anxiety neurosis. Archives of General Psychiatry, 1, 319-325.

Eysenck, M.W., MacLeod, C. & Mathews, A. (in press). Cognitive functioning in anxiety. Psychological Research.

MacLeod, C., Mathews, A. & Tata, P. (1986). Attentional bias in emotional disorders. Journal of Abnormal Psychology, 95, 15-20.

Martin, M. (1986). Influences of mood and personality on the perception of threat related material. Paper presented at BABP Annual Conference, University of Manchester, July, 1986.

Mathews, A. & MacLeod, C. (1985). Selective processing of threat cues in anxiety states. Behaviour Research and Therapy, 23, 563-569.

Mathews, A. & MacLeod, C. (1986). Discrimination of threat cues without awareness in anxiety states. Journal of Abnormal Psychology, 95, 131-139.

Mogg, K. Mathews, A. & Weinman, J. (in press). Memory bias in clinical anxiety. Journal of Abnormal Psychology.

Chapter Twenty Six

SELF-ESTEEM IN AFFECTIVE DISORDER

I. Malcolm MacLachlan

INTRODUCTION

        Several theorists have accredited low self-
esteem with a major role in depression (MacLachlan,
1985) and an abundance of evidence attests to this
relation (Ingham et al, 1986). However, MacLachlan
(1985) reported finding psychometric contamination
between the Beck Depression Inventory (BDI, Beck et
al, 1961) and the Self-Esteem Inventory (SEI,
Bachman and O'Malley, 1977) which resulted in an
inflated correlation between these measures. It was
therefore suggested that correlating these measures
violated the assumption of independent dimensions,
because some of the questions on the BDI were also
addressed to self-esteem.
        MacLachlan (1985) found that when self-esteem
items were removed from the BDI the correlation
between the BDI and SEI dropped from -0.47 to -0.05
for a small group of depressed students. For the
whole sample of 160 (depressed and nondepressed)
students the contamination effect was less dramatic;
the correlation coefficient only reducing from -0.52
to -0.45. The small contamination effect for the
whole sample indicated that low self-esteem was
associated with high levels of depression and high
self-esteem was associated with low levels of
depression, even when self-esteem related items were
removed from the BDI. However, the large
contamination effect for the depressed subsample
indicated that when the self-esteem related items on
the BDI were removed, there was no relationship
between the severity of depression (within the
depressed range) and self-esteem.
        As these results question the validity of
previous research on the relation between self-
esteem and depression (for example, Battle, 1978)

the present study sought to confirm the identification of self-esteem related items on the BDI and to investigate the contamination effect, and the relationship between self-esteem and depression in a clinical sample.

METHOD

Subjects
All psychiatric patients received a formal psychiatric diagnosis, based upon ICD-9 criterion, from a psychiatrist and this was usually the consultant in charge of the patient's care. Five groups of subjects completed the BDI and SEI: 15 subjects had a diagnosis of depressive neurosis, 36 had a diagnosis of manic-depressive psychosis and 31 had a primary diagnosis that did not involve affective disorder. This latter group constituted the psychiatric control group. There was also a hospital control group of 42 medical and surgical patients and a general population control group of 156 subjects (further details of these subjects are available in an extended report of this research).
Because of their training and clinical experience, clinical psychologists were thought to be suitable judges for the identification of items on the BDI primarily addressed to self-esteem. The subjects were drawn from an unselected list of clinical psychologists working within the Grampian, Tayside and Lothian regions of Scotland. Thirty-one of the sixty psychologists who were contacted by post (including the twelve subjects reported in MacLachlan, 1985) agreed to participate.

Procedure and Materials
The BDI is a 21-item questionnaire. Each item describes a particular manifestation of depression and has a series of four to six self-evaluative statements, with weightings from 0 to 3 to indicate severity. The depression score is the sum of these weightings; the higher the score the more depressed the person is judged to be. A cut-off of 10 on the BDI was used to distinguish depressed from non-depressed subjects (Deardorff and Funabiki, 1985, reported that this was the most commonly used criterion on the BDI). Clinicians judged, using scales ranging from 0 (labelled "This question does not measure this symptom at all") to 10 (labelled "This question is a very good measure of this symptom"), how well each of the 21 items of the BDI measured self-esteem (defined as "referring to how

one values oneself") cognitive (defined as "referring to thought mechanisms"), somatic (defined as "referring to physical aspects") and mood (defined as "referring to emotions") symptoms of depression. These symptom categories are not seen as either mutually exclusive or exhaustive. Rather the latter three symptom categories were included to facilitate conceptual distinction between low self-esteem and other symptoms of depression.

The SEI is a 10-item questionnaire requiring subjects to indicate whether they feel a particular way about themselves almost always, often, sometimes, seldom or never. These choices are weighted from 1 to 5 and there are four reverse items. The self-esteem score is the sum of these weightings with a high score reflecting high self-esteem.

RESULTS

Judge's Ratings
Criteria were established for deciding whether items were retained or rejected for the uncontaminated BDI in accordance with whether self-esteem was judged to be involved: if an item was judged to measure cognitive, somatic or mood symptomatology significantly better ($p < .05$, two tailed, Wilcoxon Matched-Pairs Signed-Ranks test) than it measured self-esteem then it was to be retained in the uncontaminated BDI. However, for an item to be accepted as reflecting self-esteem, it also had to be rated above 5 on the extent to which it was a good measure of the self-esteem symptom category. Seven items were judged to reflect self-esteem to a significant extent: items 3, 5, 6, 7, 8, 9 and 14 (analysis of only those judges whose ratings were not reported in MacLachlan, 1985, produced the same results). These items were described by Beck et al (1961) as measuring sense of failure, guilty feelings, sense of punishment, self-hate, self-accusations, self-punitive wishes and body image, respectively.

The Contamination Effect
All the correlation coefficients between the SEI and the whole and uncontaminated BDI were significant for each sample of subjects, although the uncontaminated coefficients were weaker than the contaminated ones. However, as the most dramatic results from the MacLachlan (1985) study were obtained for subjects scoring ten or more on the

BDI, we shall focus our analysis on these subjects. Table (1) shows descriptive data for the BDI and SEI, and correlations between these variables for

Table 1: Pearson correlation coefficients between the SEI and the BDI and some BDI subscales, for subjects scoring more than nine on the BDI. The means, standard deviations and ranges for these scales are given, along with the number of subjects in each diagnostic group.

GROUP		TOTAL BDI (21 items)	BDI MINUS SELF ESTEEM ITEMS (14 items)	BDI SELF ESTEEM ITEMS (7 items)	SEI (10 items)
DEPRESSIVE	r	-0.05	-0.01	-0.13	-
NEUROSIS	x	28.00	19.23	8.77	27.77
	SD	7.28	5.83	2.89	5.23
	Range	13-40	8-29	5-13	19-34
	N	13			
MANIC	r	-0.17	-0.11	-0.02	-
DEPRESSIVE	x	20.04	13.54	6.50	31.42
PSYCHOSIS	SD	8.74	6.01	4.13	6.10
	Range	10-43	5-26	1-17	20-45
	N	24			
PSYCHIATRIC	r	-0.58++	-0.26	-0.77+++	-
CONTROLS	x	21.33	14.57	6.76	33.35
	SD	8.74	5.36	4.82	9.81
	Range	10-41	6.27	0-19	12-50
	N	21			
HOSPITALISED	r	-0.26	-0.19	-0.32	-
CONTROLS	x	16.33	12.87	3.47	37.20
	SD	6.62	4.76	2.50	6.43
	Range	11-30	8-23	0-8	25-50
	N	15			
GENERAL	r	-0.48++	-0.32+	-0.54+++	-
POPULATION	x	16.19	10.67	5.52	33.90
CONTROLS	SD	5.76	4.07	2.71	5.99
	Range	10-34	4-24	0-12	15-48
	N	48			

+ $P < 0.05$
++ $P < 0.01$
+++ $P < 0.001$
BDI: Beck Depression Inventory,
SEI: Self-Esteem Inventory

subjects scoring ten or more on the BDI. Although again all groups showed a stronger SEI with total BDI correlation, than SEI with uncontaminated BDI correlation, only the psychiatric control and general population control groups showed significant SEI with total BDI correlations. In the psychiatric control group this correlation was no longer significant when the seven self-esteen items were removed from the BDI. In the general population control group the same correlation dropped one level of statistical significance. For both these groups, the seven self-esteem related items on the BDI correlated more strongly with the SEI, than did the full BDI. While the hospitalised control group showed a similar pattern of results to the above, the depressive neurosis and manic-depressive psychosis groups did not. For these two groups of diagnosed depressives there was no apparent relationship between their scores on the SEI and total BDI, or any BDI subscale.

To check whether the differential strength of the SEI with total BDI correlation between groups could be accounted for by proportionately different scoring on the self-esteem related BDI items, a two-way ANOVA (group by sex) was computed for these 7 self-esteem related items divided by the total BDI score. There was no interaction ($F(4,110)=0.23$,NS) or main effect for sex ($F(1,110)=0.02$,NS), but there was a main effect for group ($F(4,110)=4.17$, $p<.01$). A posteriori analysis indicated that only the hospital control group differed significantly from any of the other groups. They scored significantly lower($x=0.20$, SD=0.12) than the manic-depressive psychosis ($x=0.32$, SD=0.14) and the general population control ($x=0.34$, SD=0.12) groups, but not significantly different from the depressive neurosis group ($x=0.32$, SD=0.07) or the psychiatric control groups ($x=0.31$, SD=0.14).

DISCUSSION

The contamination effect

The present study has produced further evidence of psychometric contamination between the BDI and SEI: when the seven self-esteem related items were removed from the BDI, the strength of the BDI X SEI correlation decreased. Furthermore, the larger the BDI X SEI correlation (for subjects who scored above nine on the BDI), the more it was reduced by removal of these items.

Failing to control for the contamination between measures of self-esteem and depression may produce erroneously large correlations between these variables. It may also, of course, produce erroneously large between group differences, when groups are divided on the basis of one of these variables and examined for the strength of the other variable. As Levitt et al (1983) reported that self-esteem related questions were present on each of the sixteen depression inventories which they reviewed, it seems likely that some degree of psychometric contamination will be found between most psychometric measures of depression and self-esteem.

Beck and Beck (1972) have recommended the use of a shortened form of the twenty-one item BDI. This shortened version seems to be becoming popular: nine studies were published between 1982 and 1984 which used the short form of the BDI (Vredenburg et al, 1985). While seven of the twenty-one items on the original long version of the BDI were judged to reflect self-esteem, five of these items are retained on the shortened thirteen item version. Thus the shortened form of the BDI is likely to be subject to proportionately greater psychometric contamination when used in conjunction with a measure of self-esteem, than is the long form. Further, contamination between measures of self-esteem and depression may just be one instance of the contamination possibly occurring in investigations of depression and various measures of cognition. Thus as Blackburn notes " .... the correlations of the BDI with other putative depressive cognitive variables may be less meaningful than is sometimes assumed" (1984, page 306). The present study has demonstrated that such contamination needs to be taken into account, if we wish to establish the true association between related variables.

The relationship between self-esteem and depression

There was no significant relationship between the SEI and BDI scores of psychiatrically diagnosed and currently symptomatic (BDI scores >.10) depressed patients either before or after the removal of self-esteem related items on the BDI. While many theorists have noted a negative relationship between self-esteem and depression, few have considered how self-esteem may vary within the range of mild to severe depression. Cognitive therapy for depression arose from Beck's (1967) model depicting the depressed person as holding a negative view of himself, the world and the future. Given that self-esteem reflects the extent to which one holds negative views about oneself, these results imply that the components of Beck's "negative cognitive triad" may be negatively perceived to different extents. However, a recent study by Blackburn and Bishop (1983) found that negative views of the self, world and future abated at equivalent rates over the course of therapy. An intriguing aspect of these results was that, for patients who improved over the course of therapy, the pattern of symptom abatement was the same regardless of the therapeutic intervention used (that is, cognitive therapy, drug therapy, or a combination of the two). This result could be taken to suggest considerable cohesion between the various symptoms of depression. Despite this the present results are not necessarily incompatible with such a view. Inspection of the distribution of BDI and SEI scores for subjects with a primary diagnosis involving depression and who scored 10 or more on the BDI, indicated a clustering of SEI scores around the 3.0 level. The level of self-esteem associated with this SEI score may be an average lower limit for self-esteem. This lower limit for self esteem may be reached sooner by some people than others, and for some people be associated with many other symptoms of depression, while for others it may be 'one of the first things to give' and therefore be associated with fewer symptoms of depression. However, alleviation of depression may produce a lifting of symptoms across the depressive syndrome, independent of their absolute severity. Thus similar relative patterns of symptom abatement may be observed.

In conclusion, the present study has demonstrated psychometric contamination between the BDI and SEI, such that correlations between these inventories are inflated by self-esteem related items within the BDI. Future investigations should take account of such contamination and may choose to use the SEI and BDI since the sources of con-tamination between these measures have been identified. Given the importance of self-esteem in current theories of depression and the failure to demonstrate covariation between self-esteem and depression in the present sample of psychiatrically diagnosed depressed patients, further research is called for.

Self-Esteem in Affective Disorder

ACKNOWLEDGEMENTS

This research was supported by a United Kingdom MRC studentship to the author. Thanks to all the staff and subjects within the Tayside, Lothian and Grampian Health Boards who contributed to this project. An extended report of this research is available from the author who is now at the Department of Psychology, Institute of Psychiatry, De Crespigny Park, Denmark Hill, London SE5 8AF.

REFERENCES

Bachman, J.G. & O'Malley, P.M. (1977). Self-esteem in young men: a longitudinal analysis of the impact of education and occupational attainment. Journal of Personality and Social Psychology, 35 (6). 365-380.

Battle, J. (1978). Relationship between self-esteem and depression. Psychological Reports, 42(3), 745-746.

Beck, A.T. (1967). Depression: Clinical, Experimental and Theoretical Aspects. Winston-Wiley: New York.

Beck, A.T. & Beck, R.W. (1972). Screening depressed patients in family practice: a rapid technique. Postgraduate Medicine, 52, 81-85.

Beck, A.T., Ward, C.H., Mendelson, M., Mock, J. & Erbaugh, J. (1961). An inventory for measuring depression. Archives of General Psychiatry, 4, 561-571.

Blackburn, I.M. (1984). Cognitive Approaches to Clinical Psychology. In Psychology Survey 5. Nicholson, J. and Beloff, H. (Eds), The British Psychological Society, Leicester, England.

Blackburn, I.M. & Bishop, S. (1983). Changes in cognition with pharmacotherapy and cognitive therapy. British Journal of Psychiatry, 143, 609-617.

Deardorff, W.W. & Funabiki, D. (1985). A diagnostic caution in screening for depressed college students. Cognitive Therapy and Research, 9(3), 277-285.

Ingham, J.G., Kreitman, N.B., Miller, P.M., Sashidharan, S.P. & Surteen, P.G. (1986). Self-esteem, vulnerability and psychiatric disorder in the community. British Journal of Psychiatry, 148, 375-385.

Levitt, E.E., Lubin, B. & Brooks, J.M. (1983). Depression: Concepts, Controversies, and Some New Facts (2nd Ed.). Lawrence Erlbaum.

189

Associates, London.

MacLachlan, I.M. (1985). Psychometric contamination in correlational studies of depression and self-esteem. IRCS Medical Science, 13, 443-444.

Vredenburg, K., Krames, L. & Flett, G.I. (1985). Re-examining the Beck Depression Inventory: the long and short of it. Psychological Reports, 56, 767-778.

Chapter Twenty Seven

COGNITIVE THERAPY FOR DEPRESSION: MODIFYING LOW
SELF-ESTEEM

Melanie J.V. Fennell and Friederike T. Zimmer

INTRODUCTION

Self-esteem deficits form a core symptom of
clinical depression, and as such feature both in
established psychiatric diagnostic systems and in
measures of severity. In addition, an increasing
body of empirical data demonstrates an association
between depression and increased accessibility of
negative self-referent cognitions (eg Clark and
Teasdale, 1982), and tentative evidence is emerging
that self-devaluation may influence the duration of
depression and remain as a vulnerability factor
after an episode (Teasdale and Dent, in press).
Distorted negative thoughts about the self have
been identified (Beck et al., 1979, p11) as one
element of a "cognitive triad" central to the
experience of depression. Consistent with this,
recent writers on depression from a cognitive
perspective (eg Guidano and Liotti, 1983) have re-
emphasised the importance in treatment of modifying
core beliefs about the self. Two complementary
strategies are available: 1) challenging self-
devaluative cognitions and assumptions determining
self-worth; and 2) increasing the accessibility of
positive self-evaluations. Preliminary evidence
supports the immediate usefulness of both strategies
(Teasdale and Fennell, 1982; Zimmer et al., in
preparation).

1.   CHALLENGING SELF-DEVALUATIVE COGNITIONS

Beck's cognitive therapy (CT) for depression
(Beck et al., 1979) teaches the patient to challenge
situation-specific cognitions and the dysfunctional
assumptions upon which these are based. Patients

learn how to assess available evidence, search for alternative interpretations, correct errors in logic, consider the advantages and disadvantages of current ways of thinking, and carry out and evaluate behavioural experiments.

Distorted negative thoughts about the self are challenged in this way, the goal being self-acceptance based on a realistic and balanced assessment of qualities and weaknesses. To achieve this goal, however, it is necessary to determine the evidence on which self-devaluation is based, since this will vary from person to person and will determine how particular thoughts should be questioned and tested. The first author has carried out an informal survey of the content of self-critical thoughts reported by 22 moderately-to-severely depressed patients meeting Research Diagnostic Criteria (RDC; Spitzer et al., 1978) for Major Depressive Disorder. Seventeen were receiving CT, and data on these were derived from written homework and session records. Information on the remainder was gathered during a semi-structured interview.

All 22 patients reported frequent self-devaluative cognitions. These typically took the form of extreme, negative, overgeneralised judgements about the self, for example "disgusting", "lazy", "stupid", "hateful", "childish", "crazy", and "pathetic". Several categories of specific evidence were used to support global self-condemnation of this kind (many patients used evidence from more than one category).

Categories of Evidence Used to Support Low Esteem

Individual symptoms of depression

One woman saw irritability and loss of affection as signs that she was a bad mother and wife, and thus a bad person. Loss of motivation was interpreted as laziness, and low mood as "being a misery". An alternative interpretation is that these are symptoms of depression, rather than a reflection of personal worth. This idea can be tested by working on the depression and observing how symptoms change. It would also be necessary to modify the standards implied in these judgements, eg "I must be patient, loving, energetic and cheerful at all times".

Failure to overcome depression

This may be seen to reflect personal inadequacy, rather than lack of knowledge and the difficulty of the task. An alternative is to view depression as an understandable and not uncommon reaction to loss, which may be overcome using techniques which CT will provide. Putting CT methods into practice and ensuring that the patient takes credit for progress tests this idea. Underlying assumptions may relate to a perceived requirement always to be strong, competent and in control, eg "I must keep going no matter how I feel".

Past errors and failures

These may be seen as signs of worthlessness, rather than an inevitable consequence of human fallibility. Examining the context of the regretted action may show that, under the circumstances and with the knowledge available at the time, it was impossible to have acted otherwise. It would also be necessary to challenge assumptions related to perfectionism, and to the idea that one bad or stupid action makes a bad or stupid person.

Specific problems and difficulties

A particular deficit or area of weakness (for example, lack of assertiveness or being overweight) may be taken as evidence of global worthlessness. Examining the development of the difficulty may make it understandable in terms of experience rather than personality and open the way for new learning to take place. It would also be necessary to challenge perfectionistic assumptions (eg "I must be good at everything I do"), and the belief that one bad quality makes a bad person.

Comparison with others

The idea behind this is that if someone is better at something than me, that makes them a better person than me. Inferiority on a specific dimension is taken to mean global inferiority. An alternative is to accept that it is impossible to be best at everything, and that the only relevant standard of comparison is oneself. The assumption that it is possible to compare and evaluate people globally should also be challenged.

Others' problems

One woman considered herself a total failure as a mother, and therefore as a person, because her adult sons were in trouble with the police. Another had in childhood adopted a mothering role to her younger siblings and continued to feel completely responsible for solving all their problems even though they were now adult and independent. Failure to do so led to self-condemnation. In both cases, it was helpful to question how far it is reasonable to take responsibility for, and expect to control, what other people do, and whether it is indeed helpful either to oneself or them to attempt to do so.

Others' behaviour towards oneself

This may relate to the present (for example, being criticised or disapproved of) or, in cases of chronic low self-esteem, to the past. A useful strategy is to search for interpretations of the behaviour other than the preferred explanation that it necessarily and exclusively reflects one's personal worth. One woman, for example, took her mother's apparent indifference when she was a child to mean that she was fundamentally unworthy. This belief strongly affected her current behaviour, and her thoughts were much preoccupied with distressing memories of childhood. Examining what had happened provided an alternative explanation, ie that the mother's actions reflected the kind of person she was and her current circumstances, rather than the patient's worth. A similar analysis can be applied to contemporary examples. The assumptions likely to underlie use of this category of evidence often relate to the beliefs that others' opinions genuinely reflect one's value, and that it is absolutely necessary to be liked, approved of or loved.

Questioning and testing negative thoughts and dysfunctional assumptions in the way described above are core strategies of CT. They should be complemented, however, by methods designed directly to focus attention on positive behaviour and to build up self-esteem.

2. BUILDING UP POSITIVE SELF-ESTEEM

Depressed patients selectively focus on and ruminate about failures and negative aspects of themselves. These are attributed internally and generalised to form a global negative view of the self. This can cause problems for cognitive-behavioural treatments because people with low self-esteem usually do not accept external reinforcement (eg by therapists). In particular, the cognitive methods described before may in some cases initially increase the accessibility of negative self-referent cognitions and thus intensify depressed mood.

Enhancing self-acceptance by increasing positive self-evaluations deals with these problems by redirecting the patient's attention step by step towards positive and highly specific aspects of the self. This method is especially useful at the beginning of therapy and with severe chronic depression with longstanding deficits in self-esteem and feelings of inferiority.

Theoretical Background

Several theoretical perspectives may help to explain the effectiveness of the technique:

1. Adopting an information processing model, the method aims at influencing the filter for information selection, as well as the accessibility of information from short-term and long-term memory. This is done by shifting the focus of attention to present perceptions and memories which allow positive self-evaluation.

2. As mentioned in our introduction, experiments on state-dependent learning have shown that positive self-referent information is more accessible in elevated mood while negative self-referent information is more easily recollected in low mood (Teasdale, 1983). Thus, breaking the vicious circle of depression and negative thinking by shifting attention to positive aspects of the self not only leads to improved mood, but also enhances further recollection of positive experiences or aspects of the self.

3. A balance model (Roetzer, 1983a) is proposed, which assumes that the vicious circle of depression is maintained if the negative view of the self is not counterbalanced by perceived positives. Where a balance exists between positive and negative, self-critical cognitions may not have such devastating consequences. Improving positive self-evaluation may therefore have stabilising effects, even if negative cognitions are not eliminated.

4. Research on objective self-awareness (Duval & Wicklund, 1973) suggests that focusing attention on the self intensifies the predominant emotion or aspect of the self, eg depressed or elevated mood (Scheier & Carver, 1977), positive and negative self-evaluation, and internal attribution for success and failure (Duval & Wicklund, 1973). Discrepancies between actual behaviour and internal standards are brought into awareness.

To summarise, a shift in attention towards positive aspects of the self or towards memories which include positive self-evaluation or behaviour should have several beneficial effects: (1) it should produce immediate mood-elevation; (2) it should shift attention from negative information processing towards selecting positive memories or aspects of the self; (3) by focusing on new and forgotten aspects of the self, it should produce continued improvements in mood, and (4) this in turn should facilitate perception of current positive experiences. The vicious circle of negative thinking and depressed affect can thus be changed into a beneficent circle of attention to positive self-evaluation and improved affect.

The Technique of Building up Positive Self-Concept (PSC)

1. **Analysis of self-concept**: To analyse the amount and intensity of assets (eg intelligent, assertive, likeable) and deficits in self-concept, a self-concept questionnaire and information from the session can be used.

2. **Exploration of specific self-concept assets**:
We recommend starting by exploring those dimensions on which self-descriptions are most positive and then working towards more negative ones. To shift attention to positive self-evaluation, the patient is asked to remember situations in the recent past in which he or she to some degree behaved in accordance with a desirable dimension, trait or competence. (For example a woman asked for a situation relating to the dimension 'attractive' described standing in the bathroom after going to the hairdresser's and being complimented by her husband.)

The goal is to write down sentences about concrete, specific situations and behaviours related to self-concept. Different situations or behaviours can be elicited for one positive trait-word, before moving on to other dimensions (social, intellectual, body-image, competence, etc.). Sentences should include detailed descriptions, using various sensory modalities, to facilitate vivid emotional imagery. It is also helpful to break dimensions such as 'assertive' down into specific aspects (eg to refuse unreasonable requests, to express one's wishes, anger or love). One should work with recent experiences to avoid the danger of devaluing the present by comparing it with the past.

It is most important that sentences are valid and credible to the patient and can be accepted as his or her own statements. For the therapist it is like walking a tight rope: sentences should be as positive as possible (to shift attention), but as negative as necessary (so that the patient can follow). At one extreme, empathy with the patient's depressed feelings can lead not only to no change in the patient's depression, but also to increased depressed mood in the therapist (Roetzer, 1983b). At the other extreme, the main danger lies in the temptation for the therapist to be too positive. This usually leads to a "yes, but.." game, with the patient adopting a negative role while the therapist tries desperately to push forward positive verbalisations. It is helpful to include doubts and diminutions (eg "Even if I often feel unassertive, I was able to express my anger last Monday to my mother").

3. **Writing and reading:** Sentences are reformulated until they are fully accepted by the patient and then written on index cards. Patients are asked to read them regularly several times each day.

4. **Expanding:** Patients are also invited to find a new statement, or new aspects of an existing one, each day. During subsequent sessions the therapist prompts adequate formulations (concrete, behaviour-related, as positive as possible, etc.).

During the course of sessions an increase in the number of sentences should be accompanied by a shift in attention towards perceiving current positive behaviour and an increase in present-day positive self-evaluation.

Experimental Data

In a study on short-term effects with 20 severely depressed inpatients (BDI 20; HRSD 20; N-16 endogenous, RDC), 30 minutes of focusing on positive aspects of the self-concept led to significant decreases in self-reported depression (Visual Analogue Scale) and in anhedonia (Tuebingen Anhedonia Scale). In contrast, 30 minutes of exploring negative cognitions led to a significant increase in depressed mood and no change in anhedonia. In addition, analysis of video-tapes showed significantly less depressed facial expression during exploration of positive aspects of the self-concept, than during exploration of negative cognitions (Zimmer et al., in preparation).

REFERENCES

Beck, A.T., Rush, A.J., Shaw, B.F. & Emery, G. (1979). Cognitive Therapy for Depression. Guilford Press: New York.

Clark, D.M. & Teasdale, J.D. (1982). Diurnal variation in clinical depression and accessibility of memories of positive and negative experiences. Journal of Abnormal Psychology, 91, 87-95.

Duval, S. & Wicklund, R.A. (1973). Effects of objective self-awareness on attribution of causality. Journal of Experimental Social Psychology, 9, 17-31.

Guidano, V.F. & Liotti, G. (1983). Cognitive Processes and Emotional Disorders. Guildford Press: New York.

Roetzer (now Zimmer) F.T. (1983a). Interaction of Cognition and Behaviour in the Treatment of Depression. Paper given at the 14th Annual Meeting of the Society for Psychotherapy Research, Sheffield, England.

Roetzer (now Zimmer), F.T. (1983b). Die Therapeutische Interaktion in der Behandlung Depressiver. In D. Zimmer (Ed), Die Therapeutische Beziehung. Weinheim: Edition Psychologie, pp 173-188.

Scheier, M.F. & Carver, C.S. (1977). Self-focussed attention in the experience of emotion: attraction, repulsion, elation and depression. Journal of Personality and Social Psychology, 35, 625-636.

Spitzer, R.L., Endicott, J. & Robins, E. (1978). Research Diagnostic Criteria RDC) for a Select Group of Functional Disorders (3rd edition). Psychiatric Institute, February: New York.

Teasdale, J.D. (1983). Negative thinking in depression: cause, effect or reciprocal relationship? Advances in Behaviour Research and Therapy, 5, 3-25.

Teasdale, J.D. & Dent, J. (in press). Cognitive vulnerability to depression: an investigation of two hypotheses. British Journal of Clinical Psychology.

Teasdale, J.D. & Fennell, M.J.V. (1982). Immediate effects on depression of cognitive therapy interventions. Cognitive Therapy and Research, 6, 343-352.

Zimmer, F.T., Flueckiger, H., Kopittke, W. &
     Lutz, B. (in preparation). Immediate effects
     on depression of focussing attention on
     positive and negative aspects of self-concept.

Chapter Twenty Eight

OBSESSIVE-COMPULSIVE DISORDER: CLINICAL STRATEGIES
FOR IMPROVING BEHAVIOURAL TREATMENTS

Paul M. Salkovskis and David Westbrook

It is well known that, since the introduction
of effective behavioural techniques, the prognosis
of obsessional-compulsive problems has been
transformed. Previous gloomy predictions of a
chronic or deteriorating natural history have been
replaced by a reliably observed 75% success rate.
This must be one of the most impressive changes
brought about by behaviour therapy, and behaviour
therapists can be justifiably confident of their
techniques with this group. However, 75% success
means 25% failure. Foa (1979) identified those
patients who were most likely to fail in exposure
treatments: these were patients having severe
concurrent depression and patients whose ideas were
"overvalued" (meaning that they did not regard their
obsessions as "senseless"). Despite some
encouraging anecdotal reports (eg Salkovskis &
Warwick, 1985), we do not have fully validated
techniques for the treatment of such patients.
Furthermore, there are other unsolved problems.
Treatment can be very distressing to patients and
this can lead to poor compliance (also associated
with treatment failure) or even withdrawal from
treatment. For some patients, a very large number
of exposure and response prevention sessions are
required. Obsessional thoughts ("ruminations")
without obvious overt compulsive behaviour represent
a further unsolved problem; as Rachman (1983) has
pointed out, "the main obstacle to the successful
treatment of obsessions is the absence of effective
techniques".
Thus, careful consideration of the literature
on obsessional problems has led us to suggest the
following priorities for further development of
treatment approaches in obsessions.

1. Can exposure be carried out more effectively, rapidly and completely? In order to improve acceptability and compliance, the amount of discomfort experienced by patients during exposure needs to be reduced or differently attributed.
2. Can treatments be developed for obsessional "ruminations"?
3. Is it possible to apply the techniques which have proved so useful in the treatment of obsessive-compulsive disorder to disorders characterised by non-obsessional intrusive thinking?

In this paper, we will first describe ways of implementing exposure and response prevention programmes so as to maximise their likelihood of success, and then discuss the development of other strategies, based on cognitive theory, which may usefully complement traditional exposure and response prevention. Approaches to the treatment of obsessions without overt compulsive behaviour will be considered, and finally the potential for extending such treatments to non-obsessional problems will be examined.

1. Implementing exposure and response prevention (ERP) effectively

In order to gain the fullest possible benefit from exposure, factors which limit its potential effectiveness must be minimised. There are a number of ways in which the effectiveness of existing treatment approaches may be enhanced. First, it is essential that the patient should be actively engaged in a collaborative relationship with the therapist, not simply having ERP "done to" him. Second, the treatment programme must not be so aversive that the patient does not comply or drops out of treatment. These aims will be greatly assisted if the patient is adequately prepared before the active phase of treatment begins. It is important to agree on an appropriate formulation of the problems, a rationale for the treatment programme and a clear description of what will be involved. The therapist should establish the patient's understanding of these explanations through asking for feedback and questioning, and carefully deal with any doubts or questions that the patient may have. Throughout, the emphasis should be on developing a task centred relationship which is also open and trusting. For instance, the patient must be assured that no "surprises" will be sprung on him, and that all exposure will be planned and discussed beforehand. Participant modelling, where the therapist models ERP tasks for the patient prior to their participation, is undoubtedly useful in encouraging some patients to engage in the initial stages of treatment and subsequently persevere. Note, however, that modelling may serve a neutralising role by providing reassurance, as described below.

Whilst empathy and support are necessary, the therapist should not allow this to prevent firmness in the elimination of all forms of neutralising. It is often necessary to explain to patients that behaviour requested during treatment (such as not washing for prolonged periods) is not necessarily to be taken as a standard for "normal" behaviour, any more than plastering a broken leg implies that one should always wear one's leg in plaster. Thorough ERP is essential and requires a careful assessment of both avoidance and all forms of neutralising behaviour. We have found that a good way of helping patients to detect neutralising and avoidance behaviour is to ask the patient: "Try to work out whether you would be doing these particular things if you didn't have this problem (neutralising). Then try to work out all the extra things you would be doing if you didn't have this problem (avoidance)." Although overt rituals are usually the principal focus of treatment, it is often the case that insufficient attention is given to covert ritualising (such as thinking "good thoughts"); to avoidance, which can also be either overt or covert; and to reassurance seeking. We hypothesise that avoidance, cognitive rituals and reassurance are all functionally similar in preventing or curtailing exposure to the feared stimulus, and thus hindering extinction.

Some authors have suggested that reassurance may serve the same function as compulsive behaviour and that it should therefore be prevented (Marks, 1981; Warwick & Salkovskis, 1985). The cognitive model (Salkovskis, 1985) provides a clear rationale for such a view, suggesting that reassurance, like compulsive behaviour, serves to avoid responsibility and hence the attribution of blame for harm to self or others. Careful questioning about reassurance seeking should both assist in the implementation of exposure and in the facilitation of this re-appraisal of the true degree of responsibility. Table 1 is an example of how such techniques may be employed in instances where the more usual techniques, such as that described by Marks (1981, p84), are not fully effective. Such an approach must be used in conjunction with appropriate involvement of significant others in the patient's social environment.

Table 1: Cognitive manoeuvre directed at modifying reassurance seeking

---

T: You managed not to wash at all over the last two days? That's really good.

P: Yes, but I've been very worried about it.

T: Can you tell me a bit about how you coped in that time, I mean, how you dealt with the discomfort over that time?

P: Well, sometimes it hasn't been too bad, but sometimes it's just been impossible, and my family hasn't been too helpful.

T: Your family? What came up there?

P: Well, I keep asking for some kind of support and they won't give it to me.

T: Have your family found it difficult to actually help you think about other things or carry on when you're feeling uncomfortable, like we discussed with them last week?

P: Well, I just can't get rid of this worry that I'll get something awful if I don't wash.

T: Is that the sort of thing you've been trying to talk about with your family?

P: Well, I just feel sure that I'll get something, cancer or something.

(At this point it starts to become apparent from his answers that the patient is not directly responding to the content of questioning, but is obliquely seeking reassurance from the therapist in an obsessional fashion; his answers appear to be attempts to describe <u>details</u> of his <u>intrusive thoughts</u>, whilst the therapist is still attempting to elicit details of the patient's <u>behaviour</u>. This is one of the most frequently encountered (and subtle) forms of reassurance seeking within session. It also provides an ideal opportunity to tackle this particular patient's problems "in vivo".)

T: I may be wrong, but by saying these things right now, and going over the cancer thing, are you maybe worried that I don't know everything; are you hoping that I might respond to what you're

saying? Perhaps you feel that I'd respond if
there was something dangerous?

P: Yes, yes, I suppose so. I mean I just need to
know it's not going to happen. I mean, this
treatment gets the anxiety down a bit, but I
still might get it. I don't see what's wrong
with finding out whether it is going to happen.

T: I think I understand. In the last couple of
sessions, we discussed the way that washing
hands can actually continue the problem with
feeling contaminated, and the connection is easy
to see. I guess with the questions it's harder
to see the connection. Is that right?

P: Well, yes, the discomfort of not washing has
come down, and that's OK, but my mind is still
full of worries that need dealing with.

T: So we ought to look more closely at this right
now. At the moment I think you're actually
quite keen to ask me about things, for me to put
your mind at rest about this?

P: Well, I feel that you would know about it, so
why don't you tell me?

T: Obviously I should if it's going to make you
feel much better, get rid of the problem. Okay,
so, how many times would I have to reassure you
now for it to last for the rest of the week?

P: To last for the rest of the week?

T: Yes, I've got the rest of this morning set aside
because we were going to do a session with
washing. This seems more important right now
because you are managing the washing so well.
So I've got several hours in which I could
reassure you, go over things as many times as
you like really. So, how many times would I
need to do it to last for the rest of the week?

P: Well, it doesn't work like that.

T: Oh... well... how do you mean?

P: I mean if you say it lots of times, it doesn't
.... sort of build up a stock that will last
for the rest of the week.

T: Ah, I see. So if I actually try my hardest to
put your mind at rest right now, how long would
it last then?

P: Probably until the next time I touch something
dangerous.

T: You mean like the wanting to wash? It could be
as little as ten, or even five minutes? Is
that right?

P: Yes, I suppose so.

T: So is it like the washing?

P: Sort of.

T.   What are the main differences, then?
P: It might be different because I need to know
     whether I'm going to catch something.
T: So the difference is that you need to ask, and
     you don't feel like you need to wash?
P: No, they're similar in that way.
T: Can you think of any other differences?
P: I need other people to ask.
T: Do you need anything else for washing?
P: Well, I need soap and water. If you put it like
     that, it's not so terribly different.
T.   Are you sure you can't think of any other
     differences?
P: Well, I suppose the only other difference is
     asking about it makes my family even crosser.
T: Right, let's check I've got this right, we'll
     write this down as we go through it and maybe
     we can work out a plan to deal with this.
P.   Right.

Finally, it is necessary to ensure that gains
generalise from the clinic to the patient's normal
life.   Homework shold be an intensive and integral
part of treatment from an early stage; often, it
can be useful to involve the patient's spouse as co-
therapist.   At first it may be necessary for the
therapist to plan tasks in some detail, but later
the patient should take increasing responsibility
for planning and carrying out their own homework.
This is especially important for checkers, who may
experience little difficulty if they think that
tasks are the therapist's responsibility. Patients
can be asked to carry out self-directed homework
without disclosing to anyone (including the
therapist) the specific actions concerned, though
records of discomfort are kept and discussed.   This
is a difficult task to grasp, so careful explanation
should be followed by feedback from the patient to
ensure that they have fully understood.
Instructions for this "exposure to responsibility"
might be:

     "I want you to plan and carry out homework like
     we have done up to now, but with an important
     difference. This time, you'll set things up so
     that you become uncomfortable, don't check,
     record how uncomfortable you got immediately
     afterwards, but <u>don't</u> tell (or even hint to)
     anyone at all about what you've done. We'll
     discuss how you felt next session, but you and

> only you will be responsible for the task. So,
> without telling me any details of what you will
> leave unchecked, can you describe what you have
> to do for homework this week?"

2. Adding complementary psychological strategies to exposure

Given that it is possible to implement ERP to its
fullest extent, it seems likely that any further
radical advances in the treatment of obsessions will
probably involve the use of novel strategies
intended to facilitate exposure. This is
conceptually identical to the use of antidepressants
in order to enhance behavioural treatment.
Obsessional problems are normally conceptualised as:

THOUGHTS ▷ EMOTIONAL DISTRESS ▷ DISTURBED BEHAVIOUR

and would therefore seem to be obvious targets for
cognitive intervention, in which changes in thinking
patterns are utilised to reduce emotional distress.
A recent paper (Salkovskis, 1985) described a
theoretical framework on which treatment may be
based without engaging in the fruitless exercise of
"arguing with the obsession". Briefly, it is
proposed that obsessional thoughts should be
regarded as stimuli which subsequently evoke
negative automatic thoughts, which in turn result in
anxiety and discomfort. In clinical obsessions, the
content of such negative automatic thoughts concerns
being responsible for harm coming to self or others.
This element of responsibility can lead to efforts
to forestall responsibility (checking), to restore
the situation when harm may have been incurred
(washing, cognitive restitution) or to pass on
responsibility (reassurance seeking). The model
stresses the importance of behaviour in the
maintenance of obsessions, because compulsive
behaviour terminates exposure to the feared stimuli
and prevents realistic re-appraisal of
responsibility. Cognitive therapy techniques can
serve to enhance the effectiveness of exposure in
terms of rapidity, amount of discomfort experienced
and compliance. Such an approach may also be useful
in the treatment of those patients who are currently
known to be resistant to behavioural treatments
("treatment failures"; Foa, 1979). Salkovskis &
Warwick (1985) describe the successful application
of cognitive therapy in a patient with overvalued
ideation.
        Cognitive techniques need to be used within the

cognitive model as specifically applied to obsessional-compulsive disorder. The key role played by responsibility means that therapists must be particularly careful not to "take over" this responsibility, either by the over-use of direct instructions or by excessive provision of reassurance. Cognitive therapy in general uses questioning ("socratic questioning") to make particular points and the above consideration increases the importance of such an emphasis in the treatment of obsessional problems. As far as possible, the therapist should attempt to ensure that most or all information relevant to their problem is generated by patients themselves. The aim of such an approach is to allow patients to explore the inconsistencies within and between their beliefs, thoughts and behaviours. Some specific techniques are described below.

COGNITIVE TECHNIQUES

Normalising
We have emphasised above the importance of not providing reassurance, but this does not imply that one should not give relevant information which the patient lacks or has misunderstood. Early in treatment with a cognitive emphasis it is important to examine the patient's beliefs about the nature, prevalence and significance of their obsessional thoughts. It can be most useful for patients to discover that such intrusive thoughts are normal phenomena, and reading papers in this area may be helpful (eg Rachman & de Silva, 1978).

Identifying and challenging automatic thoughts
There is ample evidence that disputing with patients whether a particular intrusion is realistic or not is futile (eg Cawley, 1974). Patients already regard intrusive thoughts as unrealistic and senseless, but may evaluate their occurrence and content in ways which give rise to further (automatic) thoughts which appear to them to be realistic and sensible. Cognitive therapy is directed at these automatic thoughts, which are identified and modified through careful questioning within session (eg when obvious mood changes are observed) or by recreating the feared situation (eg asking the patients to contaminate themselves). Once patients have mastered the technique, they attempt this in vivo using thought diaries. The emphasis throughout is on thoughts which arise from

intrusions, not the intrusions themselves, e.g.

Intrusion: "I may stab my baby."

Automatic   "If I don't put the knives away it
thought: means I really want to do this."
"It would be evil not to fight this
thought." "If I don't fight it,
it might happen."

Modification of automatic thoughts can then proceed as in cognitive therapy in general: reviewing the evidence, considering alternatives, generating rational responses and devising behavioural experiments as direct tests of the thought. When negative automatic thoughts which are obstacles to ERP are identified, the "two column technique" can help the patient to generate alternative thoughts (Salkovskis & Warwick, 1985).

Decatastrophising
This technique appears to be useful in general anxiety patients (Beck, Emery & Greenberg, 1985), and has some utility for obsessional patients (see Salkovskis and Warwick, 1985, for an example). It involves deducing the worst thing which could happen, which is usually some distance removed from the obsessional intrusion (eg "a child would die from the piece of glass I didn't pick up on the pavement"). Careful questioning and belief ratings are used to clarify the actual probability of the feared consequence or chain of consequences and whether the outcome is as catastrophic as imagined. This technique should not be repeatedly used with obsessionals in the way which is possible in generally anxious patients because it can serve as reassurance.

Reattribution
The attributions made by obsessional patients with respect to the nature and origin of their thoughts can be crucial. If intrusive thoughts are considered to be odd thoughts which occur now and then to everyone, then negative automatic thoughts (and therefore discomfort) are unlikely to follow. On the other hand, if the attribution made concerning such thoughts reflects the belief that they are fundamental processes (eg "these thoughts reflect my true personality"; "these thoughts will take over if they are not resisted"), then discomfort is almost inevitable. Reattribution

usually involves examination of such thoughts in a systematic fashion: for example, "You think these thoughts mean that you are a bad person. If someone really evil had these thoughts, how do you think they would react? Would they be upset about them?" Behavioural experiments also have an important part to play in such reattribution. For instance, it is easy to show convincingly that attempting to prevent or resist an unpleasant intrusive thought makes it <u>more</u> likely, by asking the patient to try <u>not</u> to have a particular <u>intrusive</u> thought in the session. It is also useful to demonstrate that this applies to innocuous thoughts as well, eg "don't think about giraffes". The results of such experiments are used to reattribute the patient's intrusive thoughts to normal psychological processes rather than fundamental defects in personality.

Identifying and challenging assumptions

As cognitive treatment progresses, it is generally regarded as desirable to deal with dysfunctional assumptions. For example, obsessional patients may believe that "having a thought about something happening is like wanting it to happen"; someone with such an assumption who then has the thought that they could kill their children is liable to respond by thinking that they are an unpleasant person. It seems likely that failing to deal with such assumptions may lead to increased probability of relapse. A technique such as the "vertical arrow" may be employed to reveal and challenge assumptions. In this technique, a particular thought is taken to its conclusion. Table 2 gives an example of this.

Having identified the assumptions, the patient can then be encouraged to challenge the assumption itself and the evidence upon which it is based.

Behavioural experiments

One view of ERP is that it constitutes a series of behavioural experiments which result in reappraisal of feared stimuli. Setting up exposure with this end in mind can be particularly useful. Monitoring and feedback using visual analogue scales can serve an important function, in that patients will frequently predict early in treatment that discomfort will not decline as a result of exposure. Such beliefs can be directly challenged by the demonstration that (i) ERP results in decrements of discomfort within session; (ii) that this occurs more rapidly as ERP progresses and (iii) that

---

Table 2:   Using the vertical arrow to access
            assumptions

I can't control the bad thoughts
What's so bad about not being able to control them?
⬇

It's not normal to have uncontrollable thoughts
Supposing it's not normal;   what would that mean?
⬇

**I've got to get them under control otherwise I
lose control of my mind and do something awful**
Supposing you did lose control;   what would be
bad about that?
⬇

**I couldn't live with the idea that I harmed
someone when I could have avoided it.**
If you had harmed someone and could have
prevented it;   what would be bad about that?
⬇

I'd have to kill myself

---

between session decrements occur.   This data can
then be used to facilitate compliance by confirming
the therapist's prior predictions about the effects
of treatment.   It may also modify patients' beliefs
that anxiety can only be dealt with by obsessional
behaviour.

3. Approaches to the treatment of obsessional thoughts

It is well known that the treatment of obsessional
thoughts without overt compulsive rituals is
particularly problematic.   Three possible ways of
improving future treatment will be discussed here.

First, unsuccessful treatment may be due to a
failure to pay enough attention to the importance of
avoidance and other forms of neutralising when there
are no obvious overt rituals.   Some studies of the
treatment of obsessional thoughts have included
subjects who have significant overt or covert
neutralising, and it is not always clear that this
has been adequately dealt with.

Second, it is possible that it is a mistake to
consider obsessional thinking as a unitary
phenomenon, for which there will be one effective
treatment.   Various classifications of obsessional
phenomenology have been proposed, based on form
(Parkinson & Rachman, 1981;   Akhtar et al, 1975), on

content (Akhtar et al, 1975) and on affect evoked (Stern, 1978). There is no empirical evidence that these divisions have clinical implications, but a number of authors have speculated that some such classification may be relevant. Thus, Stern (1978) reports that his two cases who had "horror-disgust" obsessions were the only two who responded to satiation, whilst they did not respond to thought stopping. Emmelkamp and van der Heyden (1980) suggest that "harming" obsessions are related to difficulties in handling aggressive feelings and report that assertive training was at least as effective as thought stopping. Further research may elucidate other possible relationships between categories of thought and appropriate forms of treatment.

Finally, it may be that technical difficulties have reduced the effectiveness of habituation treatments. These treatments are based on Rachman's (1971) model of obsessional thoughts as noxious conditioned stimuli which have failed to habituate. Theory predicts that habituation will proceed more rapidly if presentations of the stimuli (thoughts) are predictable in terms of variables such as time, intensity and duration. Habituation treatments thus require patients to repeatedly elicit or imagine their obsessional thoughts, but in practice many patients find it difficult to do this in a consistent way. Tape recording the thoughts may provide a better way of carrying out habituation. The use of audiotape ensures standardised presentation and also means that the thoughts can be presented so rapidly that it is hard for the patient to carry out any neutralising. Evidence for this technique is so far restricted to single case studies (Salkovskis, 1983), but the authors are currently engaged in further controlled evaluation.

4. Generalising to other groups

A number of psychological problems show strong similarities to obsessive-compulsive disorder. That it has proved possible to develop effective treatment for obsessive-compulsive disorder, previously regarded as impervious to psychological intervention, leads to the hope that it may be possible to apply similar techniques to other problems in which similar behavioural disturbances and intrusive, upsetting thoughts are present. The possible range of such disorders is wide; upsetting thoughts have been implicated in anxiety and depression as well as obsessions (Beck, Emery &

Greenberg, 1985). Borkovec et al (1983) suggest the importance of "worry" as an extremely common complaint related to intrusive thoughts, while Salkovskis & Warwick (1986) have pointed out the strong resemblance between hypochondriasis and obsessional phenomena. They demonstrated similarities between severely hypochondriacal patients and obsessionals; in particular, the importance of neutralising behaviour was apparent. The preliminary findings suggest the importance of careful analysis of hypochondriacal patients' beliefs about the thoughts they experience since, unlike obsessional patients, they generally do not perceive thoughts of illness as senseless. As in obsessional disorder, proper treatment involves the assessment and modification of avoidance and neutralising behaviour which arises from upsetting, intrusive thoughts.

In conclusion, despite the considerable progress in treatment of obsessional disorders, further advances are possible and desirable, particularly with Foa's (1979) treatment failures and obsessional thinking. Exposure and response prevention can be refined further, and complementary techniques such as cognitive therapy are promising. We suggest that the key to more effective treatment is to be found in careful assessment of individual patients and systematic evaluation of treatment outcome, rather than uncritical reliance on the effectiveness of specific techniques.

ACKNOWLEDGEMENTS

The authors are grateful to Katie Koehler for help with the therapy transcript, and Joan Kirk, Martina Mueller and Hilary Warwick for helpful comments on an earlier version of this paper.

REFERENCES

Akhtar, S., Wig, N.N., Varma, V.K., Pershad, I. & Verma, S.K. (1975). A phenomenological analysis of symptoms in obsessive compulsive neurosis. British Journal of Psychiatry, 127, 342-348.

Beck, A.T., Emery, G., & Greenberg, R.L. (1985). Anxiety Disorders and Phobias: a Cognitive Perspective. Basic Books: New York.

Borkovec, T.D., Robinson, E., Pruzinsky, T., & DePree, J.A. (1983). Preliminary exploration of worry: some characteristics and processes.

Behaviour Research and Therapy, 21, 9-16.

Cawley, R. (1974). Psychotherapy and obsessional disorders. In H.R. Beech (Ed) Obsessional States. Methuen: London.

Emmelkamp, P.M.G., & van der Heyden, H. (1980). Treatment of harming obsessions. Behavioural Analysis and Modification, 4, 28-35.

Foa, E.B. (1979). Failures in treating obsessive-compulsives. Behavioural Research and Therapy, 17, 169-176.

Marks, I.M. (1981). Cure and Care of Neurosis. Wiley: Chichester.

Parkinson, L. & Rachman, S.J. (1981). The nature of intrusive thoughts. Advances in Behaviour Research and Therapy, 3, 101-110.

Rachman, S.J. (1971). Obsessional ruminations Behaviour Research and Therapy, 9, 229-235.

Rachman, S.J. (1983). Obstacles to the successful treatment of obsessions. In E.B. Foa & P.M.G. Emmelkamp (Eds) Failures in Behaviour Therapy. Wiley: New York.

Rachman, S.J., & de Silva, P. (1978). Abnormal and normal obsessions. Behaviour Research and Therapy, 16, 233-248.

Salkovskis, P.M. (1983). Treatment of an obsessional patient using habituation to audiotaped ruminations. British Journal of Clinical Psychology, 22, 311-313.

Salkovskis, P.M. (1985). Obsessional-compulsive problems: a cognitive-behavioural analysis. Behaviour Research and Therapy, 23, 571-583.

Salkovskis, P.M. & Warwick, H.M.C. (1985). Cognitive therapy of obsessional-compulsive disorder: treating treatment failures. Behavioural Psychotherapy, 13, 243-255.

Salkovskis, P.M. & Warwick, H.M.C. (1986). Morbid preoccupations, healthy anxiety and reassurance: a cognitive approach to Hypochondriasis. Behaviour Research and Therapy, 24, 597-602.

Stern, R.S. (1978). Obsessive thoughts: the problem of therapy. British Journal of Psychiatry, 132, 200-205 .

Warwick, H.M.C. & Salkovskis, P.M. (1985). Reassurance. British Medical Journal, 290, 1028.

Chapter Twenty Nine

TRAINING FOR COGNITIVE THERAPY

Melanie J.V. Fennell

In this paper I should like to address four
questions:

1. What is meant by "training for cognitive
   therapy (CT)"?
2. What form should training take?
3. Can the effects of training be evaluated?
4. How can CT skills be developed and maintained
   in clinical practice?

To date, systematic training programmes and
attempts to define CT and to evaluate therapist
competence have been carried out mainly in the
context of research into psychological treatments
for depression in the United States. For this
reason, I shall refer mainly to CT for depression
(Beck et al, 1979); I should emphasise however that
the points I shall make are not exclusively related
to treatment of depression. Beck's cognitive model
was originally conceived (e.g. Beck, 1976) as a
general model of emotional disorder and CT methods
are now used by clinicians with an increasing range
of problems and disorders.

1. What is meant by "training for cognitive
therapy"?
The core strategies of CT derive directly and
explicitly from "an underlying theoretical rationale
that an individual's affect and behaviour are
largely determined by the way in which he structures
the world" (Beck et al, 1979, p.3). They include:

   i) techniques such as distraction and activity-
      scheduling designed to produce immediate
      symptom-relief without necessarily achieving
      fundamental changes in thinking;

ii) techniques designed to modify perceptual biases and distorted interpretations of immediate experience, thus countering negative automatic thoughts;

iii) techniques designed to produce long-term change in underlying cognitive structures and to prevent relapse.

Is it necessary, though, to teach and practise CT as a coherent and internally consistent treatment approach, or is it legitimate, and equally effective, to learn the techniques independent of the model as a whole, and to use them prescriptively in combination with methods from other treatment approaches? The answer depends in part on the goal of training. If the aim is to produce good cognitive therapists, or if it is primarily scientific (that is, to examine the validity of the cognitive model, to evaluate CT's effectiveness and to identify the processes and mechanisms by which it achieves its effects), then training in CT as a consistent treatment approach and formal evaluation of performance are essential. If however, the aim is to produce a competent clinician, the need to learn CT as a unified treatment approach may be less absolute. Broadly-based treatment packages containing a number of different elements (including cognitive interventions) and unified by a self-control rationale have been shown to be effective with some disorders; for example anxiety (Butler et al, 1987, in press) and depression (Lewinsohn et al, 1978). In addition, most clinical psychologists, at least in the UK, learn CT as one of a number of possible treatment approaches and use it in combination with other methods and models.

Despite this, there are certain advantages to training CT as a coherent, theory-based therapeutic system, and to practising it as such with at least some patients. In particular, it encourages the novice therapist to explore the therapy's strengths and limitations to the full, rather than returning to more familiar methods when the going gets rough. Additionally, working acceptance of the cognitive model of emotional disorder, and of the principles of CT, allows a client's problems to be flexibly yet consistently conceptualised and tackled, whatever their specific content. Therapist and client may then readily generalise from what is learned in dealing with particular difficulties, and the chance of confusion resulting from a combination of different models and strategies is reduced.

2. What form should training take?

The core principles and strategies of CT may be relatively easily learned through reading and brief, intensive introductory workshops. The ability to apply CT methods successfully with a range of clients, varying in the type of problems they present and in difficulty, is less readily acquired. CT may be seen as a complex performance skill, best learned through supervised practice. Consistent with this suggestion, Shaw (1984) showed that neither scores on a written test nor performance in role-play during an intensive introductory training course predicted eventual level of competence in cognitive therapists taking part in the NIMH Treatment of Depression Collaborative Program (Elkin et al, 1985).

Training for the Program consisted of a two week introductory course, followed by 12-18 months of supervision with 4-6 depressed patients during which detailed feedback was provided on every therapy session in weekly one hour supervision sessions. As Shaw subsequently remarked: "What we have here is clearly a group of therapists who have had a lot of attention paid to them." Such an expenditure of time and money is not generally available to us in Europe, though I am aware of a similar programme currently under development at the University of Tuebingen in West Germany (Zimmer, Pers. Comm., see Notes at end of chapter).

The amount of training and supervision required to produce adequate performance in clinical practice (probably a less stringent criterion than is required for research purposes) is likely to vary from person to person and any training programme should be sufficiently flexible to adapt itself to individual needs. Previous training, for example, will influence the ease with which trainees acquire different CT skills. Insight-oriented psychotherapists may have difficulty in structuring sessions and in being directive. In contrast, medically trained novice therapists may have problems in working collaboratively and in giving and taking feedback. Shaw (1984) found that indications that feeling comfortable with short-term treatment, ability to establish a problem-oriented working alliance and a positive response to first encounters with CT might predict eventual competence. In contrast, therapists who were over- or under-directive and resistant to a phenomenological approach tended to do less well in training.

Individual differences aside, some aspects of CT are more difficult to learn than others, in particular those which are not highly specific, time limited interventions. This includes structuring sessions, formulating and carrying out an overall treatment plan, and selecting appropriate targets at different points in therapy. A good training programme must take account of individual differences in experience and of the varying difficulty of acquiring different techniques, and must sensitively monitor trainees' progress, both overall and in relation to specific skill deficits.

3. Can the effects of training be evaluated?
There are three aspects to this question:-

a. Can CT be defined and reliably measured?
DeRubeis et al (1982) have developed a 48 item scale, the Minnesota Rating Scale (MTRS), designed to discriminate between CT and another short-term psychological treatment for depression, Interpersonal Psychotherapy (IPT). They found that CT could be reliably discriminated from IPT and that the differences detected were consistent with scores given by experts in both treatment modalities as representing a "good typical" therapy session.

b. Can quality of performance be measured?
The Cognitive Therapy Scale (CTS; Young et al, 1983) is used to evaluate individual treatment sessions and consists of 6 items measuring general interpersonal and relationship factors, and 5 measuring CT techniques. Summary scores provide an overall estimate of quality of performance and of competence to take part in a clinical trial. The accompanying manual contains general instructions for use of the scale, plus detailed instructions for each item including objectives, suggestions for background reading and specification of desirable therapist strategies. Dobson et al (1985) have found good internal consistency for the scale using expert trained raters. Inter-rater reliability was generally acceptable for individual items and high for total score. Shaw (1984) has reported good construct validity, and agreement between raters on global ratings of 100%.

c. Does training affect quality of performance?
Shaw (1984) has reported increases in CTS scores in response to training both within and

across cases, and in response to discrete interventions when therapists fell below the standards required by the NIMH trial.

The evidence available suggests at least a qualified "yes" to all three questions. There is, however, an obvious need for replication, and no data are currently available on treating disorders other than depression. In Europe, it is particularly important to know how far assessments of quality can reliably be made by non-expert raters, since we need to be able to evaluate our own performance, both for research purposes and in the interests of developing CT skills in clinical practice.

4. How can CT skills be developed and maintained in clinical practice?

To some extent CT skills can be extended using books and audio- and video-taped material. By "books" I mean not only formal treatment manuals but also, for example, David Burns' (1980) "Feeling Good", a highly creative patients' guide to CT for depression. Additionally, popular psychology books like Dyer's (1977) "Your Erroneous Zones" can be a fertile source of clinical ideas. Video- and audiotapes of therapy sessions can be obtained from the Center for CT in Philadelphia. Another useful source of ideas is the "International CT Newsletter" (see Notes at end of chapter).

Material aside, supervised practice with a range of clients is undoubtedly essential. Unfortunately, few of us can afford to visit the United States for this purpose and expert supervisors with time to spare are rare in Europe. Peer-supervision, together with a willingness to experiment and to share our clinical innovations, provides a valuable alternative. Even where peer-supervision is not possible, recording and listening to one's own therapy tapes can be an invaluable learning experience.

In peer supervision and when monitoring one's own progress, it is worth following certain practical guidelines. First, there is no substitute for direct, immediate feedback on performance. Verbal reports of therapy are not enough: sessions must be taped and the tapes listened to or watched. Regular and prolonged exposure to this procedure will lessen its aversiveness! Second, it is important to be concrete and problem-oriented. General, abstract discussions are not helpful training aids. Specific goals should be defined for supervision sessions, just as they would be for therapy sessions, and progress towards them monitored. Similarly, the use of new methods and techniques, and different ways of dealing with difficulties encountered in therapy, should be practised through role-play, not merely discussed.

Besides the CTS, help in developing CT skills can be drawn from the CT Checklist (in Beck et al, 1979, pp404-407). This gives detailed criteria for therapist behaviours, including general interview procedures (such as agenda-setting and homework assignment), specific cognitive and behavioural techniques (such as eliciting and testing automatic thoughts), and personal and professional therapist characteristics (such as genuineness, accurate empathy and rapport). In conjunction with tapes of therapy sessions, it can be used to identify areas of weakness and to set targets towards which one should aim.

Peer supervision is also an invaluable way of overcoming problems in applying CT with difficult clients. A general rule is to specify precisely the nature of the problem and to deal with it using CT techniques, including an examination of the patient's thoughts, evaluation of evidence, hypothesis testing and so forth. "Cognitive Therapy for Depression" (Beck et al, 1979) contains two useful chapters on these topics ('Technical Problems' and 'Problems Relating to Termination and Relapse'). In addition, Jeffrey Young (see Notes at end of chapter), a highly experienced therapist who has worked extensively with chronic depression and characterological disorders, has identified a number of guidelines for dealing with difficult cases. These include: being aware of one's own dysfunctional cognitions and beliefs in relation to the patient and to therapy (some of these are illustrated in Table 1); refusing to buy into the patient's pessimism; maintaining a high tolerance of frustration by setting realistic goals and expecting setbacks and fluctuations in progress; maintaining a problem-solving approach to difficulties rather than blaming the patient or oneself; and recognising that CT is not the panacea for all ills and that some clients will do better with other approaches.

Table 1:   Dysfunctional Therapist Assumptions

I must succeed, even with impossible clients

If I fail with any of my clients, it must be my fault

I must not dislike any of my clients

I must avoid ticklish issues that might upset and antagonise my clients

If I fail with a client, that means I am a lousy therapist

My clients should be grateful for all I do for them

Let me close by returning to the questions I originally posed, and by summarising the answers available, given our present state of knowledge.

1. While accepting that clinicians often use CT in combination with other methods, there are advantages to learning it as coherent, theory-based, integrated treatment approach. In particular, it encourages the therapist to test the limits of the cognitive model of emotional disorder, and facilitates flexibility, consistency and ease of generalisation.

2. As a complex performance skill, CT should be taught primarily through supervised practice with a range of patients. The amount of training required will probably vary from person to person, and training programmes should take account of this variability, and should regularly monitor progress.

3. CT is an identifiable treatment modality, and quality of therapist performance can be evaluated and improved by training.

4. The core principles of CT may be acquired through reading and intensive training, but monitored experience with patients is essential to the development and maintenance of therapy skills in clinical practice.

REFERENCES

Beck, A.T. (1976). Cognitive Therapy and the Emotional Disorders. International Universities Press: New York.

Beck, A.T., Rush, A.J., Shaw, B.F., & Emery, G. (1979). Cognitive Therapy for Depression Guilford Press: New York.

Burns, D.D. (1980). Feeling Good: The New Mood Therapy. Signet: New York.

Butler, G., Cullington, A., Hibbert, G., Klimes, I. & Gelder, M.G. (1987 in press). Anxiety management and persistent generalised anxiety. British Journal of Psychiatry.

DeRubeis, R.J., Hollon, S.D., Evans, M.D. & Bemis, K.M. (1982). Can psychotherapies for depression be discriminated? A systematic investigation of cognitive therapy and interpersonal psychotherapy. Journal of Consulting and Clinical Psychology, 50, 744-757.

Dobson, K.S., Shaw, B.F. & Vallis, T.M. (1985). Reliability of a measure of the quality of cognitive therapy. British Journal of Clinical Psychology, 24, 295-300.

Dyer, W.W. (1977). Your Erroneous Zones. Sphere Books: London.

Elkin, I., Parloff, M.B., Hadley, S.W. & Autry, J.H. (1985). NIMH Treatment of Depression Collaborative Research Programme. Archives of General Psychiatry, 42, 305-316.

Lewinsohn, P.M., Munoz, R.F., Youngren, M.A. & Zeiss, A.M. (1978). Control Your Depression Prentice Hall: Englewood Cliffs, New Jersey.

Shaw, B.F. (1984). Specification of the training and evaluation of cognitive therapists for outcome studies. In J. Williams & R. Spitzer (Eds), Psychotherapy Research. Guilford Press: New York.

Young, J.E., Beck, A.T. & Budenz, D. (1983). Assessment of Competence in Cognitive Therapy. Unpublished manuscript, University of Pennsylvania.

NOTES

Center for Cognitive Therapy, Room 602, 133 South 36th Street, Philadelphia, PA 19109, U.S.A.
International CT Newsletter available from Christine Padesky, Editor, ICTN, Center for Cognitive Therapy, 1101 Dove Street, Suite 228, Newport Beach, CA 92660, U.S.A.

Training for Cognitive Therapy

Dr. Jeffrey E. Young, 111 West 88th Street,
    New York 10024, U.S.A.

Dr. F.T. Zimmer, Eberhard-Karls-Universitat-
    D-7400 Tuebingen, Universitats-Nervenklinik,
    Osianderstrasse 22, D-7400 Tuebingen-1,
    Federal Republic of Germany.

PART THREE: CARE IN THE COMMUNITY
               WHO/HFA 2000 Target three: By the
               year 2000, disabled persons should have
               the physical, social and economic
               opportunities that allow at least for
               a socially and economically fulfilling
               and mentally creative life.

               1.   Care in the Community:
                    General Issues
               2.   Care in the Community:
                    Chronic Psychiatry
               3.   Care in the Community:
                    The Challenge of Ageing
               4.   Preparing Clients for the
                    Community

Chapter Thirty

CARE IN THE COMMUNITY: AN OVERVIEW

John Hall

Clinical psychologists in most European countries have traditionally worked mainly with the psychologically and psychiatrically distressed and disabled, and in some countries have had a major contribution in work with children and young people. Where there were few clinical psychologists, arguably the best way for their scarce skills to be employed was as part of a specialist hospital or clinic, perhaps offering a regional service and thus separated from local provision. When most countries concentrated their mental health resources into large asylums, the specialist hospital was in any event the major organisational system for delivering sevices to mentally ill and mentally handicapped people.

In the mid-1980s a number of factors have changed the way in which clinical psychologists can best contribute to a comprehensive health care system. Some of these factors are organisational: large hospitals are declining in size, and are being replaced by more numerous, smaller and geographically dispersed hospitals or clinics. Many countries have changed the structure of their Health Boards, or similar bodies, so they have a prime responsibility for an identified population or community, and hence have acquired an interest in providing care for all levels of disability in the most efficient way. Some factors are epidemiological: the population of Europe is, in general, an ageing one with fewer children and more people living longer. Since many chronic conditions are age-related, this, and the success of antibiotic medication for example, has created a much larger proportion of the population surviving with major handicaps, living in domestic accommodation, for whom no specifically medical solution can be found.

A third set of factors relates to the development of
clinical   psychology   as a discipline.   New families
of   psychological   procedures   have   been generated -
notably   those   based   on   behavioural   and cognitive
concepts - in addition to the well established range
of   assessment,   psychotherapeutic,   and   special
education techniques.

Some   of   these   changes   have   been   led   by
psychologists, who thus understand them and may feel
able   to   control   them.   Other   changes,   such as
epidemiological   changes,   have not necessarily been
absorbed   into   training   courses, for example.   The
political-organisational   changes   of the philosophy
and   structure   of   health care systems - such as in
Italy   -   may   happen   rapidly,   without thought
necessarily   being given to   the   implications   for
professional staffing of new structures.

It   is   extremely difficult to generalise about
the effect   of   these   three   main   sets   of factors
across   Europe, as far as psychologists' involvement
in   community   care   is concerned.   As Hassel (1983)
points   out,   even within an individual country, such
as West Germany, the different states are relatively
autonomous   in   their   health   systems.   This
introduction   to   the   subsequent   sections, dealing
with community care of the mentally handicapped, the
chronically   psychiatrically   ill,   the   physically
disabled,   and   the elderly, can thus only provide a
loose   framework   within   which   to   place   those
sections.

The   three   chapters   in   this section have two
objectives:

i. to   introduce general concepts and basic information relating to community care;
ii. to   set the scene for more specialised material
   on community care of specific client groups.

The   first   chapter,   by   Dr.   Judy   Renshaw,
describes a   nation-wide initiative   by   the British
government   to   stimulate   the   provision   of   non-
hospital   accommodation   for   mentally   handicapped,
mentally   ill,   elderly,   and physically handicapped
people   who   are   living unnecessarily in hospitals.
The   chapter   illustrates   the   positive steps which
have to be taken to publicise these projects so that
the problems encountered in their execution, and the
solutions   of   those   problems,   can   be   widely
anticipated   and   understood.   In   addition,   the
chapter   indicates   procedures   such   as   careful
description   of   resources,   individual   client care

procedures, outcome measures, which are necessary to plan and carry out such projects.

Dr. Ann Moriarty describes the way in which psychologists are employed in Ireland to provide a community-oriented service, highlighting in particular the implications of working in a health care system with mixed voluntary and public provision, and with greatly contrasting patterns of population density within the country. Her contribution also describes practical difficulties found in other countries - the challenge of a minority language, often spoken mainly by the older members of more isolated communities, and the way in which clinical psychologists may fill a service niche not otherwise provided for - in this case a psychological service for children.

Dr. John Hall provides the last chapter in this section, examining the implications of different models of health care structure and process for health care evaluation. Service evaluation is itself a growing area of health care practice, and an area where no single pre-existing health profession has any claim to prime expertise. This chapter thus provides another example of the role expansion of psychologists which the movement to community care has produced, and provides examples of the specifically psychological issues raised by that expansion and movement.

TAKING A WORLD-VIEW OF COMMUNITY CARE

In the conference itself the above three contributions were preceded by a presentation from Dr. Sineke ten Horn, who spoke from her involvement with the World Health Organisation Collaborating Centre for Research and Training in Mental Health, based at Groningen in the Netherlands. She particularly referred to two projects with which the Centre was collaborating. One was concerned with strategies for extending mental health care into primary health care in developing countries, and another with mental health services in pilot study areas. These two projects give an even broader view of the development of community services, concent-rating on mental health services.

The first project covers seven countries - Columbia and Brazil in South America, Senegal, Sudan and Egypt in Africa, the Philippines, and India. This project has examined a number of specific issues in each country, including childhood mental disorders, knowledge of and attitudes towards mental

health by primary care personnel, and community
reactions to mental disorder.   Another aspect of
this project has been the development of a self-
report questionnaire, which among other uses may be
able to contribute to the development of guidelines
which will help governments to introduce or improve
the mental health component to their primary care
programmes.   The Centre is also acting as a resource
centre for information about training material and
intervention programmes.   The Annual Report of the
Centre for 1985 gives further details of this
project and summary articles have already appeared
(see References).

The second project has concentrated on 21 pilot
study areas in 16 European countries.   In each pilot
study area cohorts of 100 consecutive new patients
have been followed up for two years.   The results
from this project will be the first detailed and
reliable description of the development of mental
health services within Europe, and the publication
includes a separate chapter on each participating
area, as well as a comparison of services and
patterns of care throughout Europe (Giel et al,
1986).   An essential instrument in each of the
cohort studies has been a functioning psychiatric
case register, and a review of the work of such
registers over the past quarter-century has been
published (ten Horn et al, 1986).

These projects illustrate two major points of
relevance in the development of community care.
First that good "community care" is probably more
difficult to achieve than good care in institutional
settings, because of the complexity of coordination
that is required to bring it about (Hafner, 1985).
Second, that some standardisation of definition and
methodology is essential if any international
comparisons are to be made, and thus if any
international lessons are to be learned.

Care in the community is not just about care in
the community, but at least as much about care with
the community.   The "Health for all by the year
2000" strategy has major implications for the re-
orientation of professional psychology in Europe.
It "demands a much greater involvement in primary
health care, and in the prevention of physical
disorders and the promotion of health ... and that
clinical psychologists pay more attention to ways in
which appropriate advice and skills can be made
available to large numbers of people, either
directly to the public or through the training of
other professional and lay groups" (WHO, 1985).

Care in the Community: An Overview

The move to care in the community poses a major challenge   to clinical psychologists in Europe, not only to   contribute   knowledge   and   skills   they already   possess,   but   just   as much to learn new skills and new roles to face that challenge.

REFERENCES

Giel, R., Hannibal, J.U., Henderson, J.H., &
    ten Horn, G.H.M.M. (Eds), (1986).
    Mental Health Services in Pilot Study Areas.
    WHO European Series, WHO Copenhagen.
Hafner, H. (1985).   Changing patterns of mental
    health care.   Acta Psychiat.Scand.Suppl.
    No. 319, 71, 151-164.
Hassel, K. (1983).   Clinical psychology in other
    European countries.   In Liddel, A. (Ed)
    The Practice of Clinical Psychology in Great
    Britain.   Wiley: Chichester.
ten Horn, G.H.M.M., Giel, R., Gulbinat, W. &
    Henderson, J.H. (Eds) (1986).   Psychiatric Case
    Registers in Public Health: A World-Wide
    Inventory, 1960-85.   Elsevier Publishers:
    Amsterdam & New York.
World Health Organisation (1985).   Contribution of
    psychology to programme development in the WHO
    Regional Office for Europe.   Report on a
    consultation at Cologne.   WHO: Copenhagen.
World Health Organisation Collaborating Centre,
    Groningen (1985).   Annual Report, 1985.
    Obtainable from WHO Collaborating Centre,
    Oostersingel, 59, Postbox 30.001, 9700RH,
    Groningen.

(For   details   of developing countries projects, see series   of 4 articles in the November, 1983 issue of American Journal of Psychiatry, 140, 1470-1490.)

Chapter Thirty One

NEW INITIATIVES IN COMMUNITY CARE

Judy Renshaw

This paper is concerned primarily with the
British Government's "Care in the Community"
initiative in England which aims to help people
unnecessarily kept in hospital - including many
mentally ill and handicapped and elderly people - to
live in alternative settings in the community, where
this is more appropriate for them. Before
describing the initiative it may be helpful to
briefly sketch out the policy background from which
it arises.
    Services for mentally handicapped and mentally
ill people have been dominated for a very long time
by the asylums and colonies established during the
nineteenth century. This is true of Britain, of the
USA and of most western countries. Numerically, of
course, the former asylums and colonies today
accommodate only a relatively small proportion of
mentally handicapped and mentally ill people.
    In Britain, the asylums were developed with two
major purposes in mind. It was believed that both
society and the mentally ill or handicapped person
would be better off if there was a physical and a
social distance between them. First, there was the
desire to protect vulnerable individuals from the
evils of society and to allow him or her to lead a
useful life within a protected environment. Second,
there was the wish to protect society from becoming
"overrun" with what were called "defectives and
idiots".
    An important turning point in Britain came in
1946 when the asylums were handed over to the newly
created National Health Service (NHS) and were
subsequently to be designated "hospitals".
    Most hospitals reached their peak during the
1950s, with occupancy reaching well over 2,000 in
many cases. The gradual decline in numbers after

this time can be attributed to a number of factors. One reason was primarily economic. Many of the hospital buildings were getting old and were in need of repair and replacement. Their maintenance and the huge numbers of staff employed were costing a considerable amount of money. Soon afterwards institutions began to be criticised from a different angle by sociologists such as Erving Goffman, who described the restrictiveness, the rigidity and the so-called "totality" of hospital care in which people could lose their individual identity and human dignity. Further criticism of hospitals came from the publication of many reports of cruelty and ill treatment in several hospitals in Britain, and of course in other countries. Incidents of squalor, neglect and violence captured the attention of press and television during the late 1960s and early 1970s.

These <u>negative</u> reasons for the decline of hospitals were reinforced by the emergence of alternatives, in particular the notion of <u>community care</u> which began to take hold in the late <u>1950s and 1960s</u> and was specifically endorsed by the Mental Health Act of 1959. It is important to remember that promoting community care refers not just to the movement of people out of isolated hospital environments, but also removing the need to enter institutional care in the first place.

In 1962 the then Ministry of Health published "A Hospital Plan" followed a year later by what is commonly known as the Community Care blue book. The thrust of these two documents was that new District General Hospitals would replace a large proportion of hospitals nationwide, but would provide no more beds in total for the country's growing population. The slack would be taken up by an increased emphasis on care in the home and the community for non-acute illness.

Two additional developments contributed to the possibility of providing non-institutional care. The availability of new psychotropic drugs, notably the phenothiazines, for the containment of psychotic symptoms, enabled many mentally ill people to be treated in less restrictive settings. The growth of the welfare state in the years since the second world war, in particular the establishment of new systems of benefits and income maintenance, also made it possible for poor people to be helped in a less paternalistic and more independent way. Previously many destitute individuals and families had to enter institutional care in order to survive.

Later, positive arguments in favour of community care became stronger and offered clearer guidelines as to what community care should mean in practice. In particular, the philosophy of normalisation is behind much of the current thinking in service development in the United Kingdom.

Despite the continued rhetoric in favour of community care, progress over the last 20 or so years has been slow and uneven. New resources are needed for the provision of new community services. The transition itself is costly and entails additional work such as rehabilitation training, recruitment and training of staff, acquisition and conversion of buildings and the establishment of procedures and management structures. Planning and negotiation between agencies impose both financial and political costs.

An assumption of the 1970s was that responsibility for community services would gradually be handed over to Local Authority Social Services Departments from the National Health Service. Joint planning between the authorities was encouraged but putting it into practice has proved more difficult. Major differences in structure, political accountability, management and professional orientation presented considerable problems and progress in this area has been very slow. In 1976 Joint Finance was introduced as an incentive to collaborate. This reserved a portion of NHS money which was earmarked to pay for new facilities, many of which were to be managed by Social Services. Few of these facilities, however, were to provide for people transferred from hospital. Most were intended to deal with the other end of the problem, namely people already living in the community, and may have helped to prevent some from entering hospital in the first place.

In 1983 a Department of Health and Social Security (DHSS) Circular, "Care in the Community", was issued, which set out a number of changes, following a consultative document two years earlier. It was aimed specifically at helping long-stay hospital patients to live elsewhere. The new initiative made it possible for NHS resources to be transferred directly to local authorities or other organisations when long-stay patients moved from hospital into their care. Other changes included the involvement of housing and education authorities and an extension of the time period over which joint finance might be used.

In addition a sum of joint finance was

centrally reserved to fund a programme of pilot projects. The programme was intended to explore and evaluate different approaches to moving people and resources into community care, to demonstrate methods which are beneficial to the people concerned and cost-effective.

Twenty-eight pilot projects have been selected, thirteen in a first round and fifteen in a second round, which began a year later. Central funds have been made available for each project for a period of three years on the understanding that it will be continued by local funding after that time. Twelve projects are for mentally handicapped people, eight for mentally ill people, seven are for elderly and elderly mentally infirm and one is for physically handicapped people. Projects deal with a variety of services catering for those who need different degrees of support and care. These include residential care, day provision and a range of support services. Projects range in size from those which intend to move up to a hundred patients, to those which cater for only a dozen. The large projects are able to provide a wider range of facilities and will make broader structural changes to the nature of the total service offered locally.

The DHSS has commissioned the Personal Social Services Research Unit (PSSRU) of the University of Kent to publicise the initiative, to monitor the projects and to provide a more detailed evaluation of the costs and benefits to individuals. This was important to ensure that experience built up from the pilot projects might be disseminated widely and useful lessons learned from the demonstration.

The publicity role consists of a newsletter (available free of charge from the PSSRU) published twice yearly, seminars, conferences and the provision of general information in response to numerous requests. Monitoring activities comprise regular visits, special conferences for project personnel and reporting back of basic information on progress. Descriptive and narrative information about progress and problems are reported in the newsletter and at various conferences, in order that others may learn about the obstacles encountered in operations of this kind, together with some of the solutions which have been found. An important aspect of the monitoring function has been the development, in conjunction with some of the projects, of a Case Review Form, on which to record needs and service plans for individual clients. It is intended as a practice tool, to aid the processes of devising and reviewing individual care plans, and as a research tool from which information about services planned and received may be obtained.

The evaluation is concerned with a number of questions about each project:

   i. Does it improve the well-being of clients?
  ii. What does it cost?
 iii. How does it work?

The broad framework of the investigation can be subdivided into four topics: Outcomes, Resources, Process and Services in Practice. We have set out here what the topics mean in general terms. The precise implications for projects are negotiated with each one separately.

Outcomes

The essential aim here is to form a judgement about the clients' quality of life, as far as possible in comparison with their previous lives in hospital. Many different approaches to measuring this have been developed, each with its own advantages and disadvantages. But there is widespread consensus that a number of different domains of outcome should be included. We have adopted a set of multi-dimensional outcome measures with the aim of covering all the client groups included in the pilot programme, as follows:

* An interview with the client, which covers satisfaction with material situation, regime and relationships and general morale and mood;
* An interview schedule for care workers which covers communication, living skills and behaviour problems;
* A record of social contacts;
* Daily activities over two days;
* Personal presentation;
* Significant events.

A further discussion of outcome measurement is available from the PSSRU.

Process

If there are to be transferable lessons from the model projects, we need to know how they work. We have to discover which processes of intervention are associated with the most cost-effective outcomes for clients, which means we are interested in the style

and technique of working involved. Our observation
and discussion of management systems, both at the
organisational and the case level, will be a major
tool in the assessment of process, supplemented by
the questioning of key actors in each project.

Services in Practice

The picture of each project needs to be fleshed out
with details of the three main elements of the new
service. First, a description of the physical
nature of any accommodation the project provides:
the buildings, the amenities and the domestic
surroundings. Second, we need to know about the
staff of the project, their numbers, training and
experience, their responsibilities and job
satisfaction. Third, we collect information about
the social environment of the project: the degree
of choice open to clients, the amount of supervision
and privacy, their activities and daily timetable.
This we investigate with care staff and heads of
facilities.

Resources

Costing the Care in the Community initiative
involves combining estimates of the resources used
at each stage of each project for each client with
valuations of the costs of those resources. In
order that the PSSRU should be able to make those
latter valuations, we need projects to record for us
a wide range of information about the resources they
use. A key practical distinction is that they will
only be required to account to their sponsoring
agencies for some of the resources. We want to
account for all resources used, whether they are
attributable to the NHS, local education or social
services, Social Security, or otherwise, and whether
they are capital or revenue.

Hospitals and Projects

This framework will be used to investigate the
experience of discharged patients in the facilities
to which they have moved. It will also be used to
look at aspects of the original hospital. Hospitals
are interesting not only because we want to see
those clients in their initial surroundings, as the
"before" part of our analysis, but there is also
concern about the effect of moving patients on the
hospital they leave behind. We will therefore need
to make future visits to the hospitals.

From our monitoring activities we are able to
observe some of the issues and problems which have

emerged as the projects develop. A description of some of the mistakes and misfortunes of the pilot projects may provide some useful lessons for others who attempt similar enterprises.

The range of problems encountered spans financial estimates and agreements; delays in buildings and staff recruitment; resistance from hospital staff; management and accountability; relations with the neighbours; models of care; staffing and training and the relationship between the project and mainstream services. Each of these topics is worthy of a paper in its own right and most will be featured in future newsletters.

NOTE
"Care in the Community" newsletter may be
        obtained, free of charge, from the PSSRU,
        University of Kent at Canterbury.

Chapter Thirty Two

COMMUNITY CARE IN IRELAND WITH SPECIAL REFERENCE TO RURAL AREAS

Ann Moriarty

IRISH HEALTH SERVICE STRUCTURES

Compared with much of Europe the Republic of Ireland is relatively sparsely populated with an overall population density of fifty people per square kilometre. Areas with a density of eighty and over per square kilometre occur in Dublin in the east, Cork in the south and Galway in the west. Other areas, especially along the west coast, have a population of less than twenty per square kilometre.

In 1970 (McKinsey & Co. Inc. 1970) there was a fundamental re-organisation of Irish health services, which set up eight regional health boards to take over control of health services from local authorities. In the more urbanised Health Board Regions, General Hospitals, Special Hospitals (eg Psychiatric) and Community Care services are organised separately in three 'Programmes'. Rural Health Boards have only two such programmes, Hospital Care and Community Care. The structuring of health services under two or three programmes has had implications for the organisation of psychological services which will become apparent below.

Ireland has a tradition of health services (eg hospitals, child guidance clinics and mental handicap units) being set up and run by 'voluntary agencies' such as religious orders. The 1970 re-organisation of the health services incorporated services run by voluntary agencies into the overall health service structure by allocating catchment areas to them. A voluntary agency takes responsibility for delivering services to the population in its catchment area on behalf of the Health Board and receives finances to do so. Most voluntary agencies operate in urban areas and the most complex pattern of catchment area allocation occurs in Dublin. In child psychiatry a network of services for north Dublin is run by one voluntary agency, services for the south city by a second voluntary agency and services for the west administered directly by the Health Board. Adult psychiatric and mental handicap services have different and more complex divisions into voluntary agency and Health Board catchment areas. Health Board Community Care catchment areas are different again. At the other extreme, a rural Health Board, the North Western, has most services delivered directly by the Health Board.

EMPLOYMENT PATTERN OF PSYCHOLOGISTS

Traditionally the voluntary agencies, most of which run mental handicap and child guidance services, have been the biggest employers of psychologists in Ireland, partly because the lack of an educational psychological service for primary schools has thrown an extra burden on the health services for children and the mentally handicapped. Because of the relative autonomy and flexibility of voluntary agencies, they have tended to expand psychological services in response to needs and demands. As a result, in contrast with the situation in Britain and elsewhere where mental handicap has lagged behind other service areas, psychologists in mental handicap in Ireland have tended to be leaders both in terms of innovation in service delivery and in the development of the profession generally (eg nine of the fifteen elected Presidents of the Psychological Society of Ireland have worked in Mental Handicap).

Employment of psychologists by the Health Board tends to be a more cumbersome process bound up with rules and regulations governing appointments to the Public Service. First appointments were to the psychiatric service within the Special Hospitals Programme and expansion, limited though it was, occurred most rapidly in Dublin and other urban areas, there being problems in attracting psychologists to psychiatric services in rural areas. On the other hand employment of psychologists within the Community Care Programme of the Health Boards has followed the pattern of rural Health Boards making most appointments. One reason for this, of course, is that rural Health Boards have been trying to fill gaps in the services for children and the mentally handicapped which are provided in more urban areas by voluntary agencies or psychiatric services.

The development of psychological services within the Community Care Programme has been inhibited by lack of career structure. Almost all psychologists in Community Care have had temporary basic grade appointments, renewable every six months or so but usually extending for years. The psychologists have tended to focus on work with children and mental handicap, in contrast with the broader roles envisaged in the Psychological Society of Ireland's documents (eg rehabilitation, research, work with the elderly and chronically ill). However, expansion into other areas is gradually taking place. Some rural Health Boards have also made arrangements for psychological services to cross the divide between the Community Care Programme and Hospital Care which includes the psychiatric services. Current developments take place in the context of the implementation of the Department of Health's 1984 report on the psychiatric service, entitled 'Planning for the Future', which lays down proposals for a more community oriented service. This community emphasis, though not new, now has a higher profile and added momentum.

PSYCHOLOGISTS IN THE COMMUNITY

Although only a minority of psychologists are employed in the Health Boards' Community Care Programmes, many Irish psychologists see themselves as engaged in work 'in the community'. Some examples are as follows:

Mental Handicap Services
Projects in this area within one agency include evaluation of early intervention programmes (Portage, Head Start, etc); programmes to maintain children with mental handicaps in ordinary schools; home-based parental teaching and support schemes to encourage teenagers to make maximum use of community facilities; an 'out-centre project' to keep adults involved in their local community instead of transporting them into a centre.

Child Services
In the absence of a comprehensive school psychological service, some health psychologists have undertaken programmes with teachers in addition to direct work with children. Parent training has been the main focus of work for other psychologists

in Health Boards or voluntary agency child services. Typically, courses have been organised initially for parents of children attending clinics, and subsequently offered to wider community groups. Demand for these courses has been demonstrated by clients' readiness to organise facilities and by high attendance rates.

Adult Services

Among the adult community settings in which psychologists are active are:

- Day Centres, Day Hospitals, Hostels and Rehabilitation programmes for psychiatric patients.
- GP practices. Timms (1979), in a survey of the needs of GPs for clinical psychology services in rural County Wicklow, recorded high demands for treatment of marital and sexual problems in the adult population and for child treatment facilities.
- Family Planning Clinics.
- Involvement with voluntary associations such as Headway, Mental Health Association, Schizophrenia Association of Ireland, Prisoners' Rights Organisation etc.
- Working with helping agencies involved with non-hospitalised geriatrics.

Community Education

Psychologists are becoming increasingly involved in community education through various channels:

- Media work, eg television, newspapers, magazines.
- Public lecture series organised by the Psychological Society of Ireland.
- Talks to parent-teacher organisations, pre-school playgroup associations etc.
- Adult education courses, run for example under the auspices of the extramural department of the university or the adult education departments of community schools. Interesting examples are the courses run by psychologists Gerry Ryan and colleagues of the Eastern Health Board Research Department, who have conducted research (often in collaboration with other EEC countries) into topics such as long-term unemployment.

Psychologist employed as a 'Community Worker'

A psychologist has been seconded from a department of psychology within the psychiatric service to take up a post of 'Project Worker' in a Community Centre, a post which would normally be filled by a Social Worker or 'Community Worker'. One of her stated aims is 'to develop a range of services for parents and children based on a preventive model of mental health'.

THE PSYCHOLOGICAL SOCIETY OF IRELAND AND COMMUNITY PSYCHOLOGY

In 1983 the Psychological Society of Ireland set up a sub-committee to examine the role of psychologists working in the community. One of the criticisms of the Committee's report in 1985 was that it confused issues pertaining to career structures for psychologists in the Community Care Programme of the Health Boards, and issues pertaining to 'Community Psychology' as such. This led to the establishment of two further sub-committees to examine these questions separately. The sub-committee on Community Care structures for psychologists was able to report quickly and first steps are now being taken to resolve some of the problems in this area. In contrast, the task of the second sub-committee on 'Community Psychology' has proved more difficult. A survey of Psychology Society members shows that psychologists carry out a wide range of activities 'in the community' but coherent philosophies and policies have still to be arrived at.

FEATURES OF RURAL AREAS

Community psychologist services in rural areas are at an early stage of development but some features of rural Ireland which have to be taken into consideration in planning service provision include:

Population

Ireland as a whole has a young population (50% under 25 years). Rural areas have a particularly high proportion of the very young and very old, the most dependent age groups.

For example, according to the 1981 census, 33% of the population of rural County Donegal is under fourteen years, compared with a figure of 30% for the state as a whole.

Community Care in Ireland

After a steady pattern of declining population in rural areas since before the beginning of the century, the trend began to be reversed in the 1960s and 1970s. The same period saw a shift in employment patterns away from agriculture into other areas. The poor economic climate of the 1980s has led to the return of high unemployment and emigration, traditional features of Irish rural life. An additional feature of rural populations is the presence of a minority whose first language is Irish, not English. In County Donegal, 20% of the population live in Gaeltacht or Irish speaking areas.

The psychiatric hospital

Ireland has the highest number of mental health facility beds, 7.3 per 1,000 population, of the World Health Organisation member countries, but this is seen as a legacy of the past. O'Hare (1982) reported that a one day prevalence rate in 1974 for three rural Irish counties was twice that of English registers in Camberwell and Salford but the mean incidence rate of new cases was lower for the Irish counties than for Camberwell and Salford. The large psychiatric hospital has traditionally been of major importance as a source of employment for the local community, a factor which can give rise to opposition when steps are taken to close hospitals and shift care from the institution to the community. On the more positive side, this familiarity of the local population with the hospital can make for more ready acceptance of ex-patients when placed in hostels or centres in the community.

Establishing services

Health services seem to enjoy a higher public profile in rural than in urban areas, frequently a matter for discussion in everyday conversation and local newspapers and a common subject for intervention by local politicians. This community knowledge of and involvement in health services can be an asset or a disadvantage when new services are being introduced.

Because of the low density population, the establishment of specialist services is often not warranted and this may leave clients' needs inadequately met (eg placements for mentally handicapped with special needs). People are accustomed to travelling long distances for 'specialist' consultations but to make such journeys on a regular basis is not feasible.

It seems that the psychologist best equipped to provide services to a rural area is someone with a broad range of skills across many areas of specialisation (because other specialists will not be available), who has a good knowledge of the local culture, is acceptable to the local community but not personally a member of that community.

CONCLUSION

Most clinical psychologists in the Republic of Ireland have been employed in the psychiatric services run by regional Health Boards or in services for children and the mentally handicapped run by voluntary agencies, but patterns of employment are beginning to change. As psychological services have developed, they have taken on more community oriented dimensions in all areas. The community orientation is likely to be particularly characteristic of developments in rural psychological services in the near future for a number of reasons. These include the trend towards appointing psychologists to the Community Care Programme of rural Health Boards, the experience of psychologists in other services from which they can benefit, the prevailing professional philosophy and government policy favouring community-oriented health services and in particular the physical and social characteristics of rural Ireland.

REFERENCES

Department of Health (1984). The Psychiatric Services - Planning for the Future. Report of a Study Group. The Stationery Office, Dublin.

McKinsey & Co. Inc. (1970). Towards Better Health Care. Department of Health, Dublin.

O'Hare, A. (1982). Irish Psychiatric Case Registers, their Contribution to Community Health Care. Medical Informatics Europe, 82 Proceedings: Dublin.

The Psychological Society of Ireland (1985). Psychologists in the Community Care Programmes of the Health Boards. A Policy Document, Dublin.

Timms, M.W.H. (1979). A survey of the needs of Wicklow General Practitioners for a Clinical Psychologist. Journal of the Irish Medical Association, 72, No.4, 171-173.

Chapter Thirty Three

EVALUATING COMMUNITY CARE - A PSYCHOLOGICAL
PERSPECTIVE

John Hall

"Community Care" covers both a range of
specific practices and a range of philosophies. At
the most simplistic, it may be seen as simply
shifting the site on which services are delivered
from large, remote, monolithic institutions, to
small accessible dispersed institutions. More
considered sociological analysis leads to a
definition that it is "the provision of help,
support and protection to others by lay members of
societies acting in everyday domestic and
occupational settings". (Abrams, 1977, quoted in
Walker 1982). There have been several attempts at
conceptualising some of the processes within this
range of practices.

One influential attempt has been Goldberg and
Huxley (1980) in developing their theory of the
progress of an individual patient through successive
"filters" as they pass through more specialised
stages of psychiatric care. The central point about
this journey from informal care to in-patient care
is that the filters are controlled sequentially by 3
different people - by the patient, the family
doctor, and by the psychiatrist. Thus different
people contribute to the decisions about passage
through this network or maze of care, and their
beliefs and views about effectiveness and
acceptability affect that passage.

A second approach to community care is the
"ingredients" approach which involves listing the
components of a satisfactory comprehensive mental
health service. MIND (1983), the major British
voluntary body concerned for mental health, listed
160 components of such a service for all groups,
including the elderly and children. Examination of
such lists indicates that in most countries a number
of different health and social care agencies would

be involved in providing these components, indicating that comprehensive community care involves complex networks of different agencies, and the different units of service controlled by them.

Walker (1982) describes a third approach, which examines the relationship between three levels of care. Formal care is that type of care delivered by professional staff, usually in health care settings. Quasi-formal care describes the care given by social services departments, voluntary organisations and housing associations. Informal care is that given by family and neighbours - kith and kin. Walker points out that disproportionate increase in the numbers of elderly people, smaller family size, greater geographical mobility, and most importantly the growth in employment amongst women, have reduced the pool of potential care-givers, who have historically been younger unemployed women living close to those in receipt of care.

A number of other factors have modified public attitudes to community care. The increased cost of institutional care, changing political attitudes to public expenditure, and repeated exposés of institutional practices mean that increased attention has been paid to how best to care for these people. How best to provide community care for all client groups has thus become a complex and sensitive question. It involves many different facilities run by many different agencies and can no longer be sustained by an appeal to traditional patterns of family care. Different philosophies of care, such as normalisation, have become politicised so that the most basic assumptions of care givers may be called into question. Any attempt to address this issue thus requires methods that are comprehensive in who and what they cover, and are not themselves value-laden.

THE DEVELOPMENT OF SERVICE EVALUATION

A recent review by one of the leading American workers in this field (Donabedian, 1985) illustrates both the achievements and some of the continuing difficulties in service evaluation. There are a number of definitions of evaluation; one widely accepted is "the formal determination of the effectiveness, efficiency, and acceptability of a planned intervention in achieving stated objectives" (Holland, 1983). Most such definitions stress the need for specified objectives or desired outcomes which are measurable, are examinable in the light of effectiveness and acceptability and assess the efficient use of available resources.

The desired outcomes from the client's point of view within a comprehensive programme of community care will be highly individual, depending on the presenting need or problem, and the position of the individual along the path from informal to formal care. Moreover, the stated objectives of any particular set of units or facilities within a locality should be mutually consistent. The complexity of the resultant task is not always apparent from some of the literature in this field.

Hawkins and Fremouw (1981) describe an approach to programme evaluation that clearly differentiates between client and natural environment variables, pre-, in-, and post-programme characteristics, and the path from programme conception to programme delivery. In practice the enormity of mounting true service evaluation studies means studies tend to be limited to individual units or service components. Felce et al (1985) describe the transfer of profoundly mentally-handicapped adults from institutional care to small community-based houses: amongst other measures, each resident was video-taped individually for 6 hours. Garety and Morris (1984) evaluated the effectiveness of an innovative "hostel-ward" for chronic patients: several detailed measures were used, but relatively few residents were assessed. Dowell and Ciarlo (1983) reported a meta-analysis of the American Community Mental Health Centre programme along a number of dimensions; they indicated, along with other findings, the tendency for community-based services to go "up-market", and to offer a poorer service to the most disabled clients than institutionally-based services.

Two recent developments in Oxfordshire, England, have created an opportunity to evaluate changes in service pattern both for mentally handicapped people and for mentally ill people in contact with specialist services. The county, with a population of 500,000, is largely rural, with a few market towns scattered round the centrally situated major city of Oxford. Mental handicap services have been based in a hospital on the extreme west of the county, but are being trans-ferred to a number of "community units". A research project is under way both to evaluate the effects of this transfer, and to create a service-related monitoring system which will continue after the research element of the project has finished (Thomas et al, 1986. Mental illness services have been based in two early Victorian psychiatric hospitals, the larger of which is now requiring so much maintenance, apart from being unsuitable for modern care, that a decision has been made to replace the older part of the building with a more dispersed type of service. Involvement in both the planning and evaluation of these changes suggests seven distinct points that need to be borne in mind in designing an attainable, service-relevant, evaluation method with staffing resources usually available in this type of setting.

EVALUATING COMMUNITY CARE - PSYCHOLOGICAL REQUIREMENTS FOR THE JOB

1. Set up a case register
It will be apparent that an individual client or patient may pass through the care of several different agencies, though the majority of clients will be in contact only with a family doctor or other primary-care worker. Any client can only evaluate a service with which he has been in contact. The relative period of time, or frequency of contacts, with different component services is then a major determinant of what, for that client, will be the most important service as perceived by him. A minimal case register which is useable by the main different agencies, after an agreed level of "filter" has been passed, is an essential tool of the most rudimentary evaluation study.

2. Avoid reliance on skill-change measures
The search for the Holy Grail of the measure of intrinsically high reliability will fail in most community settings because of the highly variable nature of the assessment environment and because of the highly variable assessment skills of the available assessors. Attempts have been made to improve the reliability of measures such as the Wessex scales for mentally handicapped people by converting them to an interview-based measure (Caddell and Woods, 1984) but this creates as many problems as it solves. Since it is very difficult to obtain formally reliable measures of skill change in these settings, unless high levels of trained assessor time can be continuously assured, it is not advisable in community settings to select such methods as the main outcome measure.

3. Help direct-care staff to use measures correctly

In community settings the people who possess most knowledge about clients are likely to be direct-care staff - usually not formally qualified - or friends or family. They may not be highly literate, are not likely to be used to answering detailed questions or filling in detailed forms, and may not be clear why this should be important. There are a number of ways of making such records easier to complete, by, for example, the use of "readability" indices, such as FOG or SMOG, and by considering the information-processing implications of different approaches to form design (Wright, 1983).

4. Provide feedback to staff

In general, staff in a community-based service tend to be less supervised and supported than staff in an institutionally based service. It is not therefore safe to assume that a monitoring or evaluation instrument or measure will be completed, unless the staff concerned see some reason to complete it. This reason can be provided by a regular feedback system, assisted by suitable computer-based data-analysis, providing core-staff and others with knowledge of the results obtained over the previous weeks or months. A further advantage of introducing a feedback system into a monitoring and evaluation project is indicated by the increasing evidence that structured instructional and feedback packages are the main therapeutic factor in behavioural treatment regimes (see Hall and Baker, 1986). Thus introducing regular feedback as part of a management-led evaluation may be consistent with the tasks required for therapeutic purposes.

5. Choose multiple measures

The field of general medical evaluation demonstrates the continuing search for single outcome measures, such as Quality Adjusted Life Years (QALYs) or health state measures, well illustrated by Teeling-Smith (1983). In that field there are workers who do not believe it is possible to reduce several different measures to one, using a uniform formula, and who thus prefer a multi-dimensional "health profile" approach. In the field of psychiatric, mental handicap, elderly, and physical handicap evaluation it is preferable to have available several different measures, since this may reveal important differences of response between units, or between groups of clients, rather than attempt to use one combined measure.

6. Consider the clients' view

While it has often been stated that patients' views should in principle be considered, in practice their views have not been systematically heard in evaluation research. However, a significant proportion of psychologically distressed or disturbed clients have difficulties in expressing a view coherently and consistently without being unduly biased by the view or behaviour of an interviewer. A recent paper by MacCarthy et al (1986) directs attention to ways to improve the self-appraisal of such clients, and so to take more account of their views. There is an important but relatively unexplored area of research enquiry relating to the development of assessment measures with low demand characteristics which minimise assessor bias.

7. Identify possible tracer conditions

Again following the logic of the introduction to this paper, the total number of clients who could be registered in a locality could be so high that it is impossible to evaluate service delivery to them all. In such circumstances, it might be helpful to reduce the number of clients on whom detailed evaluation information is collected, possibly by looking for "tracer conditions" which act as a touchstone of the quality of the overall service. Such tracer conditions could be those which follow the most complex path through the different units, or those which are most serious. In the mental health field schizophrenia could act as a suitable tracer condition, as it tends to lead to complex patterns of service use, is a serious condition, and forms only a relatively small proportion of all cases in contact with services.

CONCLUSION

The experience of the two local development projects has suggested that many evaluation projects are conceived after the initial planning of service changes. It is important that specific service objectives are elicited by the real planners during the planning process, otherwise the desired outcome and objectives may be attributed post-hoc, and not be the objectives which stimulated change. Evaluation of community care is only one segment of an iterative cycle of doctor-patient and political resource allocation decisions, review of services, option selection and implementation. Nonetheless, it is a segment to which clinical psychologists are increasingly likely to be drawn, and which contains a number of important issues of applied psychology which still deserve attention.

REFERENCES

Caddell, J. & Woods, P. (1984). The Bryn-y-Nevadd degree of dependency rating scale: an extension of the Wessex mental handicap register. Mental Handicap, 12, 142-145.

Donabedian, A. (1985). Twenty years of research on the quality of medical care 1964-1984. Evaluation and the Health Professions, 8, No. 3, 243-265.

Dowell, D.A. & Ciarlo, J.A. (1983). Overview of the community mental health centers program from an evaluation perspective. Community Mental Health Journal, 19, 95-125.

Felce, D., Thomas, M., de Kock, U. & Saxby, H. (1985). An ecological comparison of small community based houses and traditional institutions - II. Behaviour Research and Therapy, 23, 337-348.

Garety, P. & Morris, I. (1984). Staff attitudes, organisational structure and the quality of care of long-stay psychiatric patients. Psychological Medicine, 14, 183-192.

Goldberg, D. & Huxley, P. (1980). Mental Illness in the Community. Tavistock: London.

Hall, J.N. & Baker, R.D. (1986). Token economies and schizophrenia: a review. In: Kerr, A. & Snaith, P. Contemporary Issues in Schizophrenia. Gaskell: London.

Hawkins, R.P. & Fremouw, W.J. (1981). A model for use in designing or describing evaluations of mental health or educational intervention programs. Behavioural Assessment, 3, 307-324.

Holland, W.W. (1983). Evaluation of Health Care. Oxford University Press: Oxford.

MacCarthy, B., Benson, J. & Brewin C.R. (1986). Task motivation and problem appraisal in long-term psychiatric patients. Psychological Medicine, 16, 431-438.

MIND (1983). Common Concern. Mind Publications: London.

Teeling-Smith, G. (1983). Measuring the Social Benefits of Medicine. Office of Health Economics: London.

Thomas, M., Hall, J.N. & Sharich, J. (1986). Oxfordshire Mental Handicap Service Development

and Evaluation Project: Annual Report.
Unpublished report: Oxfordshire Health Auth.
Walker, A. (1982). Community Care: the Family, the
State and Social Policy. Blackwell-Robertson.
Wright, P. (1983) Informed design for forms. In:
Easterby, R. and Zwaga, H. Information
Design: the Design and Evaluation of Signs and
Printed Material. Wiley: Chichester.

Chapter Thirty Four

SETTING UP A COMMUNITY SERVICE: IT'S EASY WHEN YOU
KNOW HOW

Len Rowland

History

The Maudsley Hospital in inner London was
founded in the era of the large, out of town asylum,
when "moral treatment" had largely lost its
psychological way. Its objective was to provide
efficient treatment locally. Not radical today,
perhaps, but nor is it far from what we aim at. It
was very much a treatment institution, if people
failed to improve they were sent to the local
catchment area hospital. It was not until the 1960s
that provision began to be made within the Maudsley
Hospital for individuals with long term
disabilities. Patients were admitted to two local
wards, into which there was some input by Maudsley
staff, and a day hospital was opened on the Maudsley
site. From the mid 1960s beds in the asylum were
run down and various initiatives set up. A range of
accommodation and work projects got off the ground.
In 1977 the first long stay beds were
established with the opening of a "Hostel ward" for
new long stay patients. In 1981 the District
Services Centre (DSC) was opened to provide the
focus of care for individuals with long term
disabilities. At the same time the day hospital, an
industrial therapy unit and the two local long stay
wards were closed down and their functions taken
over by the DSC. The Maudsley had arrived at the
point of taking over catchment area responsibility,
but without setting up new long stay wards and with
only 34 beds to provide a service for the so called
"chronic population". The service had to be
"community" in some sense, or no service at all.
Several lessons are to be learned from this
"tailored" history.

1. It took over 20 years to set up this "community" service and the process is not yet finished.

2. At each stage it was important to set up a range of complementary facilities which would fulfil <u>all</u> the functions of the resources they were superseding.

3. The development of new services was not based on the assumption that "hospitals are bad, communities are good", but rather it was guided by the principle that the hospital, or whatever resources were fulfilling its traditional functions, ought to be "community facilities" like a library or launderette. There was also the additional principle of "maximum benefit with minimum side effects".

Philosophy or model

So far so good, but having acquired a population one has to do something. First, it is important to get the philosophy clear. The service is a "rehabilitation" service. Unfortunately this seems to mean all things to all people, but what we mean is "enabling patients to function at an optimum level of independence in the context of a social environment that is as normal as possible" (Bennett & Morris, 1983).

The model is a functional, not a curative one. It espouses continuity of commitment not "through-put", (re-) training or re-settlement and not simply categorising the individual's difficulties. Depending on one's frame of mind one can regard the model as enshrining a paradox or as a balance model. People's functioning can often be improved, but at what cost to the "normality" of their environment? "Normality" can be enhanced, but at what cost for functioning? The model aims at keeping these two factors in equilibrium, to give the individual the best quality of life possible.

The approach is also community and socially orientated. That is, we do not simply "take social factors into account" but try to manipulate them. We use other community resources and aim at integrating with them to produce a comprehensive community service.

Some problems of the guidance system

"Not curing" is not enough. To set up any service one needs to start with the characteristics of the population to be served. In our case the disabilities model was adopted to help us describe our population. Whether due to pre-morbid factors, to personal or social response to psychiatric problems, to the psychiatric conditions themselves or their residual effect many people are left disabled, impaired, unable to carry out certain tasks.

Again, so far so good, careful assessment revealed that most of our clients are multiply disabled (NB multiply not universally), but the model provides no guidance as to what to tackle first, no rules for establishing priorities. One is in danger of mechanically teaching skills, of slipping into a "standardised approach" - the first step towards the dreaded block treatment. The solution seemed to be to stand the model on its head and emphasise strengths rather than weaknesses, what people can and need to do but do not. We looked at the functional levels of a range of living environments which were ordered in an eminently understandable way. Lowest functioning was associated with being in hospital and highest with living with spouse and family. All seemed to be well until we did the sensible thing and asked the question the right way around and found that 23% of our highest functioning patients were in hospital and 50% of our lowest out (Waisman, in preparation). So this functioning approach, like its predecessor, proved to be inadequate. There are obviously other critical factors not yet captured by these models.

It is easy to categorise, develop methods of assessment and devise solutions to disabilities which manifest themselves as deficits or excesses of activity. This, however, can lead to the sort of naive materialism which in its turn results in ignoring both cognitive and emotional areas as well as abstract and hypothetical variables such as apathy, motivation and dependency. One approach which, potentially, overcomes these shortcomings and appears to be in the ascendancy at present is to look at "needs". Is this our salvation? A person may not be able to cook - but does he/she need to?

Such a model makes it easier to move from a 'pigeon hole' approach to a consideration of how various areas of an individual's life interact. It copes well with the concepts of roles and functions rather than activities. For example, a person may be vulnerable to both over and under stimulation and may be unable to cook. One might teach him to cook and risk increased withdrawal as he sits at home.

Or one might identify his needs as: requiring adequate nourishment, structure to his day and some (low) degree of social stimulation. In response one might provide him with a daily midday meal (nourishment and structure), help him to budget so he can go to a local cafe in the evening (nourishment, social stimulation), and finally one might teach him to boil an egg and make tea, to allow for some variety and, perhaps, fluctuations in mood or mental state. The aim would not be merely to teach skills, improve functioning, or even meet each need, but to construct a programme in such a way that the various solutions complement each other, do not generate new difficulties or needs, and provide the individual with the best possible life style.

We have solved it - patient drive service, individual care. All is well with community care!

Despite our enthusiasm there were some rather worrying clouds on the horizon. No-one has bothered to define properly what constitutes a need. Frequently lists of needs are merely lists of problems - often less imaginative than you would come up with if you looked at disabilities and functioning. Sometimes there is a horrendous confusion between a need state and any "thing" that might alter the state: material goods, services, behaviours, skills, even alternative psychological states. At still other times there is a most worrying tendency to decide what people "need" in terms of what resources are available - they "need" medication or behaviour therapy or in-patient care. Fit the patient to the service and God help them if they are the wrong shape. To add insult to inadequacy there is no real effort to develop a theory of needs, to explain the process by which they are maintained or ameliorated. Why do they sometimes lead to dependency and apathy, and at other times to drive and motivation?

Surely, you'll say, if you know your patients well enough, you will be aware of their needs, even if there is no clearly articulated theory available. Perhaps, but Waisman (in preparation) found that patients and "normals" ranked a list of needs differently and both came up with different rank orderings, depending on whether they were asked to rank in terms of importance or satisfaction. Trivial you might respond - everyone knows all you need to do is ask the patient, besides, this is good rehabilitation practice.

I am not sure it is so simple. GPs believed they knew their patients before Ley had a look (Ley

& Spelman, 1965; Ley, 1979). Khwaja (1985a) did not find things much better in the DSC.Staff and patients agreed on the patient's problem on average on only 33% of occasions, and staff knew patient's views on only 36% of occasions. Patients knew where they ought to be (with 89% accuracy) but not why. They knew the content of plans for them on less than 40% of occasions.

Not the optimum environment for effective interventions. But we have to be careful. Why is it not the optimum situation? What criteria are we employing? What assumptions are being made? There is a tendency to assume that if you offer people what they ask for, they will take it up and all will be well. Khwaja (1985b) found that the importance of work was unrelated to the use people made of it. Its perceived importance was related to neither attendance nor effort. Providing resources is only half the problem, engagement must also be achieved.

We need to take a step back. We tend to assume that if we talk to patients, collect data and do appropriate assessments we will automatically identify their "needs". The classical model is: Information - Identification - Intervention.

There is growing evidence, however, (Rowland and Conning in preparation; Conning, 1986) that information, the needs identified and intervention are less firmly tied together than we have assumed. What people choose to discover, identify and do is determined to a substantial degree by person variables: the attitudes and the models they employ.

To make matters worse, while we have been shifting our model, the patients have stuck by the traditional model of illness and cure (Khwaja and Rowland, in preparation; Ranger, 1986).

One might be forgiven for abandoning all these fancy concepts, reverting to good, solid traditional practices, identifying groups and intervening "appropriately" (and then retiring to the bar). We thought of that too! Unfortunately we found that women (as a group) said "safety" was the most important thing, older people identified finances, widows identified household tasks, those living alone identified leisure activities, and patients identified support as the thing they most wanted. Then we noted that everyone belonged to several groups which meant....

Conclusion

The aim of this paper is not to depress, merely stress that there is no ideal service. If a service works today for a variety of reasons it probably will not work tomorrow. A good service is constantly evolving, sometimes concentrating on resources, at other times on engaging people, or how best to conceptualise and serve its population. If it does not, it is like a clock that is stopped - it is sometimes right, but when?

REFERENCES

Bennett, D. & Morris, I. (1983). Deinstitutionalization in the U.K. International Journal of Mental Health, 11, 5-23.

Conning A.M. (1986). Individual differences in designing treatments for chronic patients. Unpublished M.Phil. thesis, University of London.

Khwaja, A. (1985a). Communication between staff and patients in a setting designed to promote normal behaviour. Unpublished M.Phil, thesis University of London.

Khwaja, A. (1985b). "What patients think of work and the use they make of it". Unpublished manuscript.

Khwaja, A. & Rowland, L.A. (in preparation). Communication in a psychiatric setting? Do we listen to what they say? Do we know what they want?

Ley, P. (1979). The Psychology of Compliance in D.J. Oborne, M.M. Gruneberg & J.R. Eisler (Eds) Research in Psychology and Medicine. Academic Press: London

Ley, P. & Spelman, M.S. (1965). Communications in an out-patient setting. British Journal of Social and Clinical Psychology, 4, 114-116.

Ranger, S.M. (1986). Functioning of the multi-disciplinary team: a study of three teams in a psychiatric rehabilitation setting. Unpublished M.Phil. thesis, University of London.

Rowland, L.A. & Conning, A.M. (In preparation). Assessing the work-load of nurses caring for a chronic psychiatric population: nurses' resources versus patient needs.

Waismann, L.C. (In preparation). An investigation into needs and dependency in long term patients.

Chapter Thirty Five

A REHABILITATION DAY CENTRE IN THE NEW ORGANISATION
OF THE COMMUNITY MENTAL HEALTH SERVICES IN NORTHERN
ITALY (LOMBARD REGION)

Anna Checchi, Angelo Cocchi, Giorgio De Isabella

INTRODUCTION

A new Mental Health Act came into effect in
Italy in 1978. Its main characteristics were:

1. The local authority (the Mayor) now authorises
   compulsory admissions to hospital.
2. Fifteen-bed psychiatric wards must be opened
   in the General Hospital. No new patients are
   to be admitted to the Psychiatric Hospitals.
3. Community services are to be set up.

An uncertain period followed and the organisation of new services posed many problems: General
Hospitals were reluctant to accept the psychiatric
wards, staff had to be moved and administrators were
suspicious of interventions which occurred outside
hospitals. The complicated bureaucratic system
delayed the implementation of the law, and services
developed in different ways in different places.
Lombardy in Northern Italy passed a local law
in 1984, defining the Psychiatric Services structure
and the minimum number of staff required for its
proper functioning. It provides for updating
programmes for the staff, and organises an
information and an epidemiological system. It makes
provision to convert Psychiatric Hospitals into
Therapeutic Communities and for "experimental
initiatives" to be set up. Fifty-three local
services were set up in the region, each with at
least one community (psycho-social) centre, a
General Hospital psychiatric ward, a residential
centre where 12-20 "guests" can stay for 6-12
months, as well as "homes" or "sheltered
communities". A budget of £30 million over four
years has been set aside.

A Rehabilitation Day Centre in Northern Italy

The industrial district of Rho on the outskirts of Milan, which has a population of 240,000, has already set up two Psycho-Social Centres, one Psychiatric Service for Diagnosis and Care, five Home Communities, one Rehabilitation Day Centre and one Co-operative Society.

In this paper we will describe the activity and structure of the Rehabilitation Day Centre.

Psychosis Rehabilitation Day Centre

The centre, founded in 1980, tries to respond to the problems posed by a group of young psychotics in the new organisation of mental health services. The staff is made up of two psychiatric nurses, an occupational therapist or a social worker and psychologist.

The centre's activity is organised in two main phases, daily group activities and the formation of comprehensive plans.

Daily Group Activities

Two groups work on communication skills; the first is in social skills and the other fosters expression through action and employs non-verbal techniques (actions speak louder than words). Another integration group combines exercise and relaxation aimed at the control of anxiety reactions which contribute to the reduction of social competence. These groups, which are linked to each other by their search for more effective communication, are supported by training in daily living skills aimed at increasing the patient's personal independence.

A stimulus to the learning of social skills comes from the dynamics which develop in the group themselves, as the patient copes with the institutional reality of the centre and its rules.

The head office is located in one room in the General Hospital. For group activities we prefer to use more realistic environments free from institutional features. We use a secondary school gymnasium for relaxation therapy, and a flat in a residential area in town for other group activities.

The group activities are attended by an average of six persons. Placing a patient in a group and his/her length of stay depend on the patient's initial level and on achievement of established goals.

A Rehabilitation Day Centre in Northern Italy

Formation of Comprehensive Plans for Each Patient

This second phase involves various community activities, such as home visits and meetings with the family and in the working place.

Job resettlement has an important place in the centre's activities. Up to August, 1985, the Provincial Employment Office found work for those recognised as disabled. A quota system established in law obliged firms to offer employment to such individuals. Recent changes in economic and social conditions have made placing people in work more difficult; the centre staff has gained a good deal of experience in placing people in work. In 1984 the staff and clients of the Centre founded a Cooperative (non-profit making) Society. Nowadays the membership includes some young unemployed people from the local neighbourhood. This enterprise is involved with cleaning and gardening. It offers work opportunities, apprenticeship, assessment of work difficulties, and short-term training. It is important that these community activities must be carried out with collaboration of Local Council Social Services and that there is contact with all agencies.

Staff

The staff devote a lot of time to planning and checking individual treatment. This is carried out in cooperation with the psychiatrist. Inservice activities also include patient interviews for assessing and defining goals, analysing difficulties and crisis interventions, and daily and weekly staff meetings. Every 15 days, the staff receive supervision from the Institute of Psychology, University of Milan.

Patients

The present population consists of 20 patients aged 18-30 years, with more males than females. Their characteristics are different from those of the patients who attended the centre when it was founded in 1980. In particular, the average age has diminished substantially and the new clients have never been in a psychiatric hospital. Some have never been in a General Hospital. This new population shows serious difficulties in interpersonal skills, with a high risk of chronicity. This kind of chronicity which develops in the community, even if it sometimes resembles that which was observed in the psychiatric institution, must be considered a completely new phenomenon, which needs new analysis and specific interventions.

There are two sub-groups of "young chronics" which correspond to two types of chronicity, which we call passive marginals and active marginals.

The passive marginal group is characterised by a withdrawal from social relationships. They live with their families who can be considered to be of low expressed emotion (EE). These families have a high tolerance level and deal with all aspects of the patient's life without asking for help. Nevertheless this apparent balance and stability seems to create a relationship of pathological "mutual dependence".

There is also a sub-group with high EE levels where there is an over-involvement between the patient and one member of his/her family. These patients comply with the "sick role" in such a way as to exclude any other demands of role functioning and their repertory of behaviours displays limited social and living skills. In this situation of "institutionalisation" at home, the home visit which is intended as mere control or check up may only confirm this "sick role".

The active marginal performs the "sick role" in an intermittent and inconsistent way. Their dearth of social competence does not allow them to assume different roles. The movement from one social context to another results in the accumulation of a series of failures and of rejections. In fact, during hospitalisation, staff often come to the conclusion that the patient was admitted because he/she "had nowhere to stay", rather than anything to do with illness. The patient's difficulty in complying with the rules can lead to the staff becoming intolerant and unmotivated as a result of repeated, ineffective interventions. The relationship between staff and patient thus becomes full of conflicts which tend to spread, involving relations between staff members at all levels. In these instances even the patient role has not been performed in a convincing way.

For passive marginals the therapeutic problem lies in unbalancing the chronic relationships in which they are involved, whereas for active marginals the need is to find some stability.

With high EE families the staff can at least reduce a part of their burden, taking the family's place in making those requests which they tend to put forward too demandingly. For passive marginals belonging to families with low EE those expectations which are not expressed in the family interaction can be expressed through the staff, placing them in a realistic and coherent programme, aimed at teaching the acquisition of suitable roles.

These considerations about role situations and context bring us to the conclusion that for an effective intervention, we should search for new roles by partially moving the patient outside of the usual relationship context, in addition to trying to produce changes in rigid relationship systems within the family.

The centre itself can function as a place where it is possible to put forward alternative role demands. This happens either in the group activities, or during the planning of individual programmes, which provide occasions for the analysis of difficulties and the individualisation of goals, or patients' needs.

The Concept of Need

"Need" is an ambiguous and complex concept which refers to the individual's subjective state in relation to the social context in which he or she belongs. A need never appears in isolation, it is always mixed with other needs and, when one is satisfied, another emerges. A need is therefore part of a complex chain without a clear beginning or end. It follows that for its satisfaction we have to decide which need has priority.

The assessment of patient need implies a dynamic and dialectic approach to the problem. This can happen in many ways - let us hypothesise two different cases.

Firstly, the staff are ready to accept any request as an expression of an authentic need. In reality if the staff are part of an institution, the acceptance of the expressed need will take place in a prearranged way, with no interaction. This is likely to stifle the emergence of needs concerning autonomy and individual growth. As the limits of the institution make it necessary to predefine needs, the staff do not take on the role of representative and mediator of social reality. Instead, they abandon the dialectic function and foster opposition between the demands of the patient and the limited opportunity to satisfy needs within the institution.

In order to fulfil a dialectic mediation between patient and institution a contractual process can be used which involves examining and redefining needs. In this second case the staff pose as an active receptor of the need through a process of negotiation. This happens after discussion between staff and patient about various ways to define the expressed need. Only when an agreement is reached, shared by both, do they subscribe to the contract.

The contract, aimed at defining expressed need, is subject to verification and reformulation. This temporary definition of need defines the goal which the patient must reach to satisfy a need. It may also constitute a partial achievement which must be preserved in order to reach subsequent goals. The contract formulates a plan of the patient's evolution and, through the choice of each goal, it is possible to pin-point the needs which may be immediately achieved.

The contract outlines the method of reaching a partial goal, the role performance which staff and patient will have to assume, and the mutual behavioural expectations.

The principal instrument used to formulate contracts is the clinical interview. The centre staff and sometimes the family may be present at appropriate points in time to underline the importance of what the patient is achieving.

Clinical interviews aimed at individualising and/or stipulating needs are especially effective at the centre because we have a small staff who have been working together for some time. Direct observation during the group activities and work with families enable the staff to have a clear picture of each patient's history. This favours therapeutic continuity and allows a significant relationship between staff and patient to develop, which can mobilise remarkable aspects in the patient's personality, emphasising his/her health and fostering rehabilitation.

CONCLUSION

The therapeutic rehabilitation process described above consists of a series of interventions, carried out by the Centre with respect to the individual and his or her environment, involving an examination and definition of the patient's needs : these interventions are formulated by means of a succession of contracts. The contractual nature of the link between staff and patient puts at issue the question of patient motivation in taking part in treatment and the importance of the individual programme in the whole therapeutic rehabilitation intervention.

A Rehabilitation Day Centre in Northern Italy

An evaluation of the effectiveness of the Centre approach is currently in progress. We are doing this in collaboration with the Institute of Mental Health, Department of Medicine, University of Pavia. We await the results with interest.

FURTHER READING

Checchi, A. & Civenti, G. (1985). Lavoro e mallattia mentale. Devianze ed Emarginazione, 7, 17-23.
Cocchi, A. & De Isabella, G. (1984). Jeunes psychotiques et nouvelle strategie de travail de l'equipe: un des problemes posées par la nouvelle organisation psychiatrique italienne. Revue Pratique de Psychologie de la Vie, Sociale et d'Hygiène Mentale, 1.
Cocchi, A. & De Isabella, G. (1986). Una modalità di trattamento dei giovani psicotici, Centro Studie e Ricerche Devianza ed Emarginazione, Milano.
I provvedimenti e lo stato di attuazione dei servizi in materia di psichiatria, (1985). Notizie Sanita Regione Lombardia, 5, 11.
Leff, J.P. & Vaughn, C.F. (1985). Expressed Emotion: its Significance for Mental Illness. Guilford Press: New York.
Remocker, A.J., & Storch, E.T. (1982). Action Speaks Louder. Churchill Livingstone: London.
Shepherd, G. (1984). Institutional Care and Rehabilitation. Longman: London.
Shepherd, G. & Spence, S. (Eds) (1983). Developments in Social Skills Training. Academic Press: London.
Watts, F.N. & Bennett, D.H. (1983). Theory and Practice of Psychiatric Rehabilitation Wiley: London.

264

Chapter Thirty Six

THE BRUSSELS NIGHT HOSPITAL

G. Pieters, R. Vermote & J. Peuskens

In Belgium, the trend towards deinstitution-
alisation and community care has recently received
more support from the government. Although this
movement started later than in the UK and the USA,
and seems to proceed at a slower pace, the need to
prevent or to cut down the duration of psychiatric
hospitalisation is now generally accepted.
     The relatively generous level of provisions and
staff means that a fairly intensive therapeutic
approach is possible. However, there is a
theoretical danger that an overuse of in-patient
care will be disruptive to patients' lives and lead
to an increase in social handicaps.

A Treatment Programme for Young Psychotic Patients
Some 10 years ago at the University Psychiatric
Hospital of Kortenberg (near Leuven), it was decided
that a group of young psychotic patients should be
treated in a special programme to prevent them from
becoming long-stay patients. The treatment
programme was not only aimed at the removal of
psychopathological symptoms, but also at the
development of functional skills.
     The underlying philosophy is situated between
two extremes. One extreme views mental illness as
"brain diseases that anyone could have gotten....".
The management of insulin-dependent diabetes is the
closest analogy. The other extreme sees schizophrenia as an expression of deep rooted intra-
personal or interpersonal conflict, that can be made
to disappear by intensive individual or family
therapy. Our approach, lying between these extremes
is called "structuring therapy". By providing
external structure, balancing between over-
stimulation and understimulation, we hope to start
(anew) the process of intrapsychic structuring.

265

The Brussels Night Hospital

In the short term, we hope to be able to help patients to resume a role outside the hospital. In the long term, we hope that they will find an equilibrium between their potential possibilities and their limitations. We strongly believe in the possibility of GROWTH even for very disabled patients. We therefore believe that one should not concentrate exclusively upon the needs of the patient, but should also keep in mind the potential for growth that can be promoted in a treatment programme. Therefore, patients should be given the time to realise this potential.

The Brussels Night Hospital
In 1978, a night hospital was set up to continue the programme for those patients (one third) who did not find sufficient support and/or tolerance in the community or who did not reach a sufficient level of autonomy to be discharged.

The night hospital is sited close to the centre of Brussels. Although it is funded as a night hospital under partial hospitalisation regimen, the centre does not carry the social stigma of a psychiatric hospital and therefore seems more acceptable to patients and their families. The centre provides a place for 44 patients. About 80% of the referrals come from the University Psychiatric Centre (UPC) of Kortenberg. The main admission criteria include that the person should already be engaged in some kind of regular daily activity outside the hospital prior to admission, and have some capacity for self-management. We tend to exclude patients with toxicomania or strong antisocial tendencies. Severely mentally retarded patients are also excluded.

Patient Characteristics
On census day, 1st January, 1985, most patients were male. The mean age of our patients was 30 years, 6 months and mean duration of illness was 10 years, 9 months since first contact with a psychiatrist. The educational level of the patients and the social background of the parents of the patients was rather high. The majority of patients had a diagnosis of schizophrenia, with a reasonably long history of illness. Almost all patients had a history of several psychiatric hospitalisations before they were referred to the UPC and to the night hospital.

Staffing
There are 16 clinical staff employed altogether,

half of them are nurses and there is always someone on duty 24 hours a day, 7 days a week. Since the night hospital is relatively quiet during weekdays and at weekends, most of the staffing cover is in the evenings.

Two psychiatrists share responsibility for providing psychiatric cover and each spend an average of 10-12 hours per week there, mostly in the evenings.

We have two social workers, two psychologists and two recreational workers.

The Programme

The patients are organised into four small "living" groups (8 to 12 per group). Group members share a living room and kitchen. Patients have to participate in the upkeep of the house and cook their own meals twice a week. The small groups provide an opportunity for social interaction over routinely non-threatening issues.

Each group has a nurse appointed to it, who has particular responsibility for the group. This nurse coordinates most group activities and participates with the group in their activities when she is present. Her major role is, on the one hand, to stimulate activities and, on the other, to decrease toxic stresses by creating a non-critical atmosphere (akin to the low Expressed Emotions-concept of Vaughn and Leff, 1976).

There is a weekly meeting in each group, and a large community meeting with all residents and staff each month, where more general problems are discussed.

The daily work activity is most often arranged through the UPC. We do not see this as a mere occupation to provide a structure to the day, but consider this to be important means of enhancing self esteem. Considerable use is made of voluntary placements, much more than the use of either sheltered workshops or open employment.

The social workers have regular contacts with most places where patients are working and quite often visit these places to discuss problems. Three quarters of the patients get individual therapy with one of the psychologists.

Patients are also helped to organise their free time in and outside the centre. In the centre, a bar is open each night and is run entirely by residents and ex-residents.

In 1985, 27 patients were discharged. The mean duration of stay of these patients was 1 year, 7 months. Six patients had to return to a psychiatric hospital, four went home and eight went to live independently, several in apartments near the centre. This group, and most of the patients discharged to sheltered accommodation, continue to use the night hospital as a service centre, where they can come for psychiatric consultation, to continue individual therapy, have a chat with staff and residents or have a meal in the basement restaurant. This arrangement not only helps maintain continuity, but seems to be reinforcing for staff in that they keep in touch with their "successes".

Assessment

In the beginning the Psychiatrische Universiteits Kliniek scale (PUK) (Beyaert, 1966) developed in Utrecht was used to evaluate patient progress. The scale was completed by nurses, based on the observation of patients' behaviour. Gradually we developed our own observation scales and questionnaires to assess patient needs and capacities. In total, 250 topics are scored by simple checklists. In this way, we try to get a comprehensive coverage of the problems we consider relevant for community living. Data are gathered mostly on the basis of direct observation of patient behaviour. This information is collected continuously for regular, periodic reassessment. The data are used to determine specific forms of therapeutic intervention to meet treatment goals. The effects can then be evaluated and treatment strategy adjusted or new forms of intervention planned. In this way therapy is tailored to meet the needs of individual patients.

CONCLUSION

The night hospital in Brussels is part of a comprehensive "support system". Other elements in this system are the University Psychiatric Centre, housing alternatives and a comprehensive after-care programme. Postdischarge employment and therapeutic support, for both the individual and their families, are considered important.

Premature discharge to inadequate community care is often promoted for ideological or economic reasons, but it is not supported by scientific evidence. We think it appropriate to give these patients the opportunity to stay in a therapeutic environment, carefully designed for thorough treatment of their primary illness and for the development of functional skills. The use of highly valued volunteer work to enhance self-esteem and an indirect, "nothing personal", approach to interpersonal interactions are typical for this highly staffed night hospital.

REFERENCES

Beyaert, F.H.L. (1966). PUK Social Adjustment Rating Scales. Stenfert Kroese: Leiden.
Vaughn, C.E. & Leff, J.P. (1976). The influence of family and social factors on the course of psychiatric illness. British Journal of Psychiatry, 129, 125-137.

Chapter Thirty Seven

ESTABLISHING PSYCHIATRIC SERVICES IN RURAL NORWAY

Bodil Solberg

INTRODUCTION

In this paper, I will present my experiences in
helping to establish a psychiatric out-patient
clinic in Voss, a small community in Western Norway.
Some of these experiences have come from local
cultural characters, and some are more general.
Before going to Voss, I worked for many years in a
similar type of psychiatric out-patient clinic in
Oslo. Thus, most of my clinical background was from
the same type of work, but in totally different
surroundings - the big city as opposed to the rural
area.

During the last decade there has been a policy
in Norway to reduce the number of big mental
hospitals and to establish small out-patient clinics
and other local services instead. The ideology
behind this decentralisation of the psychiatric
services is among other things to facilitate the cooperation between the primary health and social
services, and the psychiatric expertise. The big
institutions are expensive, and in many cases their
therapeutic effects can be questioned. Therapeutic
achievement would be greater if one could intervene
and solve problems where and when they arise but,
before the big institutions decrease their activity,
there should be sufficient therapeutic alternatives
in the local district. This is a touchy question,
and causes a conflict of interest politically,
economically and professionally.

In Oslo, with a population of approximately
half a million inhabitants, there are now about ten
public psychiatric out-patient clinics, spread
throughout the city. This means that people are
able to receive psychiatric/psychological help at a

clinic close to their own homes. In the rest of Norway, however, this process of establishing small out-patient clinics just started a few years ago.

In 1982 a plan was made for the reorganisation of the adult psychiatric services in Hordaland county, which included three new psychiatric out-patient clinics, one of which was to be located in Voss. Staffed with a psychiatrist, a psychiatric nurse and a clinical psychologist, Voss out-patient clinic opened in August, 1983. It constituted a new department in the local general hospital, the first new department in the 20 years since this hospital was established. The hospital is responsible for a population of 30,000 people, living in 5 different municipalities.

Types of tasks

In addition to the normal range of psychotherapeutic activities such as psychotherpy, crisis intervention and family work, our out-patient clinic offers consultative advice to primary health and social service professionals such as medical doctors, social workers and nurses. We also give consultative advice to doctors in the other departments of the hospital (medical, surgical and obstetric departments).

Agricultural community

Voss is an agricultural community. The place is surrounded by mountains, the farms are situated high up on steep hills and down in narrow valleys. In the neighbouring communities farms are placed on the fjords, where people mostly earn their living by cultivating fruit. Farming in Western Norway means very hard work and frugality. Local communications are well developed, the journey to the nearest city, Bergen, 100 km away, takes about two hours. Nevertheless, not many years ago, going to the city or the local centre could have meant a day's journey.

Up to 1983 the local health staff and the social workers had to deal with all types of problems themselves. Local doctors in the districts were used to taking care of people with mental disorders without any assistance or interference from a local psychiatric expert. Patients with severe problems were usually sent far away from home, to a clinic or to a mental hospital. The social workers at the local social office had to make final decisions concerning complicated family affairs without any assistance.

So how did these services receive the

psychiatric out-patient clinic and the expertise we represented? We were in many ways actually interfering in a very well established system. There was a tradition, so to speak, of sending away the psychiatric problems or of concealing them with tranquillisers. Since 1983, there has been an ongoing interaction process between the staff at the psychiatric out-patient clinic and the "established" professionals. The process has run from scepticism to serious interest.

Scepticism

Having to accept the advice of the "so-called" experts who in many ways intruded on their territory was certainly difficult and perhaps also threatening for these workers. When we were about to move into the local general hospital, a proposal was put forward, saying that patients and the personnel belonging to the psychiatric clinic should use the back entrance! This was clearly a way of giving voice to the disapproval and resistance during the initial phases. We noticed this in many other ways, for instance, information about our department was left out of the new hospital brochure, planned meetings with us were forgotten, the doctors persisted in sending client referrals directly to the central institution, so bypassing us.

Perhaps the local health authorities had the feeling of being pushed by the central authorities into accepting something new? It was naturally hard for them to agree to sharing the responsibility of a patient. They were anxious too, such as the doctor who said to his patient, "Do you have to go to the psychologist to expose your soul?" People kept a close eye on the new psychiatric out-patient clinic and we often heard questions such as: "Do you really have any work to do?"

More open attitude

In spite of this scepticism, the number of referrals, mainly from doctors, started to increase. We gradually recognised a more open attitude, such as the doctor saying, "I'm almost certain that your headache is not caused by psychological factors at all, but I guess it would not hurt you to have a talk with one of the staff at the psychiatric out-patient clinic."

Serious Interest

As the time went by we noticed a serious interest in our advice and in the therapy we offered. The work load increased because of an increasing number of patients. Planned meetings with co-operating instances were no longer forgotten. The doctors, social workers etc. all had clients and problems they wanted to discuss with us.

Over the last year, we have actually had a very hard time. Everyone has complained about our long waiting list and that it is difficult to reach us on the 'phone. From not wanting to accept us openly, a demand for our services has increased to the point where we have difficulty in meeting this!

THE CLIENTS

Cultural backgrounds
For people living in these communities, the therapy which can be offered at the out-patient clinic represents a new and often unknown way of understanding and handling psychological problems. In this culture, there is no tradition of sharing emotional problems with anyone. Throughout their history, the people have been occupied with their own struggle for existence, often living in very isolated conditions. The attutide was, and still is, "you take care of yourself and your own family, and very seldom get involved in your neighbours' affairs." There is an unwritten law which says that you should not ask anyone directly about anything. This was very contrary to my experiences in urban Oslo. In the Voss-region, people are afraid of rumours, and they do not ask for help until they desperately need it. My impression is, so far, that the frequency of psychosis and psychosomatic conditions is quite high.

In our work we have encountered much doubt about the value of the help we can offer, such as: "the doctor said I should come here, but I'm not sure that it can be of any help." To be aware of and to express emotional problems is very unusual and therefore difficult.

Good reputation
Now, our clients more frequently express their satisfaction about receiving therapy. They find it possible to overcome some of their problems and can hope for a better future. Instead of having to go away for treatment, clients can stay at home; both they and their families appreciate this facility.

THE CLINICAL PSYCHOLOGIST

What is it like being a clinical psychologist in this many-sided setting? In order to succeed in this work - both as a therapist and as a consultant - one has to possess knowledge of the cultural and the local traditions. However, to be able to accept and respect the local norms and rules without being "hooked" into them is a challenge. When doing consultant work in the district, we have experienced the importance of "knowing all the rules of the game".

Intervention techniques

In the central institutions the therapy is often highly elaborate and specialised - and takes a long time. Out in the districts the therapeutic approach often has to be based on more day to day efforts, one has to work with the resources available. An important question is, who are the "key-persons" in the parish who may support our work?

The local health and social staff are also influenced by, and certainly part of, the local culture and way of life. They too are not used to expressing emotional/psychological problems verbally. "How much dare I say?" is a common question.

As a psychologist working alone in the district, one is in a vulnerable position and should have a broad knowledge about psychological processes to be able to keep on going. However, it certainly gives great satisfaction to try to master this multitude of tasks in a professional way.

PROSPECTS

In the field of decentralised psychiatric services there is much work to be done by the clinical psychologist. The medical model is of limited value. In the rural districts as well as in the general hospital, there is a need for an expansion of psychological services. In order to manage this we have to fight against economical and bureaucratic barriers. We should take time to document the effect of our work and make the "power centre" in the city aware of the need throughout the country. Perhaps through our professional organisation, initiatives should be taken to push this work forward.

Chapter Thirty Eight

LIFE WITH DISCHARGED PSYCHIATRIC PATIENTS

Eric Moss

In May 1980 a community based group in
Raanana, Israel, opened a residence for discharged
psychiatric patients, with provision that psychology
and social work students also live in the house.
Three assumptions - that the residents would benefit
from close exposure to healthy, age-similar role
models; that the students would learn about the
problems-of-living of the former patients; and that
data generated would be relevant to further
understanding of families in which one member has
had a psychiatric hospitalisation - were supported
by the results of the project. Students'
experiences could be categorised as follows:

Students' contributions
1. Students were the focal point, helping to
counter residents' withdrawal from the
community;
2. Students' presence lent security;
3. Students were positive role models for such
issues as clothing, housekeeping, etc.

Counselling by the students
Because of communal ideology, much counselling was done in groups:-
1. Crisis intervention
2. Traditional counselling
3. Social skills training

Students' changing perceptions of the ex-patients
Stage 1: Misperceptions about mentally ill
people;
Stage 2: Relief to discover that residents
seem 'normal';
Stage 3: Growing awareness of residents'
disturbance; increased anxiety

Stage 4: Students erect defensive boundaries

Stress levels
1. A high level of stress was experienced at all times
2. Students reported frequent need to leave the house to nurture their mental health
3. This aroused feelings of competition, jealousy and anger in the residents
4. This seemed to be a reflection of social inter-action patterns in the families of the residents

Boundary issues
1. Students felt constantly invaded by the residents' demands
2. The students found it hard to be both on equal footing with the residents and a professional worker
3. The students erected boundaries to defend their healthy selves and their sense of professional identity

Supervision
1. Students expressed an insatiable need for supervision
2. This paralleled residents' insatiable need for students' counselling
3. Supervision tended to concentrate on the students' own dependence/independence struggles with parents, teachers, etc.
4. This paralleled the residents' dependence/independence, struggles with parents, counsellors, etc.

With regard to the third aim of our project, we identified in the family therapy literature a tendency to "blame" families for making one member an in-patient. We find this view - after our experience of living together with discharged patients - unsympathetic to these families. Our work highlights the families' difficulties and suggests the need for rehabilitation workers to establish positive alliance with families.

FURTHER READING

Moss, E. & Davidson, S. (1984). Life with discharged patients: the experience of students living in a community group home. Psychosoc.Rehab.Jnl., Vol VIII, No. 2.

Chapter Thirty Nine

FAMILY THERAPY

Ian Bennun and Kurt Hahlweg

INTRODUCTION

This paper examines two differing approaches
when working with disturbed families. The first
approach focuses on the interaction occurring
within families containing a schizophrenic member
and behavioural family therapy techniques used with
these families in order to prevent relapse. The
second approach outlines the method developed by the
Milan associates in Italy, and the techniques used
in this approach.

Behavioural Family Therapy
There appears to be a reliable association between
family levels of expressed emotion (EE) and relapse
rate in schizophrenia and depressed patients nine
months after discharge. With regard to
schizophrenia, a number of studies (see Leff and
Vaughn, 1985) have shown that the probability of
relapse increases four-fold when the patient returns
to a family marked by high levels of criticism
and/or emotional over-involvement (high EE). In
contrast to the 50-60% relapse rate for a nine
month period among high EE families, the base rate
of relapse in families rated as low on EE is
approximately 15%.
    The treatment of schizophrenia has changed
considerably over the last 30 years. Due to the
widespread use of neuroleptic medication, the mean
length of stay in hospital has decreased
substantially. However, the relapse rate even under
continuous medication is still high, i.e. about 40%
within one year, while in contrast, the relapse rate
under placebo is 70%. In conjunction with the shift
from hospital care to out-patient treatment, the
family has become a major care giver for

schizophrenic patients.

In view of the EE findings showing that about 50% of these families demonstrate high EE and that patients are therefore at risk, several relapse prevention programmes have been developed which include the family in out-patient treatment. To date, four controlled studies have shown that family therapy in conjunction with neuroleptic treatment can be of value in order to prevent relapse (Goldstein et al, 1978; Anderson et al, 1986; Leff et al, 1986; Falloon et al, 1984). The results of the four studies are fairly consistent. In the first year, the relapse rate for patients receiving family therapy is 10%, with a 40% relapse rate for patients on neuroleptic treatment. At two years, the relapse rates are 20% and 70% respectively.

The programme described by Falloon et al (1984) is based on five behavioural principles consisting of the following components:

1. a behavioural analysis of family functioning
2. an educative component about schizophrenia
3. communication skills training
4. problem-solving training
5. behavioural strategies for specific presenting problems

The treatment for the families is home based with the patient on long-term low doses of neuroleptic medication. The therapy is usually intense with weekly sessions for the first three months, bi-weekly sessions for the next three months and monthly meetings thereafter. The main aim of therapy is to enhance the family's ability in solving their problems thereby reducing family stress and tension. Falloon's controlled outcome study showed favourable results for this type of family care when the behavioural treatment was compared with neuroleptic treatment alone. Specifically, there were clinically significant changes in social and family adjustment as well as lower relapse rates. Additional results show that the behaviourally oriented family care was success-ful in bringing about long-lasting changes in family communication. This was especially evident in reducing criticism and disagreement and in increasing problem-solving ability. In general these new family programmes are an important step in providing better care for schizophrenic patients.

The Milan Method

In contrast to the behavioural approach outlined above, the systemic approach emphasises that the family represents a functioning operational system or unit comprising a set of collected inter-related parts or sub-systems. Family functioning is determined by the relationship between members/generations / sub-systems, and as a system is organised in a self regulating homoeostatic way. The homeostatic process determines how the family deals with the external environment and, through its stabilising tendency, facilitates a steady state mode of functioning.

Pallazzoli and her colleagues at the Institute for Family Studies in Milan (Pallazzoli et al, 1977, 1978, 1980, 1985) developed a family systems approach for dealing with family conflict. For the most part the therapist spends the sessions gathering information about the problem. Prior to meeting the family, a hypothesis is generated that accounts for the function of the presenting problem. It may also describe how the family organises itself enabling the maintenance of the problem. The hypothesis is based on information contained in the referral letter, telephone contact with the referrer, telephone contact with the family, and possibly a review of existing case notes.

Originally, Pallazzoli and her colleagues worked as a foursome with the therapist interviewing the family while the remainder of the therapeutic team observed the session from behind a one-way screen. The observers interrupted the session by either offering suggestions or requesting information. Towards the end of the session, the foursome would consult, review the evidence confirming or disconfirming their hypothesis, and then present an intervention or recommendation that would be relayed to the family. This could take the form of a task/ritual for the family to carry out or a prescription as to the team's understanding of the family problem. Alternatively, the family may be given an injunction that covertly communicates a "no change" message while overtly communicating that the family can change and outlines how this may occur. Sessions are convened monthly in order to give the family time to process intervention and also to avoid the likelihood of the therapist becoming part of the family's behavioural solution.

Within this theoretical framework, presenting problems are viewed as family problems with the identified symptomatic member alerting the therapist (and family) to the family systems difficulty. The major original intervention to emerge from the Milan group is the notion that symptoms are positively connoted in as much as the family need a symptomatic member in order to preserve the cohesion of the family unit. This idea is usually linked to the prescription offered to the family at the conclusion of the session.

One useful intervention that this and related approaches use is reframing or redefining the problem with a different focus. By combining reframing and positive connotation, the presenting problem (eg an eating disorder) can be reframed as the family's solution to an as yet unidentified problem. The goal of therapy in the beginning stages of treatment would then be to identify the issue for which the (eating) problem had been presented as the solution. The symptom can be positively connoted on two counts - first, as a solution to an underlying family problem and, second, as an attempt towards family cohesion.

The role of the therapist and the observation team is to review continually the hypothesis describing the function of the symptom following particular questioning of all family members. Through circular questioning, information about differences and relationships within the family is explored. All family members are addressed; thus, the therapist adopts a neutral role by not favouring or being critical of any one member. As distinct from problem-solving therapy, the identified patient is defocused with the major therapeutic emphasis being on systemic change.

A number of research studies are currently underway evaluating this method. One study carried out in England has compared the Milan method with a behavioural problem-solving approach (Bennun, 1986). The results of the study showed that both approaches were equally effective in reducing symptoms, but that the Milan approach was superior in initiating systemic change. Future research extending the study will be directed towards testing the prediction that systemic change obtained during treatment will reduce later relapse.

REFERENCES

Anderson C.M., Reiss, D. & Hogarty, G. (1986). Schizophrenia and the Family: A Practitioner's Guide. Guilford Press: New York.

Bennun, I. (1986). Evaluating family therapy:
a comparison of the Milan and problem-solving
approaches. Journal of Family Therapy, 8,
225-242.

Falloon, I., Boyd, J. & McGill, C. (1984).
Family Care for Schizophrenia : a Problem-
Solving Treatment for Mental Illness.
Guilford Press: New York.

Goldstein, M., Rodnick, E., Evans, J., May, P. &
Steinberg, M. (1978). Drug and family therapy
in the after-care of acute schizophrenics.
Archives of General Psychiatry, 35, 1169-1177.

Leff, J. & Vaughn, C. (1985). Expressed Emotion
in Families. Guilford Press: New York.

Leff, J., Kuipers, L. Berkowitz, R., Eberlein-
Vries, R., & Sturgeon, D. (1986). Controlled
trial of social intervention in the families of
schizophrenic patients. In M. Goldstein,
I. Hand & K. Hahlweg (Eds) Treatment of
Schizophrenia: Family Assessment and
Intervention. Springer: Berlin,
Heidelberg, New York.

Pallazzoli, M., Boscolo, L., Cecchin, G. & Prata, G.
(1977). Family rituals: a powerful tool in
family therapy. Family Process, 16, 445-453.

Pallazzoli, M., Boscolo, L., Cecchin, G. & Prata, G.
(1978). Paradox and Counter-Paradox.
Aaronson: New York.

Pallazzoli, M., Boscolo, L., Cecchin, G. & Prata, G.
(1980). Hypothesising, circularity and
neutrality: three guidelines for the conductor
of the session. Family Process, 19, 3-12.

Pallazzoli, M., Boscolo, L., Cecchin, G. & Prata, G.
(1985). The problem of the sibling as a
referring person. Journal of Marital and
Family Therapy, 11, 21-34.

Chapter Forty

PROMISE OR PERFORMANCE? CLINICAL PSYCHOLOGY'S
CONTRIBUTION TO THE WELL-BEING OF OLDER PEOPLE IN
BRITAIN

Jeffrey Garland

Few clinical psychologists in Britain work
with old people.´ A small segment (an estimated 6%)
of a small profession confronts a massive challenge
from a population in which the 18.5% who are over
retirement age have high morbidity rates.
     In these circumstances it is understandable
that the small band of specialists needs to blow its
own   trumpet   to   raise   morale   and   rally
reinforcements. In the wake of Mumford & Carpenter
(1979),   the   number   of   British   papers   or   texts
promoting the potential of the profession to advance
health care of the elderly has risen rapidly and
nears thirty.
     I   shall discuss   some   of   the   main   points
relating to community care to emerge from this
literature, and shall describe two main constraints
which could make it less probable that the specialty
will be able to realise its undoubted promise in
moving   on   to   effective   long-term   performance.

Our expectations
While   some   writers   resound   with   confidence
verging on euphoria, I suggest that it is important
to have realistic expectations. I agree with the
more guarded view of Davies & Crisp (1985) who
remind   us   that   many   applications   of   clinical
psychology to the concerns of the elderly rest on
slender   evidence.   They   urge   that   a   sounder
empirical base is needed before interventions can be
applied widely in the community, "in those settings
in which the elderly naturally reside - with the
naturally   occurring   resources,   reinforcers   and
agents of change".
     Our colleagues from other disciplines also look
forward to our performance catching up with our
promise. A representative view, from a psycho-

282

geriatrician, is offered by Arie (1985):

> "Clinical psychologists have been slower to move into psychogeriatric work in Britain than in some other countries, perhaps because it features even more thinly in their professional education than in that of other health workers. The nature and level of their training make them potentially rich contributors.... they are highly trained colleagues who have yet to fulfil their potential in this field." (p.1008)

Most of the publications I have referred to give priority to the needs of old people in residential care, out-patient or day care settings. It is not surprising that as specialists who remain largely hospital-based we should concentrate our energies on this population.

Community needs

Among writers who have given special attention to the needs of old people and their carers in the community are Jeffery & Saxby (1984), Garland (1985), and Woods & Britton (1985).

Jeffery & Saxby are in no doubt about what they see as the profession's most important contribution to the well-being of the elderly:

> "What we must do is to disseminate skills and knowledge as widely as possible and so influence the behaviour and attitudes of the caregivers and service-providers. Because of their large numbers, greater contact and potential to control environments, they are much more influential with individual elderly people in need of care than scarce and expensive psychologists can be." (p.263)

Routes to improving care, they suggest, include: facilitating service functioning (enabling networks of formal or informal carers to mesh more smoothly); evaluation of quality of care taking into account expressed needs of old people; applied research, most particularly into effects of both physical and social environment; education and training to promote coping behaviours and well-being in individuals; and influencing the community by offering support to local resources for old people, influencing policies of local and national government, care agencies, contributing to projects designed to extend the contribution that the elderly make to society, and by using the media constructively in attempting to present theories and findings in a popular format.

Such an innovative approach "characterised by a preventive whole population stance with identifiable influences on the community" (Furnish, 1986), cannot but excite the ambitious professional. However, as Bennett (1986) found in an acute geriatric service, this approach is no panacea. It can be partially blocked by limitations of a busy, task-orientated general hospital system, and of a district psychology service offering only minimal sessions on a demand-only basis.

Are we in fact as well-qualified to influence the attitudes and behaviour of caregivers and service-providers as Jeffery & Saxby appear to suggest? Reviewing the state of the art for education and training of these groups I have concluded (Garland, 1985) that we have little substantial achievement to show as yet. We are reaching understanding of the complex needs which our targets have, but are still some way from evolving reliable methods to meet these needs.

In a valuable discussion of community programmes, Twining (1986) reviews interesting but inconclusive findings on support of carers and on use of volunteers. He gives a balanced account of studies of the effects of relocation ("effects may be positive as well as negative ... no justification for a policy of 'stay put at all costs'"). As he concludes: "Careful application of this knowledge could do much to enhance the lives of many older people" (p.335).

The most detailed exploration of intervention in the community is offered by Woods & Britton (1985), who set out to "examine clinical psychology's contribution to facilitating and developing the community's caring resources" (p.285). Much of their attention is given to work with relatives including psychological aspects of information-giving and practical support which interacts with provision of emotional support. They find that even in this comparatively well-researched area, studies which are large-scale or longitudinal or unbiased in sampling are still lacking. Methods for enabling volunteers to develop their psychological skills which can be achieved through collaborat-ng with agencies such as Age Concern are highlighted by these authors with notable insight (pp306-313). Woods and Britton (1985) caution that the effective-ness of primary care projects carried out by clinical psychologists with the elderly awaits thorough evaluation, although there are encouraging indications that such work is both effective for clients and refreshing for the psychologists.

Lack of manpower

From the literature and my knowledge of clinical practice I find that while we indeed merit the promise that Arie sees in us, our capacity to live up to this promise in a consistent way still needs to be established.

I note at least two major constraints on the profession's ability to translate promise into performance. The most immediately apparent of these is lack of manpower.

I have conducted a one-year survey from July, 1985, of all clinical psychology full-time or part-time posts with the elderly advertised in the British Psychological Society's Appointments Memorandum and in the Newsletter of PSIGE, the Division of Clinical Psychology's special interest group.

A total of 85 posts including 67 with Basic/Senior Grade options, and the remainder with Senior/Principal or (rarely) Top Grade establishment. During the year I was notified that in the first category 11 posts were filled (16%) and in the second category 5 (28%). Overall, 19% of posts had been filled. Most difficult to fill were sole posts at Basic/Senior Grade. Where two posts were advertised together, or a post was advertised to augment an established service, prospects for proceeding to appointment appeared enhanced, particularly where one of the posts was graded Principal or above. Where posts had been filled, it frequently was reported that there had been only one applicant, and/or that compromises had to be made on grading or number of sessions to be spent with the elderly. While some unsuccessful respondents intended to keep on trying, approximately half indicated that after several failures they had decided to postpone or cancel further attempts to recruit.

In the light of the above, clinical psychology with old people risks being caught in its own poverty trap. With resources in such short supply the profession is unlikely to make a consistent impact on a national level. Yet without wider and deeper evidence for our effectiveness, the case for increasing resources can be difficult to support. Measures are being taken to increase the output of clinical psychologists wanting to work with old people. Trainee posts with commitment to the specialty have been set up. Requirements for training placements with the elderly have been increased. Trainers are becoming increasingly aware that gerontophobia is a suitable case for treatment, responding to desensitisation beginning with exposure to relatively healthy old people, seen for example in researching compliance in community health surveys.

However, such attempts remain piecemeal and largely uncoordinated, and may need to be linked with long-term changes in the undergraduate education of psychologists. For example, modules on human development concentrate on childhood and, with rare exceptions, give comparatively little positive attention to middle and later life. Some university psychology departments do not have a single academic whose major research or teaching interest is late life (the University of Oxford currently is a case in point). Strengthened teaching on life-span human development could provide a firmer foundation for clinical specialty choice.

Building a knowledge base

A second major limitation on our prospects for developing a more effective contribution to the well-being of old people is that the knowledge base from which we operate is insecure.

Furnish (1986) contrasts the "innovative" approach proposed by Jeffery & Saxby (1984) with a "back to basics" stance advocating maintaining (but with renewed emphasis on careful evaluation) our traditional clinical activities of individual assessment and intervention, together with teaching and research. She points out that an ideal service has been depicted as a combination of these seemingly incompatible approaches, although it may be unclear how such synthesis could be achieved.

There is indeed tension within the specialty, imposed by a two-way tug between the role of applied scientist and that of clinical practitioner (Woods & Britton, 1985). Such potential conflict is not unique to work with the elderly, and the proposed resolution offered by these authors – that we work to become informed practitioners, generating and applying reliable knowledge on which interventions can be based – suggests that such tension could unify rather than divide our practice.

Progress towards a more substantial knowledge

base is being made by PSIGE, which is preparing a critical bibliography and resource list of applied psychology in relation to ageing which will be available this year. This will list not only key papers and texts, but also tables, graphs and other figures, audio and videotapes, workshop programmes, art, fiction and biography, music and films relevant to understanding the ageing process.

A national congress of gerontology is planned by the Institute of Human Ageing at Liverpool, and it is anticipated that local groups throughout the country will be developing presentations relating to distinct areas of this field of study, to lead up to this event.

I would hope that PSIGE makes a positive response to this initiative, either with its own presentation on well-being of old people, or through contributions to local projects.

The proposed congress could be the basis for a more integrated national effort in gerontological research. Wholehearted identification with such a move must benefit our long-term effectiveness.

REFERENCES

Arie, T. (1985). Psychogeriatric Services. In P.C. Brocklehurst (Ed). Textbook of Geriatric Medicine and Gerontology. Churchill Livingstone: Edinburgh.

Bennett, P. (1986). Developing acute geriatric services: some ideas from the front line. Clinical Psychology Forum, 3, 7-10.

Davies, A.D.M. & Crisp, A.G. (1985). The Clinical Psychology of the Elderly. In M.S.J. Pathy (Ed). Principles and Practice of Geriatric Medicine. John Wiley & Sons: Chichester.

Furnish, S. (1986). Provision of clinical psychology services to the elderly. Clinical Psychology Forum, 3, 11-14.

Garland, J. (1985). Adaptation Skills in the Elderly, their Supporters and Carers. In H. Davis & P. Butcher (Eds) Sharing Psychological Skills: Training Non-Psychologists in the Use of Psychological Techniques. British Psychological Society, Leicester.

Jeffery, D. & Saxby (1984). Effective Psychological Care for the Elderly. In I. Hanley & J. Hodge (Eds) Psychological Approaches to the Care of the Elderly. Croom Helm: London.

Mumford, S. & Carpenter, G. (1979). Psychological Services to the Elderly. Bulletin of the

British Psychological Society, Leicester.

Twining, T.C. (1986). The Elderly. In
    H. Koch (Ed), Community Clinical Psychology.
    Croom Helm: London.

Woods, R.T. & Britton P.G. (1985). Clinical
    Psychology with the Elderly.
    Croom Helm: London.

Chapter Forty One

PSYCHOLOGICAL SERVICES FOR THE ELDERLY
IN THE COMMUNITY: EXPERIENCE FROM NORWAY

Reidun Ingebretsen

The realities as regards the number of gero-
psychologists are somewhat less than ideal.
However, during the past decade we have seen a
stronger trend in acknowledging geropsychology in
the universities. Ten out of thirteen researchers
at our twenty nine year old institute (the Norwegian
Institute of Gerontology) are psychologists.
Through experience in Community Psychology
and Mental Health Services we have seen some of the
needs for psychological services for the elderly and
have tried out some working models through various
projects. The tasks are manifold and varied,
including:

1. Diagnosis and clinical intervention for
   different groups of the elderly
2. Consultation to caregivers
3. Milieu treatment and inservice training in
   institutions for the elderly
4. Planning and evaluation of community practice
   and prevention programmes.
   (Ingebretsen, 1984).

These tasks are not easily integrated in one
role model, and psychologists working in the
community may value them differently.

The role of the psychologist in services for the
elderly
Relatively many elderly people have mental health
problems that reduce their quality of life but few
use out-patient psychological services. This is
contrary to the principles of early intervention.
We have a poorly developed system for getting in
touch with elderly people who have mental problems.
They tend to be left alone "in peace" if they don't

289

bother others too much. Home visits are mostly carried out by nurses in the process of evaluating the need for home services, or from social workers from the service centres for the elderly.

One role model for a psychologist is, therefore, to work closely with the care givers and to be an expert on hand and available to solve problems at an early stage as well as to coordinate the intervention. This fits in with the role of a community psychologist.

A psychologist in a psychiatric out-patients' department may also work in close contact with social workers at the service centres for the elderly, home nurses and home helps. In Oslo, Hoyersten (1986) exemplifies one such role model. In addition to counselling the elderly and their families, meetings and consultations with the different helpers make up the greatest part of the job.

It appears, therefore, that there is a need for a coordinator, a person with skills in evaluating systems, interactions and behaviour, and in coping with difficult human relationships. What better person to fill this role than a psychologist?

Life changes and crises - planning, prevention and crisis intervention

Many of the problems the elderly experience are due to crises and transitions that do not necessarily require psychiatric help, but where intervention may be significant for reactions and later adaptation.

From a community point of view, the focus on life changes suggests the usefulness of special prevention programmes before retirement, or re-location etc. This is not, however, always possible. Another strategy is early crisis inter-vention and counselling connected to special stress situations like the death of a spouse or onset of illness.

Courses on preparation for retirement have become more common during the past few years. The spouses often attend together. In courses and group activities we meet elderly people who are not seeking help in a traditional way but information and teaching about ageing and the elderly may be seen as one way to prevent mental health problems and isolation. When the elderly are familiar with the psychologist it is easier to seek help when necessary.

Policies and care for the elderly need to cover a wide range of fields, not just health

care and services. These should include planning
for dwellings, traffic, meeting places for all
generations, transport etc.

Loss of a spouse - counselling services

Above the age of 70, less than 30% of the women are
married, and well over 50% are widows. Of men 70
years and over, 65% are married and about 20% are
widowers (Central Bureau of Statistics, 1982).
   The death of a life partner changes the actual
here and now, deprives the widow or widower of
sharing a common past and upsets their future plans.
In a study in Bergen, elderly widows and widowers
were interviewed by a psychologist, four, eight and
thirteen months after the loss of a spouse. Various
aspects of the grief reactions were explored and
related to coping, social networks, the marriage
relationship and illness and death of the spouse.
Various ways of giving guidance and support to the
bereaved were used when calling on them and
following them up. An "open" counselling service
for the bereaved was announced in the local radio,
news-papers and other agencies in the health care
and social security system (Ingebretsen, 1985).
This combination of research and intervention was
found to be fruitful. On the pretext of making a
contribution to research, many found it easier to
bring up their own problems. The label "help
seeking" is thus avoided and a mutual relationship
consolidated.
   A wide variety of problems was experienced,
emotional, practical, problems of concentration
and keeping the daily routines, acute confusion,
problems with decision-making, set-backs when
something happens for the first time since the
death. For a long time after the loss some need
help to express their feelings while others cry for
years without cognitively coming to terms with the
loss. More than an opportunity to express their
feelings, they need to divert their attention from
the loss and build up alternative activities and
relationships.
   Cognitive restructuring is an important aspect
of the intervention repertoire after a loss. It is
also necessary to keep a family and network
perspective even though the grief seems like the
most lonely experience. For some the most serious
problem is not the grief, but the totally changed
life situation.
   As a consequence of this, a social contact
forum has been established with social gatherings

and group activities, like songs and poetry, keep fit, needlework, theatre visits and dancing.

Health check-ups and rehabilitation

Another way of coming into contact with elderly people potentially in need of help is by offering health check-ups. The health problems of the elderly are in their own right a natural focus of concern for psychologists as well as for physicians.

Typical of the illnesses of the elderly is their chronic nature. It is, however, too easy to limit rehabilitation aims and practices with the elderly, for example in connection with strokes, amputations, fractures and other sudden or gradual reduction in capacity. Specific neuropsychological inquiries as well as training programmes and counselling with the patient, the family and potential helpers about their reactions, hopes and resignation regarding future adaptation may be relevant.

Psychological services to nursing homes and residential homes

I cannot point to a well founded role for psychologists in Norwegian institutions for the elderly. Most of the experience is drawn from research projects or more limited contact through in-service training or consultation, but also from a psychologist in full-time employment in a nursing home.

From a project in a combined nursing and residential home, I drew the conclusion that the tasks for a psychologist in an institution for the elderly may include: individual diagnosis and therapy, group work and milieu treatment, counselling for the relatives, consultation and in-service training for the staff, evaluation of the personal and social resources of each elderly person applying for admission to the institution and preparations for relocation.

This role calls for a realistic, but still optimistic attitude - a rather patient impatience, the ability to listen to the points of view of residents and staff members together and the motivation to get things done in spite of long-lasting routines and resignation. If things are "swinging", keep a role as the "resource person in the background" rather than the "fixer in the front line", but be ready for a fight when necessary.

Conclusion

The tasks for psychologists in this field are numerous. We are only at the beginning of the process of "shaking hands" with these challenges, which call for enthusiasm in developing our knowledge and clinical tools.

To help improve the situation of the elderly, the mental health service system has to become more easily available, located closer to the clients. Close co-operation with primary helpers is crucial both for referrals and consultation.

REFERENCES

Central Bureau of Statistics of Norway (1982). Population by Age and Marital status.

Hoyersten, J. (1986). Verbal Communication. Oslo.

Ingebretsen, R. (1984). Eldres psyckologi-virkelighetsforankrede fremtidsvisjoner. In P.A. Holter, S. Magnussen & S. Sandsberg (Eds), Norsk psykologi i 50 ar. Norsk psykologforening, 1934-1984. pp 175-199. Universitets-forlaget: Oslo.

Ingebretsen, R. (1985). Jeg har level ved din side. Oslo: Norwegian Institute of Gerontology, Report 8/1985.

Chapter Forty Two

WORKING WITH VOLUNTEERS: WHAT CAN THIS ACHIEVE?

Sally Furnish

It has been argued that clinical psychology cannot afford to be concerned solely with the assessment and treatment of individuals (Hawks, 1981). Nowhere is this more apparent than in work with the elderly; the number of psychologists for the post-retirement population is even more in-auspicious than for other client groups. It is also emerging that the traditional psychological role models for intervention with older people have relied too heavily on mainstream academic clinical psychology, leading to psychologists working at the wrong level of clinical practice (Jeffery & Saxby, 1984). Organisational change, policy and planning should have greater emphasis, and not just within the confines of the National Health Service. For example, it may be more desirable for older clients to seek help from agencies outside the NHS to avoid medicalising life stresses such as adaptation to loss, retirement, poor health, reduced social circumstances and confronting death (Furnish, 1986). The ultimate aim of 'giving psychology away' is overall population screening and a more preventive approach for practitioners.

Volunteers are frequently cited as an additional source of informal community support and a necessary supplement to statutory services by, among others, the Government, Health Advisory Service, and critics of domiciliary and after-care facilities. In fact, only a small proportion of elderly people living at home receive a volunteer visitor, the highest estimate in community surveys in Great Britain being 4% to 5% (Bond & Carstairs, 1982). An over-reliance on informal community carers leads to patchy care provision, non-preventive health policies and inefficient monitoring of services.

Working with Volunteers: What Can This Achieve?

Unfortunately, the role of psychologists working with volunteers and voluntary organisations has received little attention. Ryder (1986) refers to the choice between working with a professional team or a voluntary group in the addiction field. Our small numbers mean that such decisions are being taken, whether or not they are made explicit. In care of the elderly we may offer a service to a community psycho-geriatric nursing team or a local Alzheimer's Disease Society, to a Social Services day centre or one run by Age Concern. Ideally, these decisions should be made on the basis of how quickly and appropriately client needs can be met rather than the expectations of other staff or the constraints imposed by the job description. There may be less bureaucracy to overcome with volunteer agencies (Feldman, 1981).

The rationale for choosing to work with volunteer groups rather than elsewhere deserves careful consideration. Psychologists should be selective, not lending credibility to woefully inadequate schemes, and using similar methods of intervention and constructive criticism as in other care systems. Ryder (1986) cautions against those voluntary organisations which display an unscientific approach to helping problems. Some self-help groups are in danger of advising newcomers from the personal experience of existing members alone. Here, modelling of group counselling methods might be an appropriate role for a psychologist. Hit-and-run teaching sessions are as unlikely to be effective as elsewhere (Jeffery & Saxby, 1984) and a preferred method would be guided practice and ongoing supervision, as used by several branches of CRUSE, the voluntary organisation for bereavement counselling.

In order to help elderly clients find more adaptive solutions to problems, any service should seek, at the very least, not to undermine the existing care network of the client. The delicate balance between over and under-provision is too often neglected when services move in or clients are whisked off to new placements. My own experience of the Crossroads Care Attendant Scheme is that it can be an acceptable way of providing extra practical support to carers without usurping their role. Informal carers are the most reliable source of essential support needing frequent, personal contacts. In the absence of relatives to perform this function, the East Kent Home Care Scheme (Challis & Davies, 1980) used the frequent visits of volunteers, supervised closely by social workers, to maintain elderly people in their own homes who would otherwise need admission to residential care. However, such schemes are far from widely available, are dependent on the efforts of a few innovative field workers, and, hardest of all, require a restructuring of the system of social service provision, to give social workers direct access to sufficient funds and immediate alternative care in a crisis.

The political and ethical implications of professionals offering support to the voluntary sector have been more thoroughly examined in the social work and social studies literature (e.g. Darvill & Munday, 1984). One of the most dangerous routes social work could take is exemplified by the Barclay Report (1982), which recommended a new role of 'community social worker' acting as a gatekeeper of informal and voluntary resources. The report went on:

> "Public services to the needy will be limited to the rescue of casualties who fall through the net of family and community self-help and whatever charitable bodies supply ..."

This is advocating a crisis-intervention, non-preventive stance which would seriously jeopardise the welfare of already vulnerable sections of the population like the elderly. Proclaiming itself as the 'Safety Net' approach, the Barclay Report stands in direct opposition to the aim of reinforcing the existing support system, since it proposes that help should be given only when the care network has disintegrated. It also undervalues staff in all services who are left to pick up the pieces, with the attendant problems of staff recruitment, low morale, high absenteeism, and increasingly poor quality care.

Darvill & Munday (1984) present an alternative approach, the 'Welfare State/Collaborative' model, which emphasises a partnership between statutory, voluntary and self-help groups with the state retaining control and responsibility. The probation service is quoted as having a long tradition of close collaboration with voluntary organisations in providing good quality prison after-care. Ultimate state control could detract from the flexibility and autonomy permitting agencies such as MIND to pioneer new developments. Pressure groups presumably need freedom to make their maximum contribution. Close collaboration can also lead to a situation where, for example in running support groups, neither professionals nor volunteers wish to disrupt arrangements with the other by taking the initiative for change so that the service fails to grow.

If volunteers do have a place in the provision of care to the elderly, their role and limitations can only be established by thorough investigations. Sadly, such research is poorly funded and seldom encouraged. A review of studies on volunteer visiting and hospital discharge schemes (Furnish, 1984) demonstrated the inadequacy of most research on these topics. Crucial steps in the process of data-collection were omitted, and the descriptive methods used were unclear, inconsistent or open to bias. Client requirements were often assessed incompletely, and seldom were the clients themselves consulted about the schemes. Referring agencies used schemes more as a last resort than as an additional source of support.

Insufficient attention has been paid to the volunteer's role in a particular scheme, despite the implications for recruitment and training of volunteers and for the publicity and objectives of the scheme (Goldberg & Connelly, 1981). In practice, the volunteer may attempt to fulfil one or both of a befriending role or a task-orientated function, although this duality is not usually made explicit. In the care of the elderly, few volunteers are trained in counselling techniques, although their role is often assumed to encompass this complex activity. There are frequent mismatches between client needs and volunteer activities, leading to misunderstandings and lack of preparation of volunteers. In a study of an Age Concern hospital discharge scheme, volunteers appeared to underestimate the importance of their role in listening and talking to clients, preferring to emphasise the practical tasks they performed, whereas all clients mentioned socialisation as one of the main activities carried out during the volunteers' visits (Furnish, 1984). It may not always be appropriate for volunteers to perform practical tasks for their clients, e.g. when the individual needs to regain coping skills.

One of the most useful investigations of a volunteer scheme was conducted by Power et al (1983). The authors questioned residents and staff of elderly people's homes and members of the general public about what volunteers might do to help residents in the Local Authority homes. Opinions were similar in all three groups; residents, staff and public alike believed that a friendly, individual contact could be made and gradually extended to taking residents out. A group of residents was studied before and after receiving a volunteer and compared to a control group. No significant differences were found in residents' CAPE scores and there was a non-significant trend on a life satisfaction index showing a positive effect for residents receiving volunteers. However, spontaneous comments from residents suggested that these measures were not sensitive enough to the positive effect of friendship and concern, and a later study showed that elderly residents visited by volunteers reported experiencing significantly less loneliness and were getting out more than controls. This illustrates the importance of consulting clients themselves.

Outcome studies would appear not to be the best means of evaluating volunteer schemes (Goldberg & Connelly, 1981), and in fact there has been little demonstration of objective changes in clients after contact with professionals. With appropriate supervision and training, the evidence suggests that paraprofessionals are at least as effective, if not more, than workers with a full professional mental health background. If clinical psychologists wish to help elderly people with minimum disruption to their existing coping skills and everyday lives, volunteers may be a potential and as yet largely untapped source of manpower to this end.

REFERENCES

Barclay Report (1982). Social Workers - Their Role and Tasks. Bedford Square Press: London.

Bond, J. & Carstairs, V. (1982). Services for the Elderly. Scottish Home and Health Department: HMSO.

Challis, D. & Davies, B. (1980). A new approach to community care for the elderly. British Journal of Social Work, 10, 1-18.

Darvill, G. & Munday, B. (1984). Volunteers in the Personal Social Services. Tavistock: London.

Feldman, M.P. (1981). The Employment of Clinical Psychologists: Present and Future. In I. McPherson & A. Sutton (Eds) Reconstructing Psychological Practice. Croom Helm: London.

Furnish, S.A. (1984).   Investigation of an Age
    Concern Hospital Discharge Scheme.
    Unpublished dissertation: British
    Psychological Society.
Furnish, S.A. (1986).   Provision of clinical
    psychology services to the elderly:
    where to begin?   Clinical Psychology Forum,
    3, 11-14.
Goldberg, E.M. & Connelly, N. (1981).   Voluntary
    Action.   In E.M. Goldberg & N. Connelly (Eds)
    The Effectiveness of Social Care for the
    Elderly.   Heinemann: London.
Hawks, D. (1981).   The Dilemma of Clinical Practice
    - Surviving as a Clinical Psychologist.   In
    I. McPherson & A. Sutton (Eds) Reconstructing
    Psychological Practice.   Croom Helm: London.
Jeffery, D. & Saxby, P. (1984).   Effective
    Psychological Care for the Elderly.   In I.
    Hanley & J. Hodge (Eds) Psychological
    Approaches to the Care of the Elderly.
    Croom Helm: Beckenham.
Power, M., Clough, R., Gibson, P. & Kelly, S.
    (1983).   Helping Lively Minds: Volunteer
    Support to Residential Homes.   Research Report,
    Social Care Research Team: University of
    Bristol.
Ryder, D. (1986).   'Giving Psychology Away':
    two models from the addiction field.
    Clinical Psychology Forum, 1, 4-7.

Chapter Forty Three

DEMENTIA AND CARE IN THE COMMUNITY. EXPERIENCES
FROM CLINICAL PSYCHOLOGICAL WORK IN NORWAY

Per K. Haugen

INTRODUCTION

Dementia in old age occurs most frequently in
the oldest age-groups. In the coming years we must
expect an increase in the number of these patients,
since relatively speaking, the population increase
will be greatest in the group over 80 years of age.
A rough estimate shows that in Norway there will be
an increase in the numbers of people with dementia
with approximately 40% to 50% from 1985 to 2000.
    In Norway very little attention has been given
to diagnostic problems and the potential treatment
for patients with memory problems. There is also a
lack of knowledge of the family situation of people
with dementia. This was the background for a
research project at the Norwegian Institute of
Gerontology.
    The study was aimed at developing methods for
assessment of dementia, to include evaluating
changes in mental capacity over time, methods for
discrimination between dementia and functional
disorders and methods used in connection with
therapeutic measures for people with dementia.

METHOD

    A psychological battery of tests was given to
161 persons aged 75 years, living in Oslo. The
clients were also given somatic, psychiatric and
neurological examinations which included
computerised cerebral tomography. Fifty-nine of
those interviewed had a normal mental capacity,
while 102 had memory and disorientation problems.
Of these 102, 60 were diagnosed as suffering from
dementia of Alzheimer's type (DAT), 23 had multi-
infarct dementia (MID) or a combination of DAT and

MID. Thirteen had organic brain disorders other than DAT and MID, two were diagnosed as having confusion as a result of somatic illness and four had a psychiatric illness.

The battery of tests included the Mini Mental State (MMS), tests from Geriatric Mental Status Examination (GMS), Wechsler's Adult Intelligence Scale, the Revised Kendrick Battery and the Revised Visual Retention Test (Benton).

RESULTS

The results from the study showed that psychological testing is an important tool in differentiating people suffering from dementia from the normal group. Psychological testing was also shown to be of great value in diagnosing other illnesses that might result in memory problems not caused by dementia. In our study psychological testing was particularly important in relation to old people with depression, confusion and aphasia/apraxia and brain disorders other than DAT and MID.

We found that the greatest diagnostic problem was the differentiation between dementia and aphasia/apraxia, confusion and pseudo-dementia. Aphasic clients are often difficult to detect from patients with dementia because language difficulties are also important symptoms in dementia. In psychological testing, however, differences between the two groups occur, for instance, in naming and word order.

Symptoms of depression may also resemble symptoms in dementia. In psychological testing, assessment of concentration, consciousness, memory and language are of special importance. Symptoms in relation to confusion may also resemble symptoms in dementia, both when somatic illness and when psycho-social conditions are the cause of the mental problems.

It is also important to get a picture of preserved functions which may be useful in practical management of the clients. The results of the psychological assessment are also of importance when deciding measures for treatment and in giving advice to families and personnel facing the difficult behaviour of the clients.

DISCUSSION

Our study has shown that "screening-tests" for

dementia are useful tools as a starting point in testing. However, as diagnostic tools, screening-tests have a very limited value. Mini Mental State (MMS) is the most frequently used screening-test for dementia in Norway and other countries. The MMS can give an indication whether a patient has a reduced mental capacity or not, but it gives little information about the cause of this. MMS gives, for instance, no information as to whether the patient has an early dementia or depression.

In psychological testing of dementia it is necessary to do a comprehensive investigation of psychological variables such as attention, concentration, orientation, memory, language, visuo-spatial ability and abstraction. Psychological tests are not standardised for the oldest age-groups. For instance, testing an elderly person of 80 years of age represents quite a different situation from testing a client of 65. Our study shows that evaluation of mental capacity of old people based on quantitative data alone can indeed give a very wrong picture. Observation of how the client is functioning in the test situation and the way problems are solved is important in evaluation of psychological functioning.

In our research project we have also looked at the families taking care of elderly demented relatives living at home. Twenty-nine families were interviewed. One conclusion from this study is that families are getting little support from the public health service in solving their emotional problems in relation to the elderly with dementia. It is necessary that family members who are taking care of people with dementia have access to psychological consultation.

Our study has clearly shown the need for psychological services in connection with dementia in diagnostic work and in consultation both with families and staff members in public health service. In Norway such psychological services are seldom available. It is important to develop models of community health services where psychologists also have the opportunity to work with these groups of people.

As a result of our study and similar studies in Norway and Sweden, we are now opening the first gerontopsychiatric unit in Norway for people with confusion and memory problems where the cause is unclear. The unit will have an interdisciplinary staff which includes two psychologists. The unit is

in the County of Vestfold, to the southwest of
Oslo and will serve a population of 200,000 people.
The work at the unit will be concentrated on
diagnostic investigation. It will also give
consultation to families and staff in the community
health service. The unit has 14 beds, and
can, if further investigations are necessary,
offer accommodation for four to six weeks.

FURTHER READING

Glorstad, S. (Ed) (1986). Informasjon om
    Gerontopsykistrisk untreningsavdeling.
    Granli Senter: Sem.

Chapter Forty Four

RESIDENTIAL CARE AND QUALITY OF LIFE FOR PEOPLE WITH
DEMENTIA
Robert T. Woods and Per K. Haugen

Introduction

This theme is relevant for at least three
reasons:

  a. Despite 'Community Care', there are and will
     continue to be many residential facilities for
     people with dementia.
  b. Psychological interventions are often overwhel-
     med by the influence of institutional factors.
  c. In the UK many opportunities are arising to
     create a better future, with finance becoming
     available from the closure of large mental
     hospitals. The mistakes of the past must not
     be repeated!

Institutions - as they are and as they should be

Townsend (1962) identified a number of features
associated with institutional living for elderly
people at that time. Indeed, he recommended the
gradual closure of all such institutions! Recent
research (reviewed by Woods & Britton, 1985, chapter
9) demonstrates the continued relevance of such
concerns. Lack of activity continues to be a
predominant feature; residents continue to have
little in the way of meaningful social interaction;
choices continue to be denied; not enough is done
to help the person maintain their sense of identity;
homes remain geographically and/or functionally
isolated from the person's family and friends and
the wider community. Although the institution
cannot bear the whole responsibility for these
features, too often the institution maintains the
person's loss of activity, of conversation, of
identity and so on.

Residential Care for People with Dementia

Although it may be hard to imagine an 'ideal' institution, efforts to improve quality of life should be based on an explicit set of values and principles. The principles of normalisation are a useful starting point. For the person with dementia, their life-time of experiences, interests, attitudes and opinions can help guide those involved to a better understanding of experiences that would be valued by that particular individual. A King's Fund (1986) paper 'Living well into old age' develops these ideas further, basing its discussion around the following key principles:

1. People with dementia have the same human value as any one else, irrespective of their degree of disability or dependence.
2. People with dementia have the same varied human needs as anyone else.
3. People with dementia have the same rights as other citizens.
4. Every person with dementia is an individual.
5. People with dementia have the right to forms of support which don't exploit family and friends.

Here we consider two aspects; the individualisation of care (principle 4) and the provision of care for the person with dementia in the mainstream of society (an important implication of principle 2). So community care is seen not as care by the community or even care in the community, but being cared for as a member of the community. This involves as a starting point much more integration of residential care with the community.

Individualisation of care

In the endeavour to improve the quality of life it is important to maintain a perspective on how the individual is affected by the home. Their control over their environment must be safeguarded, so that, for example, in an effort to increase activity levels patients are not coerced into activity! The aim must be to increase opportunities, choices and scope for mastery, not to enforce conformity. The person with dementia needs an environment geared to their individual needs and resources in view of their reduced adaptability.

It is instructive to consider the situation of a particular elderly person with dementia about to enter a residential unit. What questions would we want to ask to ensure the person's individuality, dignity and rights were safe-guarded? The questions might well depend on our perspective on the situation.

If we were a member of a visiting service evaluation team we might ask about the choices available, the amount of structure in the home and the opportunities for continued interests and contact with family. Would regular reviews of progress be held (involving the family), and would care be planned on an individualised basis? How would the home balance the person's rights against the possible risks, for example in relation to the danger of falls if free mobility is allowed?

From the point of view of the person's daughter, we might be concerned about having a particular person in the home to contact and we would want to know what the other residents would be like. Perhaps we would also be keen that our father should have some privacy and that his special needs be catered for.

If we were the patient our first question might be more poignant. 'Can I go home again if it doesn't work out?' We would probably be concerned regarding privacy and the safety of our possessions, freedom to continue our interests, and the arrangements for regular contact with our family. Would staff take the time and trouble to understand our efforts to communicate? Will they help us non-judgementally with our self-care?

Looking at the institution through the eyes of individual residents is a powerful way of getting to grips with the many difficult issues relating to quality of life, and can be recommended as an exercise for all staff involved in the provision of care.

Integration of residential care with the community

How could a residential home be integrated with the community in practice? The scale of provision is a limiting factor - the smaller the unit, the easier integration will be. In an existing larger unit having attractive facilities in the home for community use (eg a bar, resource centre, rooms for meetings etc.) might help bring people in. The siting of the home is another vital factor, so that it is accessible and in the area from which the residents have come.

Changing the institution

It is possible then to describe some of the qualities that residential facilities for people with dementia should have in the future. It is encouraging that individual differences between institutions can be identified, and these can help in the identification of targets for change. But how can change be brought about in the existing homes and hospitals? Often it seems that psychological interventions have little impact compared with the influence of institutional factors.

For example, in a study reported in detail by Haugen (1985), two psychiatric nursing homes were the setting for a comparison of two types of psychological intervention involving group therapy and in-service staff training respectively. The results were apparently clear-cut. Positive changes in both staff and patients occurred in the home where group therapy was implemented, whereas in the home where staff had received additional training regarding dementia and its management hardly any changes were apparent in staff or patients. Group therapy is clearly the way forward!

However, closer analysis suggested it was not simply the interventions that differed between the homes. Some of the factors identified are relevant to many settings and are listed here:-

1. The relative number of staff, the amount of time available for interaction with patients and the other duties (such as domestic chores) that are expected of them are limiting factors in bringing about an individualised approach.
2. The layout of the ward or home is also significant; in this case a large single ward was compared with a home divided into small units, where it proved much easier for staff and patients to get to know each other.
3. The provision of time in staff rotas for meetings between staff to ensure consistent approaches and facilitate good staff communication is important.
4. The support and interest of senior staff is important to encourage and reinforce the efforts of staff on the ward (it is not sufficient on its own!).
5. The relevance of the intervention to the home or ward, in relation to previous developments, should be considered. For instance, in one of

the homes extending the existing OT programme would have enabled the intervention to build on existing resources and to have been less of a major change in direction for the home and so more readily accommodated. In contrast, the group therapy intervention helped to consolidate and extend what had already been achieved in the other home.

The following suggestions for encouraging change emerged from the project.

1. Staff need help to avoid 'burn-out' in their work, to find reinforcement in what can be a difficult and demanding job. Often the results achieved seem rather small, the same problems and the same questions occur repeatedly.
2. A small intervention (like the group therapy in this project) may become a catalyst for other changes, under the right conditions.
3. Generalised training (eg concerning the nature of dementia) may not be as helpful as training based on the staff's own practice. Training is better centred on for example a care-plan for a particular resident with whom the member of staff is working.
4. If a professional (eg a psychologist) from outside the institution is involved in the intervention, then there must be full consultation with staff and the joint responsibility of staff with the professional must be emphasised beforehand. Arrangements for the handover of responsibility and the withdrawal of the professional, perhaps to an advisory role, need to be made well in advance.
5. Staff should be encouraged to systematically obtain information about the person's earlier life and interests. This gives them an opportunity to see the person 'behind the diagnosis'. Previously unnoticed qualities and characteristics - their relationships, their humour, their outlook on life - become evident. New ideas emerge for working with the individual patient and sometimes behaviour which seems meaningless can be better understood viewed through the person's past.
6. Changes in function in people with dementia will be small in view of the nature of the disorder. Systematic record keeping regarding the person's functional capacity is valuable in giving staff feed-back on their work. It also

helps focus attention on what the individual patient may, or may not, be able to do and helps highlight the differing perceptions of different staff members.

Developing good quality residential care for people with dementia is not an easy task. With the development of new facilities and with increasing pressure on existing residential facilites it is a vital task, in which clinical psychologists must play their part, despite the attractions of working 'in the community'.

REFERENCES

Haugen, P.K. (1985). Dementia in old age – treatment approaches. Norsk gerontologisk institutt, Report 5/85, Oslo.
King's Fund (1986). Living well into old age – applying principles of good practice to services for people with dementia. King's Fund, London.
Townsend, P. (1962). The Last Refuge. Routledge & Kegan Paul: London.
Woods, R.T. & Britton, P.G. (1985). Clinical Psychology with the Elderly. Croom Helm: London.

Chapter Forty Five

CLINICAL PSYCHOLOGY AND THE CARE OF THE
NEUROLOGICALLY IMPAIRED

Barbara Wilson

This paper is concerned with people whose
physical handicap results from neurological
dysfunction. Besides their physical impairments
these people are likely to experience cognitive,
emotional and behavioural disorders which in many
cases are more handicapping than their motor
problems. Return to the community and continuing
independence from institutional care may depend on
the successful reduction and management of these
problems. Clinical psychologists have an important
role to play in helping physically handicapped
people, their relatives and their therapists to cope
with and possibly reduce the range of problems
associated with neurological dysfunction. It is
also possible in some cases for the psychologist to
carry out effective treatment of the motor and
sensory impairments.

The Patients

Among the common neurological conditions which
give rise to physical handicap are severe head
injury, cerebral vascular accidents (strokes),
degenerative diseases such as Parkinson's disease
and multiple sclerosis, trauma to the spinal cord
and cerebral or spinal tumours. The diagnosis will
determine, to some extent, the nature of the
problems and the type of treatment required. For
example, a severe head injury is likely to lead to a
combination of physical, cognitive and behavioural
disorders associated with diffuse brain damage. A
stroke, on the other hand, is likely to cause less
diffuse but more specific cognitive difficulties
such as dysphasia or unilateral neglect.

The Care of the Neurologically Impaired

Interdisciplinary Collaboration

There are several ways in which clinical psychologists can work with people who have physical handicaps. These range from giving information about the disease or condition to modifying the attitudes of certain sections of society. The main purpose of this paper, however, is to describe how clinical psychologists can work with other therapists (particularly physiotherapists, occupational therapists and speech therapists) to enable the physically handicapped to improve their functioning in the community. Such collaborative work is achieved through interdisciplinary treatment programmes which aim to tackle motor, sensory, cognitive, emotional and behavioural disorders.

ASSESSMENTS

In every treatment programme detailed neuropsychological and behavioural assessments are required to determine whether each problem is:

a. a direct result of neurological dysfunction (e.g. unilateral neglect);
b. a learned behaviour indirectly related to the neurological deficit (e.g. screaming for attention after a severe head injury);
c. unrelated to the neurological disorder (e.g. fear of the hydrotherapy pool in someone who has always been afraid of water).

Designing Treatment Programmes

Following assessments, clinical psychologists can combine their skills with the skills of other therapists in order to design an appropriate treatment regime. Motor difficulties, for example, are usually considered to be the province of physiotherapists, and psychologists would not have the skills to deal with muscles and joints, flexor and extensor patterns, spasticity or increased tone. However, psychologists do know how to improve learning and how to evaluate procedures they have put into operation. In particular, single case experimental designs help us to determine whether improvement can be explained by natural recovery or whether intervention has been responsible. Motor problems are likely to be a direct result of the neurological damage, although in some cases failure to improve may be maintained by behavioural consequences such as attention or rest following disruptive behaviour. In other cases previous physical handicap, such as rheumatoid arthritis, may be superimposed upon a head injury or stroke.

Sensory problems, including visual handicap and tactile sensory loss, are common after many neurological conditions. Again, some individuals may exaggerate the handicap in order to obtain certain kinds of positive reinforcement. Others may have sensory problems predating their neurological damage.

Cognitive deficits may also be a direct consequence of the neurological insult, learned after it, or predating it. The same is true of emotional and behavioural disorders. The treatment selected will depend, in each case, on the analysis of the problem and the extent of additional handicaps. However, a whole range of treatment approaches have been used successfully in the rehabilitation of the physically handicapped, including biofeedback, shaping, desensitisation, reality orientation, modelling, chaining and portage programmes. (For a further discussion of these see Wilson and Staples (1987)).

Clinical Examples

The following examples illustrate interdisciplinary treatment programmes for physically handicapped people. They were designed to help people return to the community and/or maintain independence from institutional care.

Case One: <u>Treatment of a motor problem</u>. The patient in this case was a young woman who sustained severe brain damage resulting from anoxia. She was left with several problems including very pronounced apraxia. Apraxia is a term which refers to a variety of movement disorders which cannot be explained by paralysis, weakness or poor comprehension. Thus the young woman was able to walk, talk and understand language. She had a full range of movements but she was unable to plan or coordinate her movements. The degree of apraxia was so acute that she could not feed or dress herself. When attempting to put on her coat, for example, she would not know how to begin. Sometimes she gripped the coat fiercely and pulled inappropriately. Sometimes she leaned right over to put her arm in the armhole but missed and almost touched the ground.

A programme was designed to help her become more independent. Each task was broken down into a series of steps and a system of graded assistance instituted for each step. She learned within a few days to drink from a cup unaided and to pull her chair towards and under the table. At a later date she learned to dress and undress herself, and to make herself coffee, carrying out all the steps alone apart from pouring the boiling water (see Wilson, in press, for a description of the treatment procedure).

Case Two: <u>Treatment of a sensory problem</u>. This treatment was designed for a man whith spinal injuries and a partial paraplegia. His sensation was impaired and he had no feeling at all in his buttocks. Because of this, together with the fact that he spent long periods seated in a wheelchair and refused to lift himself often enough, he developed a sacral pressure sore. His physiotherapist, nurses and doctors made considerable efforts to persuade him to cooperate with the recommended skin care regime but were unsuccessful. When a second sore started to develop he was referred to clinical psychology and a treatment programme was designed by the psychologist which involved the cooperation of the physiotherapist, occupational therapist and nurse.

A feedback procedure was adopted. As a first step the team had a piece of electronic equipment made which consisted of a sensor pad to place beneath the cushion of the man's wheelchair and a box containing a device to count the number of lifts made (see Carr and Wilson, 1983). A lift was recorded when the man's buttocks left the seat of the wheelchair for four seconds. One lift every ten minutes was considered to be the minimum number of lifts required for good skin care. Every time the man's buttocks left the seat for at least four seconds the counter in the box registered a lift.

Baselines were taken in four different settings to see how frequently the man was lifting prior to the introduction of treatment. He made a total of two lifts in eight baseline sessions. A multiple baseline across settings design was employed, the equipment being introduced in one setting at a time. The equipment was first used during the man's daily woodwork sessions. He was shown the equipment and told that it would count the number of lifts made so that he would know if he was lifting enough. At the end of the session he was told how many lifts he had made. The following week the equipment was used in the dining room during the lunch break in addition to the woodwork sessions. It was then used during coffee breaks and finally it was used on the ward.

The introduction of the treatment was staggered to see whether increased lifting was due to treatment or to some other factor. Increased lifting was directly related to the introduction of the electronic equipment. He showed no increased lifting until the equipment was used. When it was in place his lifting increased dramatically and, even more importantly, his sores started healing.

Case Three: <u>Treatment of an emotional problem.</u>
This example involves a young woman who was injured in a road accident when she sustained a severe head injury and was unconscious for three months. She was very handicapped physically and needed considerable treatment from the physiotherapy department to reduce contractures and prevent further contractures and painful bony growths developing. Unfortunately, because of the pain and distress involved she beacame very frightened of her physiotherapy sessions and exercises. Without appropriate treatment it would have been almost impossible for her family to have her home again as they would be unable to transfer her from her wheelchair to the toilet or her bed or into the car.

The young woman's physiotherapist and clinical psychologist decided to tackle the case in the following way. Firstly, observations were made of the young woman's behaviour to see (i) which particular exercises she feared most and (ii) how long she spent at each exercise before giving up, crying and becoming panic stricken. Knowledge was also needed of any exercise she liked doing.

Of the exercises she found most frightening, her physiotherapist selected three for treatment, namely, long sitting (sitting with one's legs straight out in front), trunk rotation and bridging (moving oneself forward rather like a caterpillar). The young woman spent between one and two minutes on each exercise before becoming agitated and fearful. There was, however, one exercise she enjoyed - head balancing - presumably because she found this easy and painless.

A multiple baseline across behaviours design was employed. In this design one problem at a time is tackled and the introduction of treatment is staggered to tease out treatment effects from natural recovery or non-treatment factors. Long sitting was tackled in the first week, trunk rotation was added in the second week and bridging added in the third week. When treatment began the young woman was told how long she had spent on that exercise the day before; encouraged to spend a little longer than the previous time; given verbal and visual feedback (in the form of a chart); and allowed to spend some time doing head balancing exercises if she 'beat her record'. This procedure was used initially only for long sitting although baselines were taken on the other disliked exercises. She steadily improved her tolerance for long sitting each day but spent no longer on the untreated exercises than she had in the pre-treatment period. The following week she was encouraged to increase the time spent on trunk rotation exercises and the same steps were followed. Again she increased steadily the length of time spent on this exercise once feedback and reinforcement (in the form of head balancing exercises) were introduced. Finally, the same treatment was used for bridging and in this area too her tolerance increased. Furthermore, the physiotherapist was able to introduce more intensive and active therapy, suggesting improvements as far as physical problems were concerned, and the pain distress decreased.

All three patients described above returned home and have remained free from institutional care. Had space permitted, other examples of successful interventions by clinical pyschologists could have been cited in support of the main premise of this paper, which argues that there are many ways in which clinical psychologists can help people whose physical handicap results from neurological impairment. Furthermore, the nature of this help is such that the subsequent improvements to everyday living can enable a person to leave institutional care and return to the community. Treatment programmes designed with this aim in mind are likely to be most effective when psychologists work closely with other rehabilitation therapists.

REFERENCES

Carr, S. & Wilson, B.A. (1983). Promotion of pressure relief exercising in a spinal injury patient: multiple baseline across settings design. Behavioural Psychotherapy, 11, 329-366.

Wilson, B.A. (1987). Rehabilitation of Memory.
    Guilford Press: New York.
Wilson, B.A. (in press). Remediation of apraxia
    following an anaesthetic accident. To appear
    in J. West and P. Spinks (Eds.) Case Studies in
    Clinical Psychology. John Wright & Sons Ltd:
    Bristol.
Wilson, B.A. & Staples, D. (1987). Working with
    people who are physically handicapped. To
    appear in J.S. Marzillier & J. Hall (Eds.),
    What is Clinical Psychology? Oxford University
    Press: Oxford.

Chapter Forty Six

MENTAL HANDICAP SERVICES IN THE NETHERLANDS
AND ENGLAND. LEARNING FROM THE CONTRASTS

Mary-Honor Richer-Auping

Comparing Dutch and English Mental Handicap
Services is not easy. The Dutch system is complex,
fairly comprehensive and evolved, but at least it is
well laid out in a publication entitled Vademecum –
zorg voor Geestelijk Gehandicapten (Vademecum – Care
for the Mentally Handicapped) (Manen, Daans et al,
1985). This gives information on provisions,
organisations, law, training etc., and is intended
for all associated with the mentally handicapped,
including the handicapped people themselves. The
English system is difficult to describe because it
is fast changing, not coherently organised or
planned and not summarised in a work similar to the
Vademecum although two publications of value do
exist (DHSS, 1980, 1985).
Let me give a potted history of the Dutch
experience and then compare it with the English.
In the Netherlands before 1950, the care of the
handicapped child rested on the family. From the
mid fifties but especially in the sixties, fast
developments took place. Parents got together in
parents' associations; they started to influence
the type of provisions for their children. Also
the Sociaal Pedagogische Dienst – the Social
Pedagogical Service – was properly established.
This service had started in the 1930s looking at
mentally handicapped school leavers. In 1957 it
received subsidy from the government. This
interaction between parents and care givers led to a
new approach and better chances for the mentally
handicapped. Developments of central importance
were Day Care Centres for children and adults and
Gezinsvervangende Tehuizen (family replacement
homes). These GVTs have no clear equivalent in
England; the people who live there go out to work or
to a day centre during the day and in the evening

take care of themselves with the help of a few
staff. Their wages, if they work, largely pay for
the upkeep of the homes. There are over 400 at the
moment with another 100 or so under construction.

This expansion was guided by the principle that
the mentally handicapped ought to be integrated into
the community.

In the new regulations of 1968, work within
these social pedagogical services was seen as
specialised social work. Currently this has
developed into a service called the Social
Pedagogische Zorg (Social Pedagogical Care) which
forms a link between the family and the organised
care for the Mentally Handicapped. There are 50
such places in the Netherlands with a total of 400
social workers who specialise in mental handicap.
These social workers work closely with a
psychologist, a doctor and an orthopedagogue. I
shall explain orthopedagogy later; it has no direct
equivalent in England, but roughly speaking, the
training is a mixture of psychology, especially
developmental, and special education.

In Britain it is only over the past few years
that District Handicap Teams and Community Mental
Handicap Teams have been set up with the awareness
that a multidisciplinary approach at the earlier
stage would be appropriate. When this development
occurred in the Netherlands, some 10-15 years
earlier, there existed a sort of "treatment
optimism" (Zijderveld, 1986) and the mentally
handicapped were thought of as people with
potential. First and foremost, the approach was to
ask what the mentally handicapped _were_ able to do
and not of all those things they _were_ _not_ able to
do.

Since then in the Netherlands, there has been a
continuous development of seeing the mentally
handicapped as an individual with his or her own
potential. This optimistic attitude also influenced
the development of Sociale Werkplaatsen ("social
work places"). These are only superficially
equivalent to Adult Training Centres in Britain. In
1969 a Wet Sociale Werkvoorziening (Social Work
Provision Law) was introduced which gave these
people the same rights as people working in ordinary
employment. Take pay for instance; previously,
only pocket money had been given and this I gather
still pertains in England, but now in the
Netherlands proper wages are paid. It is expected
that the person works regular hours (8 per day) and
has a work output at least equivalent to one third

of the output of an ordinary worker doing the same job. All people start off with a minimum income (about £6,500). Those people who cannot produce the required output but benefit from work get 75% of the minimum income.

There are three main areas of work, industrial, outdoor manual work and simple office work. These social work places take people with all types of handicap, mental and physical and psychiatric. In 1983, 79,058 handicapped people were employed in these work places and 29% (21,889) were mentally handicapped.

These 'Social Work Places' are difficult to compare with the ATCs. About 76,000 people in England and Wales are currently attending Adult Training Centres or Social Education Centres (Independent Development Council for People with Mental Handicap, 1985). Originally the ATC was designed to provide opportunities for occupation and to train service users for sheltered or open employment. In 1977 the National Development Group produced a pamphlet - No.5 "Day Services for Mentally Handicapped Adults" - with the major recommendation that the focus of activity should shift from "training for work" to "education in its broadest sense".

This is a concept I find difficult to grasp: education for what? It seems to me to deny the adult mentally handicapped person the opportunity and the dignity of contributing to the work of the nation. Whilst a small percentage of mentally handicapped individuals in England perform "real" jobs, the majority do not, unlike in the Netherlands.

So, underlying all this seems to be a difference of philosophy, a difference in the status and dignity of the mentally handicapped person in England and in the Netherlands.

Training Staff

Let me now turn to the issue of training staff in the field of Mental Handicap. The Dutch system is quite different from the English system.

Nearly all the 130,000 people working with mentally handicapped people in the Netherlands have undergone some specific training. In England, about 80% of care staff are untrained (is this the English belief in the amateur?). The Dutch courses range from those for day care staff to university courses. In the past, as in England, working with the mentally handicapped was seen as custodial.

However, the change of attitude towards the mentally handicapped and the increase of provisions led to a vast expansion of training courses. These different courses have several points in common. Firstly, although very adequate, none train people just to work with the mentally handicapped. However, some courses are now being reorganised into courses dealing specifically with mental handicap. Secondly, all courses are recognised by the Ministry of Health and/or by the Ministry of Culture, Recreation and Social Work. Thirdly, and I think this is a very important point, all courses spend a great deal of time on the personal development of the student. It is recognised that the non-specific skills are as, if not more, important than the specific skills. It is often said in English education that the hidden curriculum is as important as the explicit curriculum. In the Netherlands, this curriculum has been brought out of hiding, and the students' own personality development, their feelings and attitudes are attended to. In order to explain this more fully, I shall describe some courses in more detail which as far as I know have no equivalents in England.

The MBO-IW (MBO - Institutional Worker) course takes 3 years and its level is probably equivalent to basic nurse training in England. The course has a very broad curriculum. It is a form of welfare work characterised by its own methodology for working with groups at any age. The goals of the course include gaining a knowledge of human development and behaviour, normal and abnormal, the behaviour of groups and how to handle groups, relevant ethical, statutory and administrative considerations, and relationships between institutions and the community at large. The student will study psychology, a little medicine, drama and art therapy, legal sociology, theory and practice of residential work and "agogiek" which has no direct translation but means how to work with people to promote their personal development and well-being. After this course it is possible to progress to the HBO-IW which is a 4 year part-time course. This course used to be the recognised training for the post of management of several groups plus their leaders but this role is now filled by someone with an even higher qualification, VO. The requirement for a higher qualification in the same job has been a consequence of the glut of people trained to work with the handicapped, quite the reverse of the English predicament.

Nurse Training

In England, most people working directly with the mentally handicapped are nurses or (untrained) nursing assistants. In the Netherlands, a much smaller percentage of those who are trained to work with the mentally handicapped are nurses. Dutch nurse training, like other training, emphasises personal development which appears to be largely neglected in most English courses. In moving away from the emphasis on nurse training, the Dutch are casting doubt on the relevance of specific nurse training to cope with the mentally handicapped.

Psychologists and Orthopedagogues

In Britain there is an overall shortage of clinical psychologists for most client groups, but the shortage is greatest in mental handicap. The number of psychologists currently employed in the Netherlands is estimated at approximately 8,000, of which, more than 4,000 are working in the clinical field. Most are employed by psychiatric hospitals, mental health centres and general hospitals and only a small number in mental handicap (Strien et al., 1987). Those psychologists who are employed in mental handicap in the Netherlands do mainly diagnostic work. Other work is done by orthopedagogues. An approximate translation of the term pedagogy is the science of "upbringing" which involves the study of developmental psychology, care taking and other interactions between children and adults, including professional services for children.

Orthopedagogy is one type of pedagogy and, as the prefix "ortho" implies, it is the study of correct, or rather correcting, development. One speciality within orthopedagogy is training for working with the mentally handicapped. An ortho-pedagogue working in mental handicap often works next to a psychologist and a social worker. The main role of a psychologist is a diagnostic one. The orthopedagogue sets up and supervises treatment programmes amongst other things, and is often responsible for managing group leaders. The social worker, as mentioned before, is the main link between the family and other provisions. So, in the Netherlands, psychologists and orthopedagogues are often directly involved with with the mentally handicapped individual and the trained care staff. For them, the issue of influencing and developing provisions, which is such an important part of the psychologist's work in Britain, is hardly applicable in the Netherlands because fairly satisfactory provisions already exist.

Another major issue in Britain at the moment is the sharing of skills - teaching skills to non-professionals, parents, etc.   However, since most staff are extensively trained in the Netherlands they already have the skills that British psychologists would want to pass on. This means time can be devoted to other tasks.

Underlying cultural and economic differences

One simple economic difference between Mental Handicap provisions in the Netherlands and Britain is that the Dutch have spent more money on this. The Government collects revenue specifically for the chronically ill and handicapped - 4.3% of the income tax revenue is earmarked for these groups by law.   In the most part, money is not spent directly by government institutions, since most institutions are privately run and receive government grants after their first year of operation, providing certain conditions are met.

Although the Dutch had more money to spend in the 60s and 70s this does not explain why they chose to direct that money into Mental Handicap. That was a result of basic cultural attitudes. In Britain, as well as in the Netherlands, it is fully recognised that all mentally handicapped people are individuals with special needs, but in the Netherlands there is more of a complete acceptance of the mentally handicapped individual's dignity and rights. Although many in Britain have been aware of the principle for some time, it has taken a long time to be widely assimilated (Wilcock, 1984).

As the (OHE) Mencap report published only last week noted (The Times, 17.7.86), progression towards providing services for mentally handicapped people in Britain has been "disappointingly slow" partly, it was felt, through a lack of political will. Why has it taken the British, only a few miles across the North Sea, so long to come to these same conclusions? Part of the answer lies in the cultural differences between the Netherlands and England. The Netherlands is less elitist and less class conscious and this aspect of the culture has some of its roots in the Protestant Calvinist tradition.

Conclusion

It has been impossible in this brief paper to give

more than a flavour of the contrasts between Dutch and English provisions for the mentally handicapped. I have concentrated on the Dutch system, partly because I suspect that it will be less familiar to many people than the English system, but mainly because it is more advanced in its provisions, its staff training and its underlying philosophy. This is not to belittle current English advances, everyone has to find their own solutions, but it is perhaps characteristic that the English have not often looked across the North Sea to discover if there is anything there to be learned. However, this attitude is changing as this Canterbury conference symbolised.

REFERENCES

DHSS (1980). Mental Handicap: Progress, Problems and Priorities. A Review of Mental Handicap Services in England since the 1971 White Paper. DHSS: London.
DHSS Study Team (1985). Helping Mentally Handicapped People with Special Problems. DHSS: London.
Independent Development Council for People with Mental Handicap (1985). Living Like Other People - Next Steps in Day Services for People with Mental Handicap. King's Fund Centre, London.
Manen, N.Y. & Van Daans, Y. (Eds) (1985). Vademecum - Zorg Voor Geesteljk Gehandicapten. Samson: Alphen Aan De Ryn.
National Development Group (1977). Day Services for Mentally Handicapped Adults. Pamphlet No. 5. N.D.M.G.H.: London.
Strein, P.Y., Dewolff, C.J., & Takens, R.J. (1987, inpress). The Netherlands. In A. Gilger (Ed), International Handbook of Psychology.
Wilcock, P. (1984). Special Issue on Mental Handicap. Division of Clinical Psychology Newsletter, 43, 8-9.
Zijderveld, B. Van (1986). Samenleving En Geestelijk Gehandicapten De Laatste Vijftig. Jaar Maandblad Geestelijke Volksgezondheid, 41, 3, 233-251.

Chapter Forty Seven

THE CONNECTIONS PROJECT: THE DEVELOPMENT OF A
MULTI-LEVEL BOARD GAME FOR TEACHING LIFE AND SOCIAL
SKILLS TO MENTALLY HANDICAPPED ADULTS

Alastair Ager and Nan Samways

The CONNECTIONS project involved the development of a board game teaching activity for mentally
handicapped individuals. The aim was to provide a
structure for teaching a wide variety of relevant
life skills and to encourage and enrich patterns of
social interaction. Major considerations in its
design were that it should:

(a) involve age appropriate activity for mentally
    handicapped adults;
(b) be flexible enough to allow individuals of
    varying ability to play together;
(c) fit in with the staffing constraints of units
    such as Social Education Centres in allowing
    group participation and (eventual) independ-
    ent activity.

To ensure age-appropriateness, a 'content-free'
structure was adopted for the game itself, with
differing sets of playing cards available to provide
the core material. Card sets correspond to one
particular theme of life skills education, eg FOOD,
MONEY etc. Further, the card sets were designed to
represent objects and situations in a lifelike
manner. High-quality photographs have been used
throughout, and a wide and realistic range of
pictures have been used with regard to each theme.
    The necessary flexibility in the game was
obtained by two major means. First, the task set
each player at the start of the game can be of
varying difficulty (eg one player is asked to
collect four apples, another to collect four items
that may be bought at the butcher's). Thus the game
can accommodate differing playing abilities in the
group of students playing CONNECTIONS at any one
time. Second, the game has a threefold compendium

structure which allows even greater flexibility of use.

In order that players might eventually play the game independently of a teacher or instructor, it was considered vital that the central rules of the game were minimal and its central concept fundamentally simple. A central concept of collecting cards was thus linked through all three levels of the game. Rules were minimised to a basic structure for moving, and taking and replacing cards.

With regard to the fundamental goals of CONNECTIONS, early evaluation data are encouraging. The game does appear to encourage individuals to learn useful skills relating to the theme of a particular card set. Also, interactions between clients are clearly both increased and enriched whilst playing the game. Further evaluation and development of CONNECTIONS is planned, and it is hoped that it will shortly be made commercially available.

Chapter Forty Eight

CLIENTS AND TREATMENT AT A PRISON SYSTEM MENTAL
HOSPITAL

Lawrence V. Annis, John H. Dale, and
Christy A. Baker

SUMMARY

Prison populations are generally reported to
suffer greater incidence of emotional disorder than
does the general public. One state in the USA
has taken the atypical step of creating a special
combination mental hospital and close custody prison
to care for its most disturbed prisoners. The state
corrections department is charged with security and
admissions for this free-standing prison for inmates
drawn from a 28,000-bed penal system, while the
state human resources department is responsible for
treating these inmate-patients. Recovered inmates
are typically discharged to other prisons in the
corrections network. The present paper describes
the clients and treatment at this unusual program.

INTRODUCTION

Researchers and clinicians have consistently
reported that prison inmates display more frequent
and intense parasuicidal behavior, bizarre acting
out, apparent responding to internal stimuli,
withdrawal from interpersonal contact, and other
indices of emotional disorder than do non-
incarcerated persons of equal age and education
(Aadland & Schag, 1984; Lombardo, 1985). People
with active mental illness enter confinement and
even inmates with no history of tenuous reality
contact may decompensate during the stress of
incarceration.

Emotionally disabled prisoners are typically
treated by mental health staff in regular prisons,
or transferred to secure treatment facilities in
what are essentially civil hospital settings. A
less frequent option, transfer to a special prison

326

offering elaborate treatment services, seems generally avoided for fear that inmates' rights may be especially abused due to the physical and social isolation and general dearth of external account-ability that historically characterise institutions of this sort (Arboleda-Florez & Chato, 1985). Given the considerable treatment needs of prisoners and the often competing requirements for security, some intensive therapy programming seems essential for the welfare of the inmates and the community, and to protect the integrity of the correctional setting.

In recent years, the burgeoning population in Florida's thirty-one prisons included numbers of severely disturbed and chronically mentally ill inmates. A 1982 survey by the state Department of Corrections estimated that in excess of six thousand inmates in the state presented signs of mental illness, and about three per cent of the state's 28,000 inmates could likely benefit from in-patient psychiatric treatment. Pressures of caring for these severely disabled inmates considerably distracted the Department of Corrections treatment resources from their principal out-patient mission.

Florida's response has been to combine the security consciousness and close management practices of the state Department of Corrections with the mental health expertise of the Florida Department of Health and Rehabilitative Services. The state legislature recently authorised in-patient treatment at a new Corrections Mental Health Institution for prison inmates recommended for admission by their facility's mental health staff, typically by a psychologist and a psychiatrist, as in need of intensive care due to mental illness, and committed by a circuit judge. This law (Florida Statute 945.40) defines "Mental illness" as:

"an impairment of the emotional processes, of the ability to exercise conscious control of one's actions, or of the ability to perceive reality or to understand, which impairment substantially interferes with a person's ability to meet the ordinary demands of living, regardless of etiology, except that, for the purposes of transfer of an inmate to a mental health treatment facility, the term does not include retardation or developmental disability, simple intoxication, or conditions manifested only by antisocial behavior or drug addiction."

This paper describes the program that evolved and

the clients it serves.

CLIENTELE

The Corrections Mental Health Institution, commonly known by its acronym (CMHI), received a total of 154 new admissions from its opening in March, 1985, through June 1, 1986. Only four former CMHI patients were re-admitted, but the recidivist rate is expected to climb considerably in the future.

Gender
Female inmates have been about twice as likely to be admitted as were males. Comprising just 5% of Florida's prison population, women account for 12% (N=19) of total CMHI admissions.

Age
Ages at admission have ranged from 19 to 60 years, but the vast majority have been between ages 20 and 40. Mean age is 32 years, and the median is 31.

Race
The state inmate population as a whole is 51% white and 49% black. By contrast, whites account for 59% of CMHI admissions (N=89) and blacks for 41% (N=63).

Principal offence
The majority of CMHI clients entered Department of Corrections custody following conviction for violence directed at another person. Compared to the balance of the state's penal population, a male or female inmate at CMHI was three times more likely to be a convicted murderer (28% of admissions). Male CMHI inmates were twice as likely as males incarcerated at other prisons to be rapists or child molesters (15% of admissions). Only 32% of the inmates admitted to CMHI carried a crime against property as their primary conviction. By contrast, property crimes were the primary conviction of 51% of prison inmates state-wide.

Incarceration
Given the seriousness of the crimes for which clients were convicted, one would expect substantial penalties to have been imposed. This is indeed the case. The most accurate assessment of duration of incarceration needs to be based on probable dates of parole, which are typically much earlier than an

inmate's end of sentence. A death sentence was
carried by one client, who had been found
incompetent for execution, and 20% of the inmates
were serving terms of natural life. Other sentences
ranged fron 2 to 60 years, with a median of 10
years. Time served prior to CMHI admission was 4
years, ranging from as brief a period as 4 months to
as long a term as 20 years, with a median of 4
years.

Diagnosis
Many admissions were diagnosed both psychotic and
and personality disordered (see table 1). Among
those assessed as schizophrenic, most were
considered chronic undifferentiated.

Table 1:   Diagnoses of Admissions

Diagnosis	%
Schizophrenic	60
Schizophrenic-like	7
Affective disorders	17
Other psychosis	2
Adjustment disorder	12
Organic syndromes	7
Personality syndromes	46
Paraphilias	2
Mild mental retardation	2

PROGRAM

    The Corrections Mental Health Institution is
located on the grounds of a 1500 bed state mental
hospital and adjoins a 400 bed medium security
prison. The facility is managed by the Florida
Department of Corrections, which has responsibility
for internal and external security and supervises
admissions and discharges. The state's Department
of Health and Rehabilitative Services (DHRS)
provides treatment programs, including mental
health, medical, education, recreation, dental, and
related support services. Like other treatment
staff, the five psychologists assigned to CMHI
remain HRS employees, but are provided offices at
CMHI. A Department of Corrections psychologist at
CMHI directly coordinates treatment and corrections
activities.

Clients and Treatment at a Prison Mental Hospital

The Corrections Mental Health Institution contains a total of 135 beds in one-person, three-person, and four-person rooms. Room assignment is based on a combination of earned privileges and treatment need. One wing, containing fifteen beds in one-, three-, and four-person rooms, is assigned to female inmates, making this the only co-educational prison in Florida.

Admissions
Inmates are customarily admitted from the four state prisons possessing in-patient mental health operations.

Treatment Programs
As indicated above, inmates admitted to CHMI are a varied group. They represent a wide range of emotional, social and medical difficulties. The particular needs of a single inmate change considerably over the course of confinement, thus requiring a wide variety of rehabilitative activities.

Treatment is necessarily highly individualised. Elements of each inmate's therapy are selected and then modified to suit their changing special requirements. Treatment goals are customarily addressed by several programs at once. Inmates are typically offered:

psychotropic medication;
individual and group psychotherapy;
short-term counselling, especially in crisis
  situation;
training in assertiveness and other social
  skills;
organised occupational therapy, including art,
  music, crafts, and weight training
academics, from literacy skills to assistance
  with college correspondence courses;
library services;
indoor and outdoor recreational activities.

Few clients participate in all possible treatment programs, but most are involved in at least some rehabilitative activities. More difficulties are encountered in encouraging poorly motivated inmates to participate than in lack of opportunities for productive use of energy and time. Access to special privileges and recommendations for gain time are partly contingent upon participation in rehabilitative pursuits. Room restriction is avoided as much as possible, since self-isolation is detrimental to the social education and emotional well-being of many clients. Virtually all CMHI inmates receive psychotropics.

Discharges

The interagency/multidisciplinary treatment team reviews each client's case 30 days after admission and no less than every 60 days thereafter. The degree to which an inmate meets the statutory requirements for continued placement is addressed at these reviews, and formal reports are periodically issued to the court and the Department of Corrections. The team's assessment of need for continued hospitalisation has typically focused on two issues: continued mental illness and the need for services at CMHI as opposed to care at another prison. The principal factor used in the evaluation has been theinmate's behavior in the housing area and adjunctive activities. Appropriate socialis-ation displayed in a variety of situations and with a number of persons across a significant period of time appears to be the best predictor of post-treatment adjustment. Compliance with regulations and with treatment team recommendations, especially taking prescribed medications and participating in some off-ward treatment program, seem to indicate the likelihood that the inmate will comply with requirements for effective out-patient treatment at another correctional facility. Due to the chronic nature of most of the inmates' emotional disorders, the severe stressors typically associated with incarceration, and the lengthy duration of many remaining sentences, as many as 50% of the inmates transferred to other prisons are expected to eventually return to CMHI before final discharge from the state correctional system.

For those inmates completing their sentences, a procedure similar to that indicated above is followed. The client is recommended for admission to a state in-patient civil facility when substantial emotional handicaps remain or when a period of adjustment from the total-control prison environment is called for, or when discharged from state custody if only out-patient services are indicated. Of the 92 CMHI inmates thus far discharged, 88% were transferred to another prison to complete their sentences (some had only a few weeks remaining in custody), 11% transferred to state mental hospitals for their catchment areas, and one person was released to the custody of the county sheriff for prosecution on charges of assaulting a staff member a few days before his sentence was due to expire.

DISCUSSION

The Corrections Mental Health Institution is an unusual venture. The combination of security-oriented corrections and a treatment-focused human services agency in a single, free-standing special prison has considerable potential. Careful analysis of clients and treatment may eventually discern the most effective matches of program and inmate-patients. Currently, however, CMHI offers one potential model for creative integration of divergent approaches into a single integrated program to meet important individual and community needs.

REFERENCES

Aadland, R.L. & Schag, D.S. (1984). The assessment of continued threat to the community in a mentally ill offender program. Journal of Criminal Justice, 12, 81-89.

Arboleda-Florez, J., & Chato, F. (1985). Issues regarding admissions from a correctional facility to a hospital forensic unit. International Journal of Offender Therapy and Comparative Criminology, 12, 43-62.

Lombardo, L.X. (1985). Mental health work in prisons and jails. Criminal Justice and Behavior, 12, 17-28.

DETAILS OF CONTRIBUTORS

Dr. Alastair Ager, Lecturer in Clinical Psychology,
Department of Psychology, University of Leicester,
Leicester LE1 7RH, UK.

Lawrence Vincent Annis Ph.D., Senior Clinical
Psychologist, Corrections Mental Health
Institution, Chattahoochee, Florida, U.S.A.

Ms Juliet Auer, Senior Social Worker, Churchill
Hospital, Oxford, UK.

Christy Adele Baker, M.S., Graduate Student,
Department of Sociology, Florida State University,
Tallahassee, Florida, U.S.A.

Sukhwant Singh Bal, Researcher, Department of
Psychology, University of Birmingham, UK.

Maria Barreda-Hanson Ph.D., M.A., B.A., APS Mem.,
Clinical Psychology (USA), Senior Psychologist,
Department Child Psychiatry, Queen Victoria Medical
Centre, Melbourne, Victoria, 3000, Australia.

Dr. Ian Bennun, District Department of Clinical
Psychology and Exeter Community Mental Health
Centre, Larkby, Victoria Park Road, Exeter, U.K.

Prof. Norman R. Bernstein, Professor of Psychiatry,
University of Illinois, Chicago, U.S.A.

Rooshmie Bhagat, Ph.D., District Clinical
Psychologist, Airedale General Hospital,
Keighley, BD20 6TD, UK.

Judith Bullerwell-Ravar, Psychologist, Centre de
Psychologie de l'Enfant, Université de Paris X,
France.

Michael Calnan, Social Psychology Research Unit,
Beverley Farm, The University, Canterbury, Kent, UK.

Anna Checci, Senior Social Worker, Unita
Operativa di Psichiatria, Via Settembrini 1,
20017 RHO (Milano), Italy.

Angelo Cocchi, Head of Psychiatric Service,
Unita Operativa di Psichiatria, Via Settembrini 1,
20017 RHO (Milano), Italy.

Professor Raymond Cochrane, Department of
Psychology, University of Birmingham,
Birmingham B15 2TT, UK.

333

Details of Contributors

John H. Dale Ph.D., Human Services Program Director,
Corrections Mental Health Institution,
Chattahoochee, Florida, U.S.A.

Helen R. Dent Ph.D., Lecturer in Psychology,
Clinical Psychologist, University of Leeds, UK.

Giorgio De Isabella, Clinical Psychologist,
Unita Operativa di Psichiatria, Via Settembrini 1,
R H O (Milano), Italy.

Dr. René Diekstra, Professor and Chairman,
Department of Clinical Psychology, Subfaculteit der
Psychologie, Rijksuniversiteit te Leiden, Holland.

Gabriela Duglosz, Faculty of Education and
Psychology, Silesian University, Katowice, Poland.

Dr. Melanie Fennell, Psychological Treatment
Research Unit, Warneford Hospital,
Oxford OX3 7JX, UK.

Sally A. Furnish, Clinical Psychologist (Care of the
Elderly), Gwent Health Authority, St. Woolos
Hospital, Newport, Gwent NPT 4SZ, UK.

Dr. Jeffrey Garland, Clinical Psychologist,
Rivendell Assessment Unit, Radcliffe Infirmary,
Oxford OX2 6HE, UK.

Dr. R. Gokal, Consultant Physician, Renal Unit,
Manchester Royal Infirmary, Manchester, UK.

Elina Haavio-Mannila, Department of Sociology,
University of Helsinki, Finland.

Dr. Kurt Hahlweg, Research Fellow, Department of
Psychology, Max Planck Institue of Psychiatry,
Munich, West Germany.

Dr. John Hall, Department of Clinical Psychology,
Warneford Hospital, Warneford Lane, Headington,
Oxford OX3 7JX, UK.

Jocelyn Handy, Department of Behaviour in
Organisations, School of Management and
Organisational Sciences, Gillow House, University of
Lancaster, Bailrigg, Lancaster LA1 4YX, UK.

Prof. Per Kristian Haugen, Special Psychologist in
Gerontology, Granli Senter, Sem, Norway.

334

Details of Contributors

Dr. J.H. Henderson, Medical Director, St. Andrew's Hospital, Northampton, U.K. (Lately Regional Officer for Mental Health, WHO Regional Office for Europe, Copenhagen, Denmark).

Irena Heszen-Niejodek Ph.D., Assistant Professor, Faculty of Education and Psychology, Silesian University, Katowice, Poland.

Dr. V.F. Hillier, Senior Lecturer, Computational Methods in Medical Science, University of Manchester, UK.

Reidun Ingebretsen, Norwegian Institute of Gerontology, Oscargt. 36, Oslo, Norway.

Dr. Marie Johnston, Academic Department of Psychiatry, Royal Free Hospital, Pond Street, London NW3 2QG, UK.

Martin van Kalmthout, Ph.D., Clinical Psychologist and Psychotherapist, Department of Clinical Psychology and Personality Theory, University of Nijmegen, Holland.

Dr. John Kincey, District Psychologist, Central Manchester Health Authority, UK.

Thomas Koehler Ph.D., Assistant Teacher, University of Hamburg, Department of Psychology, Von-Melle Park 5, 2000 Hamburg 13, Germany.

Marina B. Kuyper, M.D., General Practitioner, Department of Family Medicine, University of Amsterdam, Holland.

Jacqueline Lees, Psychology Student, South Birmingham District Psychology Service, c/o Monyhull Hospital, Monyhull Hall Road, Kings Norton, Birmingham B30 3QB, UK.

Dermot A. McGovern, MB.ChB., M.R.C.Psych., Consultant Psychiatrist, Bromsgrove and Redditch Health Authority, U.K.

Dr. I. Malcolm MacLachlan, Department of Psychology, Institute of Psychiatry, De Crespigny Park, Denmark Hill, London SE5 8AF, UK.

Details of Contributors

Dr. Colin MacLeod, Research Clinical Psychologist,
Department of Psychology, St. George's Hospital
Medical School, University of London,
London SW17 0RE, UK.

Prof. Dr. Stan Maes, Professor of Health
Psychology, Tilburg University, The Netherlands.

Dr. Shamim Mahmud, Senior Clinical Psychologist,
St. James's Hospital, Portsmouth, Hampshire, UK.

Dr. Theresa Marteau, Academic Department of
Psychiatry, Royal Free Hospital, Pond St.,
London NW3 2QG, UK.

Dr. Derek Milne, Regional Tutor in Clinical
Psychology (Northern), University of Newcastle upon-
Tyne & Northumberland Psychology Service, Otterburn
House, East Cottingwood, Morpeth NE61 2NU, UK.

Ann Moriarty Ph.D., Senior Clinical Psychologist,
North Western Health Board, General Hospital,
Letterkenny, Co. Donegal, Eire.

Eric Moss Ph.D., Clinical Psychologist, Shalvata
Mental Health Center, PO Box 94, Hod Hasharon,
Israel.

David Mushin MBBS, FRANZ(C), Dip. Child Psych.
(Toronto), Clinical Director, Department of Child
Psychiatry and Chairman, Divison of Psychiatry,
Queen Victoria Medical Centre, 172 Lonsdale Street,
Melbourne, Victoria, 3000, Australia.

Dr. Desmond Oliver, Consultant Physician, Renal
Unit, Churchill Hospital, Oxford, UK.

Roger Paxton Ph.D., District Psychologist,
Northumberland Health Authority, Otterburn House,
East Cottingwood, Morpeth, Northumberland NE61
2NU, UK.

J. Peuskens, Psychiatrist, Psychosocial Centre St.
Alexius, Brussels & University Psychiatric Centre
St. Jozef, Kortenberg, Belgium.

G. Pieters, Psychiatrist, Psychosocial Centre St.
Alexius, Brussels & University Psychiatric Centre
St. Jozef, Kortenberg, Belgium.

Details of Contributors

Lyn Quine, Research Fellow, Institute of Social and Applied Psychology, University of Kent at Canterbury, UK.

Dr. Judy Renshaw, Research Fellow, Personal Social Services Research Unit, University of Kent at Canterbury, UK.

Mary-Honor Richer-Auping, Clinical Psychologist, Aylesbury Town and Wing Community Mental Handicap Team, Manor House Hospital, Aylesbury, Bucks, UK.

L.A. Rowland, Lecturer in Psychology, Institute of Psychiatry, University of London, Honorary Clinical Psychologist, The Bethlem Royal and Maudsley Hospitals, UK.

Dr. Derek Rutter, Social Psychology Research Unit, Beverley Farm, The University, Canterbury, Kent, UK.

Paul M. Salkovskis, Research Psychologist, University of Oxford Department of Psychiatry, Warneford Hospital, Oxford OX3 7JX, UK.

Ms Nan Samways, Graphic Designer, 111 Coleridge Close, Hitchin, Herts, UK.

Dr. Maryanne Schlosser, Research Fellow, Health Psychology, Tilburg University, The Netherlands.

Miss L. Gail Simon, Social Worker, Regional Social Work Team, Manchester Royal Infirmary, Manchester Social Services Department, UK.

Bodil Solberg, Psychologist, Psyckiatrisk Poliklinikk, Fylkessjujehuset pa Voss, N-5700 Voss, Norway.

John Cramer Spensley, FRACP, MBBS, Honorary Paediatrician to Birth Centre, Queen Victoria Medical Centre, 172 Lonsdale Street, Melbourne 3000 Victoria, Australia.

Mrs. Janis P. Stout, Team Leader, Regional Social Work Team, Social Work Department, Manchester Royal Infirmary/Manchester Social Services Department, UK.

Ms Anne-Marie Toase, Clinical Psychologist, North Warwickshire Health Authority, District Psychology Services, Coleshill Hall Hospital, Gilson Road, Coleshill, Birmingham B46 1DW, UK.

Details of Contributors

R. Vermote, Psychiatrist, Psychosocial Centre, St. Alexius, Brussels & University Psychiatric Centre St. Jozef, Kortenberg, Belgium.

Louise M. Wallace, Ph.D., Principal Clinical Psychologist (Physical Health), South Birmingham District Psychology Service, c/o Monyhull Hospital, Monyhull Hall Road, Kings Norton, Birmingham B30 3QB, U.K.

David J. Westbrook, Clinical Psychologist, Department of Clinical Psychology, Warneford Hospital, Oxford, OX3 7JX, UK.

Dr. Barbara Wilson, Senior Lecturer in Rehabilitation, Southampton General Hospital, Tremona Road, Southampton SO9 4XY, UK.

Dr. R.T. Woods, Lecturer in Clinical Psychology, Institute of Psychiatry, De Crespigny Park, London SE5 8AF, U.K.

Mrs. Helen Yu, Psychological Technician, Central Manchester Health Authority, UK.

Dr. Friederike Zimmer, Elsehard-Karls-Universitat Tubingen, Zentrum fur Psychiatrie und Neurologie, D 7400 Tubingen 1, Nervenklinik, Osianderstr. 22, W. Germany.

For Product Safety Concerns and Information please contact our EU
representative GPSR@taylorandfrancis.com
Taylor & Francis Verlag GmbH, Kaufingerstraße 24, 80331 München, Germany